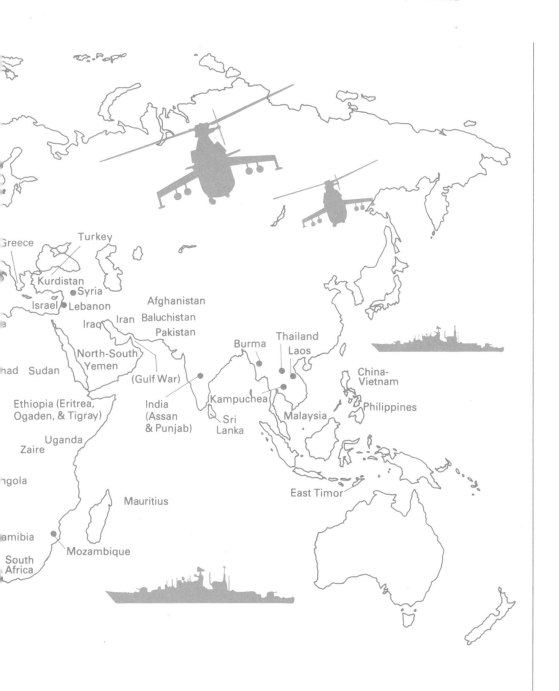

WAR
ANNUAL 2

A Guide to Contemporary Wars and Conflicts

Brassey's titles of related interest

LAFFIN, J.
Brassey's Battles: 3,500 Years of Conflict, Campaigns and Wars from A–Z

LAFFIN, J.
War Annual 1

MASON, R. A.
War in the Third Dimension

SIMPKIN, R.
Race to the Swift: Thoughts on Twenty-First Century Warfare

By the same author

Military

Middle East Journey
Return to Glory
One Man's War
The Walking Wounded
Digger (The Story of the Australian Soldier)
Scotland the Brave (The Story of the Scottish Soldier)
Jackboot (The Story of the German Soldier)
Tommy Atkins (The Story of the English Soldier)
Jack Tar (The Story of the English Seaman)
Swifter than Eagles (Biography of Marshal of the R.A.F. Sir John Salmond)
The Face of War
British Campaign Medals
Codes and Ciphers
Boys in Battle
Women in Battle
Anzacs at War
Links of Leadership (Thirty Centuries of Command)
Surgeons in the Field
Americans in Battle
Letters from the Front 1914-18
The French Foreign Legion
Damn the Dardanelles! (The Story of Gallipoli)
The Australian Army at War 1899-1975
The Israeli Army in the Middle East Wars 1948-1973
The Arab Armies in the Middle East Wars 1948-1973
Fight for the Falklands!
On the Western Front: Soldiers' Stories 1914-18
The Man the Nazis Couldn't Catch
The War of Desperation: Lebanon 1982-85
Battlefield Archaeology
Australians at War
The Western Front 1916-17
Holy War

General

The Hunger to Come (Food and Population Crises)
New Geography 1966-67
New Geography 1968-69
New Geography 1970-71
Anatomy of Captivity (Political Prisoners)
Devil's Goad
Fedayeen (The Arab-Israeli Dilemma)
The Arab Mind
The Israeli Mind
The Dagger of Islam
The PLO Connections
The Arabs as Master Slavers
Know the Middle East

And other titles

WAR ANNUAL 2

A Guide to Contemporary Wars and Conflicts

by

JOHN LAFFIN

BRASSEY'S DEFENCE PUBLISHERS
(a member of the Pergamon Group)

LONDON · OXFORD · WASHINGTON · NEW YORK · BEIJING
FRANKFURT · SAO PAULO · SYDNEY · TOKYO · TORONTO

U.K (Editorial)	Brassey's Defence Publishers, 24 Gray's Inn Road, London WC1X 8HR
(Orders)	Brassey's Defence Publishers, Headington Hill Hall, Oxford OX3 0BW, England
U.S.A. (Editorial)	Pergamon-Brassey's International Defense Publishers, 8000 Westpark Drive, Fourth Floor, McLean, Virginia 22102, U.S.A.
(Orders)	Pergamon Press, Maxwell House, Fairview Park, Elmsford, New York 10523, U.S.A.
PEOPLE'S REPUBLIC OF CHINA	Pergamon Press, Room 4037, Qianmen Hotel, Beijing, People's Republic of China
FEDERAL REPUBLIC OF GERMANY	Pergamon Press, Hammerweg 6, D-6242 Kronberg, Federal Republic of Germany
BRAZIL	Pergamon Editora, Rua Eça de Queiros, 346, CEP 04011, Paraiso, São Paulo, Brazil
AUSTRALIA	Pergamon-Brassey's Defence Publishers, P.O. Box 544, Potts Point, N.S.W. 2011, Australia
JAPAN	Pergamon Press, 8th Floor, Matsuoka Central Building, 1-7-1 Nishishinjuku, Shinjuku-ku, Tokyo 160, Japan
CANADA	Pergamon Press Canada, Suite No. 271, 253 College Street, Toronto, Ontario, Canada M5T 1R5

Copyright © 1987 John Laffin

First edition 1986

Second edition 1987

Library of Congress Cataloging in Publication Data

Laffin, John.
War annual 2.
Bibliography: p.
1. Military history, Modern—20th century.
2. Military art and science—History—20th century.
3. World politics—1985–1995. I. Title. II. Title: War annual
II. III. Title: War annual two.
U42.L342   1987   355'.009'04   87–21868

British Library Cataloguing in Publication Data

Laffin, John
War annual 2.
1. War
I. Title
909.82   U21.2

ISBN 0–08–034751–7

Printed in Great Britain by Richard Clay Ltd,

Contents

WAR TRENDS

Introduction

WAR ANNUAL 1 justified the confidence of the author and publisher in its concept as the first book to describe all the world's wars currently in progress. Reviews in several countries variously assessed it as 'valuable', 'necessary' and 'essential' to students of war at every academic and professional level.

In the year since the first **WAR ANNUAL** was published it remains all too clear that there is no shortage of wars; in fact, the number has increased. Some conflicts have been brief. The operational phase of the conflict between the United States and Libya in May 1986 lasted between 11 and 12 minutes. The brief but violent action had consequences not only for the two principals but for the world at large. Longer wars continue their perennial course without any sign of a truce, let alone a peace. Other wars just 'erupt'. In many parts of the world men's instant recourse in a crisis is to rush to arms.

I try not to take sides in my descriptions of wars but the term 'terrorist attack' must sometimes be used. A bomb planted in a city bus station and which kills hundreds of people is not an act of warfare, even if it takes place during a war. Similarly the cold-blooded shooting of bus passengers after they have been forced to alight can only be called a massacre. Such deaths cannot be dignified by the conventional war term of casualties.

In contrast to **WAR ANNUAL** 1, in **WAR ANNUAL** 2 I give many of my sources but it is not possible to state all of them. The lives of some of my many contacts in countries at war would be at risk if I gave their names; others would certainly lose their jobs. Yet others—notably diplomats—would be embarrassed at least and perhaps compromised if I were to name them. I could not write this book without information from trusted sources who trust me and I am grateful to them.

Terrorism, unless it occurs during a conflict considered to be a war, is not included in this book. If it were to be included then many European countries would be on the list of those at war. In the period 1986-87 acts of terrorism occurred in France, Spain, Portugal, Italy, Belgium, West Germany, Yugoslavia, Greece, Turkey, Corsica, Cyprus, Eire and Holland. In Northern Ireland terrorism is part of life and, at least for the Irish Republican Army and the Irish National Liberation Army, it is also part of a war. The leaders of the IRA and the INLA have declared themselves to be at war.

It is not correct to say—as an American State Department official has said—that the driving force behind all war is the Soviet Union. The Soviet Union is certainly a combatant in some of the world's major conflicts, notably Afghanistan. It is deeply involved in Angola, Ethiopia and in parts of Central America. But to see the Russians everywhere involved in war is to overlook many wars which have no link to the Communist bloc. Conflicts in or related to India, Pakistan, Bangladesh, Lebanon and Ireland are sectarian or religious. Some wars in South America are wholly 'civil' wars. Others in the same continent are aggravated by the narcotics traffic. The fighting between South Africa and some of its neighbours is racial. Many conflicts concern border disputes.

Some wars have changed their character. For instance, that between Iran and Iraq started as a war over territory; it is now largely religious—a holy war. The war in Uganda began—or so one side would claim—as a war to overthrow a tyrannical government; it is now much more a tribal war. A few wars are genocidal. It is difficult to see Indonesia's war against the people of East Timor as anything but genocidal.

Almost without exception reviewers of **WAR ANNUAL** 1 confessed surprise at the large number of wars. The armaments manufacturers are not surprised; they know exactly where wars are taking place and where they are likely to take place. The manufacture and sale of arms and military material is by far the world's most lucrative business. Some of the largest companies cannot keep up with the demand for more and better weapons. The morality involved is not part of this book. The simple fact is that there is an insatiable demand for the tools of war. As I commented in **WAR ANNUAL** 1, judged by its frequency, war is normal.

London   JOHN LAFFIN

The Wars — 1986-87

Soviet-DRA operations north of Kabul, July 1986.

SOVIET UNION

IRAN

KONAR PROVINCE

WARDAK'S AREA OF OPERATIONS

Kabul
Jalalabad
Asadabad

Ali Kel
Khyber Pass

HAZARAJAT

Ghazni
NANGAHAR PROVINCE

Gardez
Parachinar
Zhawar

AFGHANISTAN

PAKTIA PROVINCE
Miram-Shah
Urgun

Mashad

KANDAHAR

PAKISTAN

Quetta

0   Miles   200

Afghanistan Resistance War

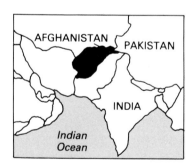

AFGHANISTAN   PAKISTAN

INDIA

Indian Ocean

Afghanistan Resistance War

THE SOVIET UNION'S VIETNAM?

Background Summary

The Soviet Union invaded Afghanistan in December 1979, ostensibly to help the Afghan government and army to 'maintain control over rebellious elements'. President Hafizullah Amin was killed in the fighting and Babrak Karmal succeeded him. Opposing the Soviet and Afghan regular army were groups of Mujahideen or holy war warriors, mostly tribesmen from the hills. While the Soviet and Afghan armies controlled large parts of Afghanistan and caused a large-scale refugee flow to Pakistan they were unable to subdue the Mujahideen.

(*For full details of earlier fighting see* **WAR ANNUAL** 1.)

Summary of the War in 1985

With the Russians and their Afghan puppet government on one side and the Mujahideen or Islamic freedom fighters on the other, the war was more bitter in this period.

The Soviet command introduced an indoctrination programme to instil in the Russian soldiers fear and hate for the Afghan tribesmen. This was not difficult as some groups of Mujahideen had tortured and mutilated Russian prisoners. In addition, the Russians frequently carried out ground and air operations against Mujahideen groups operating from Pakistan. The Pakistan government protested against the consistent violation of their territory but, as the Soviet leaders had judged, the Pakistanis stopped short of military reprisal.

Soviet tactics indicated a degree of desperation at not being able to finish off the war. The Russians 'resettled' large parts of the Afghan population in places where they could give the fighting men little help. A policy of calculated terrorism was adopted to dissuade the villagers from supporting the guerrillas. This reached serious proportions with the killing of 1,000 civilians in two raids in eastern Afghanistan and in the systematic destruction of large parts of the irrigation system. Without irrigation Afghanistan's agricultural yield dropped by 40% in 1986-87.

Meanwhile the Afghan government tried to pacify the country by a propaganda campaign to show that the guerrillas were traitors to their own country. In addition, following Soviet advice, the government sent large numbers of children to the Soviet Union for 're-education'. The long-term aim of this programme is to produce pro-Soviet Afghanis who will then change the attitude of their fellow-countrymen towards the Russians. At least, this is what the Soviet government and the regime of the 'Democratic Republic of Afghanistan' (DRA) hopes.

Despite all their efforts the Russians and the DRA army held no more than 35% of the country at the end of 1985.

They made many attempts to cut the supply lines bringing in weapons from Pakistan, the West and from some Arab states, notably Egypt and Saudi Arabia. They also stepped up the use of airpower, to spot guerrilla posts, to intimidate and to attack. It is only through increased use of airpower and airborne troops that the Soviet forces can cover all the 200 mountain passes between Pakistan and Afghanistan.

That the Russians intended to stay was evident from the vast military infrastructure which they built during 1985. They planned to use Afghanistan as a strategic base for expansion of Soviet influence throughout South-east Asia and the Middle East. The language of expansion was apparent from an article in *Pravda* in March 1985. Soviet troops were stationed in Afghanistan, according to a government-employed author, to 'defend Soviet borders from the approach of hostile imperialist and pro-imperialist forces'.

In any case, by December 1985 the war was six years old and the Russian leaders could not end it without losing immense military prestige and political influence.

The War in 1986-87

During 1986 some writers described the war in Afghanistan as a continuation of Rudyard Kipling's 'Great Game', a reference to the imperial British-Russian confrontations and Intelligence plots of the nineteenth century for control of the route to India through the Khyber Pass.

While there are indeed similarities between the 'great game' then and now, the theory overlooks some major factors. For instance, it does not take into account Islamic *jihad* or holy war. In the nineteenth century Islam and its followers, the Muslims, were merely pawns in the game. Today they are important players. Islam is one of the world's great political and military forces and the Mujahideen of the Afghan Resistance, all Muslims, are fighting a *jihad*.

The Soviet military doctrine in Afghanistan is based on three 'preconditions for victory'. They are:

● Neutralisation of the leadership, command and control of the guerrilla organisations through the deep penetration and manipulation of these groups. Murder of the primary leaders and of commanders is considered vital.

● Destruction of the popular base of the revolution by inflicting intolerable suffering on the civilian population. This forces civilian evacuation of friendly areas and destroys the economic base of the revolution.

● Isolation of people in the 'suppressed area' from safe havens. The surviving fighters and their civilian supporters then feel deserted. In isolation the organization itself cannot revive and cannot replace its commanders, weapons and supplies.

There is nothing new in this doctrine. In the nineteenth century the Imperial Russians defined such a doctrine for the suppression of a Muslim insurgency and the subjugation of Central Asia.

By early 1987 the Russians believed they were close to achieving their first and second preconditions, especially away from the Pakistani border areas. For instance, in 1984 the murder of the popular leader Zabiullah brought the gradual collapse of resistance in the Mazar-i-Sharif area. By 1986 the economy of the interior was broken and the civilian population was brought to starvation point.

The Russians have found that by subjecting the population and locally based resistance to intense psychological warfare they incline them to cease fighting and to concentrate on the revival of the social and the economic infrastructure of the region. This campaign comes under loose control of the Afghan army and is completely out of reach for the Resistance. Psychological warfare is waged by infiltrators who spread rumours, issue false orders, carry out sabotage and ambush Resistance forces, while themselves masquerading as resistance fighters.

The very existence of the country-wide resistance depends primarily on the ability of the political leadership in Peshawar, Pakistan, to infiltrate commanders, instructions and weapons into the interior. Only in this way is it possible to exercise control over the suppressed population and incite them into reviving and maintaining the *jihad*. This vital operation, in turn, is entirely dependent on the functioning of the few centres of logistics in Paktia near the Pakistani border, especially Zhawar. Without these logistics centres it would be virtually impossible to support and sustain the entire country-wide resistance.

Populated villages are important assets to the guerrillas; the people provide food, shelter and vital information on Soviet military movements. With the villages depopulated and farms destroyed some areas of Afghanistan are free-fire zones and therefore dangerous for guerrillas carrying out hit-and-run operations.

The Russians' confident expectation of victory does not indicate a collapse of the Resistance. Certain events during 1986-87 were humiliating for the Russians. The Mujahideen's prolonged resistance and the inability of the Soviets, backed by the DRA forces, to kill or capture any of the rebel leaders embarrassed the Soviet leadership. In other parts of the Third World, where the Russians have made progress, they realise that people are critical.

Among the Mujahideen leaders prominent during 1986-87 are Abdul Huq, Ismael Khan, Rakhim Wardak, Jaluddin and, the most famous of all, Ahmad Shah Massood.

Abdul Huq, a bright and cunning young commander of the *Hezb-i-Islami* group, was an irritant to the Soviet army throughout the period. One of his coups was the blowing up of a major ammunition dump near Kabul. Massood commands the *Jamiat-i-Islami* faction in the strategic Panshir Valley north of Kabul; during 1986-87 his fighters persistently threatened Soviet supply lines and convoys.

Ismael Khan prevented the Russians from completely overrunning the city of Herat in the north-west, while Jaluddin was the key figure in keeping Mujahideen supply routes open into Afghanistan from Pakistan. A secret of Mujahideen leaders' success was their ability to adapt their tactics to the changing attempts of the Russians to subdue and eliminate them.

Impatient with Babrak Karmal's lack of success in dealing with the Resistance, the Soviet High command replaced him with Muhammad Najibullah, who prefers to be known as 'Comrade' Najib. Najib, who was only 39 when he took over in May 1986, had been head of KHAD, the security police. The Russians marked his accession to power as General Secretary of the People's Democratic Party of Afghanistan (PDPA) with a massive show of force in Kabul.

Najib was chosen because of his military and security experience and his evident ability to 'deal with' the tribes and nationalities which make up Afghanistan. Information from Western embassies in Kabul stresses that he was not selected because of any likelihood that he could make the Soviet presence any more acceptable to the people of Afghanistan. Najib is a member of Afghanistan's largest tribal group, the Pashtuns. His professed respect for Islam and for Afghan traditions is suspect because of his Marxist credentials and reputation for brutality.[1] Karmal was retained as President—a meaningless position in Afghanistan—while Sultan Ali Keshtmand was confirmed as Prime Minister.

Najib's policies,[2] the same as Babrak Karmal's though pursued with greater vigour, include:

- The strengthening of Afghanistan's depleted and demoralised armed forces and stepping up of the campaign against the Resistance; new conscription measures have been introduced.
- Trying to unite the country and extend the regime's hold through more effective activity by the Communist party and such mass organisations as the National Fatherland Front and through the staging of local elections, with the aim of creating a 'new historic society'.
- 'Broadening the social bases of the revolution' by including (reliable) non-Party figures in the administration and 'political forces outside the country' who are ready to participate in constructing a 'new' Afghanistan, as endorsed by Gorbachev on 28 July 1986.
- Winning over the tribes and nationalities through a mixture of force, financial inducements and lip-service to Afghan traditions—*eg* the convening of *jirgas* or councils at all levels. They are viewed with great scepticism by the mass of the people.
- Protestations of the regime's respect for Islam and of its leaders' Islamic beliefs.
- Assertions that there is no intention to impose 'Socialism' in Afghanistan, but only 'national democracy'.

Najib's rise to power was accompanied by more determined efforts, political and military, to extend the basis of the regime's control and support in the country, and by Soviet efforts to persuade the international community to believe that a lasting political settlement does not require an early and complete Soviet with-drawal—which would put the regime in Kabul at risk—but instead is dependent on cessation of 'external interference'. The Soviets have also concentrated on projecting Najib as a figure of genuine national reconciliation. But his harsh reputation, the continuing bitter war waged by Soviet and regime forces and the trials of resistance leaders living abroad all point to the same overall objective— achieving a 'settlement' in Afghanistan only on the Soviet Union's terms.

Najib has blamed all sorts of shortcomings on the Party and the administration, including inertia and corruption. His campaign against them often reflects Gorbachev's style. At Soviet prompting, Najib maintained Babrak Karmal's efforts to reduce the rift between Parchamis (now dominant) and Khalqis within the PDPA, but these differences and personal rivalries continue.

During 1986 the Soviet Union tried to cut the cost of the long war by making

Kabul's embattled government work harder for the aid it received. Development aid, an integral part of overall Soviet strategy, no longer came without strings, as it did following the pre-war Communist coup in 1978.

Many officially declared non-military projects such as road repairs actually support the war effort while others, such as boosting natural-gas exports to the Soviet Union, are needed to help Kabul pay off its mounting debts to Moscow. The Kremlin gradually cut off Kabul's hard-currency earnings by taking larger amounts of its prized fruits, carpets and Persian lamb pelts in barter deals.

The Soviet Union's costs in Afghanistan are a state secret but the Stockholm International Peace Research Institute (SIPRI) has estimated that the Kremlin was spending US$3 billion a year fighting in Afghanistan and had given about US$800 million in aid.

Najib complained of the Soviet financial squeeze in a speech in Mazar-i-Sharif in June. 'The Russians don't leave enough gas for us', he said. 'They took more than 2.4 billion cubic metres of our gas from the northern fields . . . Our total yield was only 2.6 billion cubic metres.'

Moscow pays US$300 million a year for this gas but then takes it all back to cover Kabul's debt repayments. The Soviet is developing a US$500 million copper mine in the Logar Valley, an area south of Kabul where government troops tried several times during 1986 to flush out guerrillas.

Repairs to strategic roads churned up by tank tracks, army-escorted truck convoys and mines rank high among Soviet goals. Moscow is paying for improvements to the two-mile Salang Tunnel which runs through the Hindu Kush mountains north of Kabul. It is expanding the port town of Heirston, at the Afghan end of a new bridge linking the two countries over the Amu Darya river, and is repairing on credit the Salang Highway that is Kabul's umbilical cord to the Soviet Union. All these are mainly military projects.

Defection Provides Mujahideen Propaganda Coup

A significant propaganda coup for the Mujahideen was the defection from the Afghan-Soviet army of Colonel Mirash Matullah, commander of the 3rd Corps of the Afghan Army. With his wife and family, he left Kabul on a trip to the south-western border province of Paktia. Here agents of *Hezb-i-Islami* organised safe passage for the party to Pakistan. Having obtained political asylum from the Pakistan government, he announced that he intended to use his 22 years of military experience to help the Mujahideen in their *jihad*. Colonel Matullah had controlled insurgency activities against the Mujahideen in Paktia province. His reports provided some of the most revealing details about the relationship between the Soviet and Afghan armies.[3] Groups of Kabul soldiers were deployed as a human shield in front of the Soviet soldiers as each attack began, he claimed.

The Afghan armed forces amounted to 90,000 in December 1979. According to Matullah, by the end of 1986 they had decreased to 30,000. Afghan casualties were 10 times those of the Soviet troops and to reinforce the government units teenage boys were being press-ganged, given a few weeks' basic training and thrown into combat.

Matullah gave evidence of the army's low standard of efficiency. About 600 Afghan army paratroops were dropped into Paktia province to seize the

Mujahideen base at Jawar, near the Pakistan border. The attack was a disaster and all the Afghanis were either killed or captured.[4]

A Soviet commando force later took Jawar but Colonel Matullah said that the Russians suffered some of their heaviest losses of the war, including 25 aircraft shot down. Matullah claimed that the Russians planned to send specially-trained mountain commando units into Afghanistan.

Geneva Talks—Without the Rebels

In July 1986 United Nations-sponsored peace talks on the Afghan war were held in Geneva. Afghanistan was represented by officials of the Democratic Republic of Afghanistan (DRA). The DRA is not democratic nor does it represent the people of Afghanistan. The talks were doomed to failure because they failed to observe the fundamental principle on which they were called—as direct negotiations between the warring parties. The UN negotiations excluded the Mujahideen, a major 'warring party'. Senator Gordon Humphrey, co-chairman of the US Congressional Task Force on Afghanistan, said that 'the fate of nations being decided in the absence of their legitimate representatives is reminiscent of Yalta'.

At the talks the Soviet Union insisted that before any Russian troop withdrawal could take place all aid to Afghan guerrillas must be cut off and Pakistan must officially recognise the puppet regime in Kabul. Senator Humphrey said that the 'bedrock criteria' of the United States in any settlement of the Afghan war had to include withdrawal of the Soviet forces, the return of the Afghan refugees and self-determination for the people of Afghanistan. At the time the Senator was critical of the US administration because it had, he said, endorsed the dishonestly structured talks in Geneva.[5]

According to American and Pakistani Intelligence estimates nearly one million Afghans had been killed; five million, or one-third of the population, were refugees in Pakistan and Iran; and another million were internal refugees, their villages and towns having been destroyed by Soviet air and ground attacks. More than 300,000 people had been forcibly moved from the mountainous Paktia, Kuner and Laghman provinces near the border to desert regions in south-west Afghanistan.

The only reason that any negotiations at all took place was because the people of Afghanistan were resisting.

Kurt Lohbeck,[6] a television producer with deep experience of wartime Afghanistan, complained that American policy-makers appeared to be playing poker while their Soviet counterparts were playing chess. 'Poker is a game of bluff and hidden resources where each hand is played separately; chess is more complex and intricate and each move, while seeming to be insignificant, is all part of the master game plan.'

Iranian Involvement in Hazarajat

Another part of the 'chess game' became apparent at the end of 1986 with the first reports from the Hazarajat, the mountainous central part of Afghanistan, concerning the activities of radical pro-Iranian guerrilla groups.

According to one source, up to 25,000 Afghan civilians and Mujahideen had been killed by the pro-Iranian groups, which include the *Sepah-e Pasdaran* and *Nesr* factions. They are said to operate with the support of the Communist Tudeh Party in Iran. This party was banned in Iran in 1983 and its leaders were arrested on charges of spying for the Soviet Union. However, the Teheran government has long since patched up its relations with Moscow. The Soviet puppets in Kabul are probably backing the pro-Iranian groups in the Hazarajat.

Their involvement initially began in 1980 when about 300 agents disguised as *mullahs* or Muslim priests arrived in the area, supposedly to take part in the *jihad* against Soviet occupation forces and to provide religious education. But soon after their arrival they began to denounce local Mujahideen leaders to the DRA authorities.

They now claimed that Ayatollah Khomeini had said that the main fight was against the Sunni Muslims of the region. Khomeini, a Shi'a Mulsim, had declared war against the Sunni Muslims. For as long as this war continued, he said, it was not permissible to fight against the Soviet Union. The radicals, ever growing in strength, went from village to village, plundering the households of landlords and others labelled 'oppressors'. Thousands of people were killed, thousands more forced to abandon their homes. Several former members of parliament, who were in office before the Communist takeover in Kabul in 1978, were assassinated.

Mujahideen guerrillas defeated a DRA army sent into the Hazarajat by Hafizullah Amin when he was President. Since then Soviet and DRA forces have rarely bothered to commit units to the central provinces; the pro-Iranian radicals are keeping the region subdued for them.[15]

Pakistan the Key to all Resistance

Late in 1986 there were strong signs that Moscow and Kabul, in their efforts to undermine the Islamic resistance in the Pashtun tribal belt along the Afghanistan-Pakistan border, were laying the groundwork for the possible dismemberment of Pakistan. Some analysts consider that the ultimate Soviet objective is a lethal blow to the heart of the Islamic world through Pakistan and/or Iran, once these countries are sufficiently destabilised to make such a move feasible.

A two-pronged strategy became clear. One prong was to depopulate border areas inside Afghanistan through repeated aerial and artillery bombardment of villages on which the resistance fighters depend for support; the other was to incite tribesmen on the Pakistani side to stir up unrest against the anti-Soviet Afghans. The argument was something like this: 'If the Mujahideen win the war Afghanistan will be in the grip of the *mullahs* and Afghanistan will be just like Iran. If we join the Communists we will all be equal and prosperous.'

In Pakistan there was growing domestic pressure on the government in Islamabad to cut off support for the Mujahideen and make a deal with the Kabul regime and its Soviet mentors. This pressure was created by the Afghan secret police, the KHAD, with a campaign of bombing attacks within Pakistan together with frequent cross-border raids by DRA forces. Understandably the many Pakistanis who suffer as a result of this form of terrorism want their government to stop giving refuge to the Afghan Mujahideen.

There is an even a more serious result of the Soviet-Afghan violence in Pakistan—it encourages the Pashtun separatist elements in the Pakistani border areas who want to establish a Pashtunistan state, independent of Pakistan. This idea is supported by Kabul.

Late in 1986 'Comrade' Najib and other senior Party officials organised a big political rally in Kabul's Pashtunistan Square to express support for the dissident tribesmen in Pakistan's North-West Frontier Province (NWFP) and in Baluchistan. The number of Pakistanis at this rally was larger than at any previous similar occasion.

The Kabul government, at Soviet urging, distributes arms to Pakistani tribesmen ready to cross the tribal territories. Pakistani police sources claim that the Afghan government has given 300,000 Soviet-made Kalashnikov automatic rifles to Pakistani dissidents who might fight the Mujahideen.

The Soviet-Afghan tactics are clear. Unable to control the Mujahideen guerrillas themselves, they are hoping that the Pakistani separatists will do so. Kabul is offering other incentives to bring Pashtuns from Pakistan over to its side. More than 1,000 Pakistanis from NWFP are studying in the Afghan capital, having been offered free education by the Communist government.

The Russians and their Afghan puppets are keenly aware of one of Pakistan's main weaknesses—the 'provincial question'. Apart from the disputed Kashmir region, Pakistan is made up of four provinces—Punjab, Sind, NWFP and Baluchistan, each of which is the home of different ethnic groups. The Punjabis alone make up 60% of the country's population and thus tend to dominate the government, the armed forces, commerce and industry. This places a serious strain on the national social fabric.

The Soviet 'Withdraws' Troops

On 28 July 1986 the Soviet leader Mikhail Gorbachev announced that six Soviet regiments—at most 7,000 troops—would be withdrawn from Afghanistan. In mid-October 1986 the Soviet and DRA gave great publicity to the actual withdrawal. In fact it had minimal military significance and left over 110,000 Soviet troops in Afghanistan.

'Comrade' Najib's claim that the withdrawal was proof that the combined Soviet-Afghan armed forces were being successful had little bearing on the military situation and was nothing more than a conciliatory gesture by the Kremlin timed to coincide with the opening of the Afghan-Pakistan talks in Geneva, under United Nations auspices. The units withdrawn were three air defence regiments, two motor rifle regiments and a tank regiment. Since the Resistance movements have no aircraft the removal of air defence regiments meant nothing. The timing of the withdrawal also coincided with the bi-annual rotation of Soviet forces all over the Soviet bloc.

There can be little doubt that the Soviet Union will announce further reductions in the number of troops in Afghanistan; equally there is little doubt that most of them will be secretly replaced.

Despite their reverses, the Mujahideen were probably more successful during 1986 than in any other year. They inflicted heavy losses on Soviet and DRA forces, particularly on their convoys travelling to and from the Soviet Union. Also, they disrupted the reinforcement of garrisons within the country. In and around Kabul they attacked Soviet and regime installations and they controlled large areas of the countryside.

The new-found ability of the various Resistance leaders to co-ordinate military activities and to attack and capture DRA fortifications was shown by the successful operation against Farkhar in north-eastern Afghanistan. Massoud, leading a mixed group of fighters, caused many casualties, blew up supply dumps and carried off arms and ammunition.

The Mujahideen achievements were all the more militarily impressive because the Soviet leaders' strategy and tactics have become more sophisticated and competent and because the High Command increasingly uses the highly trained, mobile commando units, the *Spetsnaz*.

Ruthless Soviet retaliation campaigns have followed nearly every Mujahideen success. For instance, the Resistance captured three senior Afghan regime officers at Istalef in the Shomali area, north of Kabul. In October 1986 Soviet forces retaliated with heavy bombing which killed many civilians and destroyed crops.

Lieutenant Dubovik's Documents

From time to time valuable documents fall into the Mujahideens' hands and through them the Resistance leadership—and eventually the West—has learnt more about the Soviet army in Afghanistan. During June 1986 Ahmed Shah Massoud came into possession of such papers. In the Khelob Valley in the north-east Massoud attacked a Soviet hill post of about twenty men, commanded by Senior Lieutenant S. Dubovik. All were killed and two Mil Mi-8 Hip transport helicopters were also destroyed.

Massoud, knowing that Soviet reaction to an attack is rapid, quickly ordered his men away from the devastated post. However one guerrilla sprinted to it and snatched up Dubovik's map case just as Soviet helicopter gunships arrived and began firing. From the map case it was found that Dubovik was second-in-command of the Scout/Diversionary Company of an Airborne Attack Regiment—a commando unit. He was carrying colour maps, a list of personnel signal charts, written orders and a diary.

The find was of great military value. It showed the Mujahideen that the Russians and the DRA commanders had good intelligence about rebel positions. The grid chart for encoding signals was even more valuable. The unit roll reveals the ethnic origins of soldiers. In Senior Lieutenant Dubovik's company were Central Asians, Ukrainians and White Russians. Dubovik and his commander, another Senior Lieutenant, were Ukrainians.

An order from the Chief Political Directorate instructed the officers to take action to curb 'irregular non-regulation relationships', which apparently refers to homosexuality. The officers are told greatly to increase soldiers' workloads as a means of overcoming the problem. In addition, physical abuse and humiliation of soldiers by officers was to cease.[7]

Soviet—DRA Tactical Developments

It took the Soviet High Command several years to learn an obvious lesson: an offensive was best launched to coincide with the Resistance's massive spring resupply effort. At this time the guerrillas must necessarily expose themselves in large numbers along well-established trails. By attacking them the Russians and DRA disrupt the Resistance as it tries to recover from the winter and launch its summer operations.

The Soviet-DRA command laid their plans well for their offensive in March 1986. From Kabul, through Gardez and from Ghazni they made three simultaneous attacks, largely with DRA forces and militia, many of whose troops were former resistance men. In close and strong support were airborne troops (VDV), *Spetsnaz* commandos, artillery and helicopters. The DRA troops made up 75% of the task force. Units included the 37th and 38th Commando Brigades, 466 Brigade, 87th Infantry Division, 50th Regiment, 212 Reconnaissance Battalion, 2nd Border Brigade and the Kabul Police Brigade.

In mid-April, by which time the guerrillas were largely disorganised and defensive, the Soviet-DRA forces launched another offensive from Kandahar to break up the resistance concentration north of the city. On this occasion, too, a regiment of élite Soviet troops, *Spetsnaz* and airborne troops stiffened the DRA.

The Russians used fleets of helicopter gunships to strafe Mujahideen positions; foreign observers counted 16 in action at the one time east of Kabul. At times Soviet together with DRA soldiers mounted major campaigns to clear whole areas of rebel fighters. One of the biggest offensives involved two and sometimes three co-ordinated campaigns. For instance, in September 1986 34,000 Soviet and Afghan troops pushed about 1,000 Mujahideen from the Paghman district, north of Kabul. Tanks, Sukhoi-Su-25 Frogfoot fighter-bombers and helicopter gunships were used. Regrouping in the Shomali region, the Mujahideen were attacked by a Soviet-Afghan force of 15,000.

It amounts to the Soviet military commanders manipulating the Resistance into taking an active part in its own destruction. They confront the Resistance leaders with a threat which they cannot ignore and cannot absorb—as with the assault on its most important base in Zhawar. The Resistance leaders must activate all their units in the region, thus exposing them to the enemy. At the same time inadequate co-ordination and lack of sophisticated radio communication make it impossible for the leaders to concentrate the attacks of their groups.

During 1986-87 the Soviet army increased its number of headquarters to improve communication at top level and therefore to achieve more rapid and effective co-ordination.

One aspect of the Soviet propaganda campaign deserves special mention because of its military implications. Several Mujahideen leaders were offered senior positions in the Afghan regular forces; this allowed them to bear arms and to retain control over their local areas. This was a shrewd Soviet-DRA move and some guerrilla leaders accepted the offer because it gave them a degree of control and influence within their own areas which is denied the Mujahideen groups operating from Peshawar.

The Soviet army uses a vast number of booby-traps disguised as innocent objects such as brightly painted toys and cassettes; some are miniature booby-traps, such as pencils. All explode when handled and are designed not so much to kill as to maim and demoralise. The object is to produce casualties so as to discourage civilians from remaining in areas which the Soviet and the regime would like to clear. Many victims of these booby-traps are taken to hospitals in Pakistan.

Chemical Warfare

At the end of 1986 Western diplomatic sources in Kabul reported that the Russians were using chemical weapons. There had been reports of chemical warfare in 1985 but these were unconfirmed. By artillery shell and from aircraft, gas was used against guerrillas at Paghman and, further west, at Chesmilbubul. In one incident five Afghan army soldiers and two officers were accidentally killed by gas meant for the Mujahideen.

On another occasion, also near Paghman, gas canisters were dropped into irrigation shafts and tunnels used by Mujahideen—and civilians—as shelters. People near tunnel entrances were seen to emerge with blue-coloured hands and vomiting; this suggests cyanosis, a symptom of respiratory failure.

Another development, also at the end of 1986, was the appearance of air-delivered anti-personnel mines. The Russians are using them prolifically and the guerrillas, who are handicapped by the lack of suitable mine detectors, have great difficulty in clearing them.

Missiles for Resistance Could Change the War

The increasingly successful use of Stinger and Blowpipe missiles could change the progress of the war. The first use of Stingers in October 1986 was dramatic, with an 80% success rate. The Americans, who train Resistance fighters in the use of missiles at a camp near Islamabad, provide two more missiles for every enemy aircraft brought down. All Soviet jets and helicopters within the supposed four-mile range of a Stinger are vulnerable. Many posts throughout Afghanistan may have to be evacuated. Huge resources will have to be devoted to making air bases secure and preventing the Mujahideen infiltrating to within firing distance.

The greatest effects are likely to be psychological and political. The Russians' unquestioned technological superiority keeps many Afghan leaders on their side, or neutral, because the Resistance is seen as incapable of forcing a Soviet withdrawal. If the Mujahideen can protect territory from bombing raids these leaders may think again. Also, some of the millions of refugees may return to their villages, once again giving support to the Resistance forces.

Soviet Annexation of Wakhan Corridor

Under an agreement, which has never been made public, the Kabul government has permitted the Soviet Union to annex the Wakhan corridor, the thin strategic finger of Afghanistan which reaches east to the Chinese border. This has given the Soviet Union a 288 km, border with Pakistan and has cut off China from Afghanistan. The Chinese, who relinquished their own claims to the area in 1963, have protested strongly about the Soviet annexation. The Russians had been seeking to annex the Wakhan for a century and the Pakistanis say they are unlikely to give it up, even if they withdraw from Afghanistan. Soviet forces in the corridor do not operate under command of the 40th Army HQ, which directs the Afghan war from Termez in Uzbekistan. Wakhan is under the Pamir Military District in Murghab, Tadzhikistan, which is part of the Southern Strategic Theatre at Tashkent.

The army has positioned FROG 3 and SCUD B surface-to-surface missiles in the Wakhan, capable of reaching deep into Pakistan. New weapons being tested in the Wakhan include a high-altitude version of the heavily armoured Hind helicopter. Five strongpoints have been built near passes that lead through the Hindu Kush into Pakistan.

A Chinese source says that 4,000 Soviet troops are in the Wakhan while the Pakistan Institute of Strategic Studies reports the presence of a motor rifle regiment with a strength of 2,300 men, supported by 120 mm mortars and tactical short-range missiles.[8]

Soviet domination of the Pamirs puts the Russians not only astride the Wakhjir Pass to China but within 50 km of the Pakistan/China Karakoram Highway through the Khunjerab Pass. This is a route along which the Chinese can send arms to the Afghan Resistance during the short summer season. It also puts Soviet forces in position to block Mujahideen supply routes by which weapons, ammunition, mortars and rockets can move by mule through western passes from Chitral, Pakistan, into the adjacent Afghan provinces of Kunar and Badakhshan.

Fighting by Sectors: 1986-87[9]

The change in Soviet-Afghan regime military tactics (first noted in **WAR ANNUAL** 1) towards the use of smaller units and mobile helicopter-borne troops, including *Spetsnaz* forces in an attempt to cut off Mujahideen supply lines was confirmed in 1986-87 and seems to have brought some success. But Resistance activity continued at a high-level and the Soviet-DRA forces were unable to seal off the Afghan borders and could not exert lasting control over many rural areas and some towns.

Kabul

Defensive rings of mines and outposts surrounded Kabul in 1984-85 and Kandahar and other towns in 1986-87. Nevertheless, the fighting around Kabul has been generally intense. Rocket attacks by the Resistance reach targets within the city and there are frequent gun battles there. Mujahideen slip through the defensive cordon around the city and open fire on Soviet vehicles. A large car bomb narrowly missed the visiting Soviet First Deputy Prime Minister. The size of the Soviet presence in Kabul early in 1987 was indicated by the 90 minutes it took a Soviet-Afghan regime convoy to pass by; it was followed the next day by the passage of 230 trucks loaded with military supplies.

On 26-27 August 1986 Mujahideen rockets started a fire in the area of the barracks at nearby Kharga which led to a huge explosion at an ammunition dump there and further fires and explosions. Fighting in the Kabul area was particularly intense at Paghman, from which major Resistance attacks are launched on the capital. The town was flattened by bombing and house-to-house searches are common in the surrounding villages, but the Mujahideen remain there. They are said to have overrun five or six Soviet bases of 100 men in the area. Around 4,000 Soviet troops were reported to be engaged in fighting at Paghman from 29 July to 4 August 1986, often supplied by air drops. After setting fire to the town on 5 September, Soviet troops returned to Kabul. A column of Soviet lorries was attacked in Paghman in mid-September, and 40 Soviet troops were captured by the Mujahideen. In their Kabul operations the guerrillas used 122 mm missiles, a heavier weapon than the 107 mm weapons they had used in the past.

West Afghanistan

In Herat, where there was intermittent heavy fighting throughout 1986, the regime claimed to have gained the upper hand. More than 20,000 Soviet-Afghan troops backed by tanks and aircraft hit rebel groups in Herat and the rough country between Herat and the Iranian border, 70 miles away.

However the policy is to allow unarmed columns of refugees to proceed to Iran; for the Soviet planners the greater the number of refugees the better.

North Afghanistan

During 1986 and into 1987 Soviet convoys on the main Salang road connecting Kabul with the Soviet frontier were attacked by the Mujahideen at a number of places. A large fuel convoy was held up at Khenjan (north of Salang) in May and many vehicles were destroyed. Mujahideen attacked Soviet-DRA forces in the Panjshir Valley in April with some success. The Russians bombed the area soon afterwards in retaliation. Soviet-DRA attention switched in May to the town of Shakadora in the Shomali area, and heavy fighting ensued and has continued there. A convoy was intercepted in May. In early July, four helicopters bombarded the town, causing 20 civilian deaths a few days before local elections were due to be held.

Bagram air base, north of Kabul, was attacked by Mujahideen on 4 July. An ammunition dump there blazed for two days afterwards. Charikar, nearer the capital, was the scene of frequent gunfights. Fierce battles were reported there on 25-26 August, after which trucks filled with wounded Soviet-DRA troops were seen returning to Kabul.

South and East Afghanistan

Soviet-DRA forces continued to focus many operations on targets near the Afghan-Pakistani border, such as Resistance transit bases. These forces captured the Mujahideen supply base at Zharwar in Paktia and publicised their 'great victory', but the Mujahideen later returned. Both sides suffered heavy casualties.

Spetsnaz units spearheaded the penetration of Zhawar to ensure that any intelligence material was retrieved and exploited. The haul was valuable, since it included communications systems, documents, reports, correspondence of commanders, Resistance analysis of its own operations, names of commanders and lists of stores and depots. Large quantities of weapons, including ground-to-air missiles, fell into Russian hands. After destroying tunnels and storage sites the Russians evacuated the rubble, leaving behind wide areas of minefields and booby-traps. The Resistance, having no mine-clearing equipment when reoccupying Zhawar, used Afghan army prisoners to clear the minefields by hand. Several were killed or wounded.

In addition to Zhawar, the Soviet-DRA troops destroyed 20 secondary bases and positions and captured more supplies of weapons and ammunition. The loss of quantities of diversified anti-aircraft weapons was a heavy blow to the Resistance.

Rakhim Wardak, a senior Resistance leader, described the Soviet-DRA attack on Zhawar as 'the heaviest since the invasion . . . the air attacks were terrible'. In their advance the Soviet-DRA used massive firepower—tube artillery, multiple-barrelled rocket launchers, tanks, helicopters and other aircraft—to suppress the Resistance, while landing troops by helicopter.

These drenching rocket, shell and bomb attacks are calculated to force the Resistance fighters into open areas which the Russians know as 'hunting zones'. Here they can more readily be shot down by troops landed on local ridges. Most of those fighters who stay behind are destroyed by the incessant air strikes.

One observer[10] believes that the occupation and destruction of the Resistance complexes in Zhawar by the Soviet and Afghan forces could be the turning point in the war, but I disagree with him.

Khost, near the Afghan-Pakistan border, was besieged by the Mujahideen and fighting continued for months. In one month 900 DRA troops were reported to have defected to the Mujahideen. Ghazni was the scene of bitter fighting for much of 1986.

In the important city of Kandahar, DRA and Mujahideen forces periodically ousted one another from control of the town centre and surrounding countryside. Eventually the Russians ringed the city with defensive mines and outposts, but this did not stop Mujahideen activity. Shooting was often heard all day and a curfew was imposed from 1400 hours; the shops shut at noon in case of gunfights. Water, electricity and other supplies are uncertain.

During 1986 American-made Stinger anti-aircraft missiles reached the rebels. They already had the older British Blowpipe and some captured Soviet-made SA-7s but the Stingers made the guerrillas' air defences more formidable. The Russians lost several aircraft, mostly to Stinger missiles; near the Pakistani border nine Soviet and two regime helicopters were shot down in the space of a few weeks.[11]

Refugees

Between a quarter and a third of the country's pre-invasion population has left Afghanistan for neighbouring countries since 1979. Once source claims that the population of Afghanistan late in 1986 was only 7 million, half living in towns and half in rural areas; the 1977 census figure was 15.2 million.[12]

In Pakistan, over 350 refugee camps accommodate whole families, but there are always newcomers who wait, sometimes in large groups, for registration before being admitted. Numerous international agencies help the Pakistan authorities to run and provide services to the camps. The British Government has given about £40 million in aid to Afghan refugees since 1980. The European Community has also provided substantial support.

Gorbachev's Appraisal— 'A Bleeding Wound'

It is known that Mikhail Gorbachev sees Soviet involvement in Afghanistan as an obstacle to improved East-West relations; at the Communist Party Congress in Moscow he described Afghanistan as 'a bleeding wound'. This comment does not indicate an imminent general withdrawal. The Soviet commitment is total and permanent.

By October 1986 the Soviets had suffered 25,000 casualties, including 10,000 killed, since December 1979. They lost 500 aircraft in the same period.[13]

During 1986 and into 1987 the political leadership of the Mujahideen became more cohesive. The formation of *Ittihad-i-Islami* Mujahideen Afghanistan, an alliance of seven major resistance parties, showed that the need for a united resistance was understood. Despite the political and religious differences between them the seven appeared to be co-operating, especially in the military sphere. A majority of the world community, led by the Islamic Conference Organisation, tacitly recognises this 'government in exile'.

As long as the Resistance can maintain some organised communication between Peshawar and the interior of Afghanistan the Russians cannot win the war, but disease and hunger among the rebels might well eventually produce the victory which has eluded them.

Amnesty Alleges Torture

Soviet army officers in Afghanistan are taking part in torture sessions which have been 'widespread and systematic' for six years, according to an Amnesty International report.[14]

Torture in Afghanistan is only one of its concerns, Amnesty reported. Others included extra-judicial executions 'carried out by Soviet troops supported by Afghan military personnel'; the imprisonment of thousands of political prisoners; and the use of the death penalty. More than 100 death sentences were officially reported in a two-year period.

'Some of the victims of extra-judicial executions are armed opponents of the government,' Amnesty noted, 'but many others are apparently non-combatants suspected only of sympathising with armed opposition groups.' Amnesty's evidence was derived from former political prisoners whose accounts have been checked and confirmed by former government officials.

On the involvement of Soviet personnel, Amnesty says that the state security service, KHAD, has Soviet advisers at its main offices and that many of the testimonies given to Amnesty refer to a Soviet presence during torture sessions.

The torture is said to include regular beatings, electric shocks to the body, burning with cigarettes and hair being torn from the scalp. Women are tortured and also made to watch men being tortured. Among those held are former government officials, teachers, business people and students, many of them women.

Amnesty's allegations are supported in a report for the UN Human Rights Commission by Felix Ernacora of Austria. It was submitted to the General Assembly in December 1986.

The Opposing Forces in 1986

Afghan

Army: 35,000: nominally the army has three corps HQ, three armoured divisions, 11 infantry divisions, 11 mechanised infantry formations, mostly brigades; 1 commando brigade of three battalions, and 2 mountain regiments.

The army is composed almost entirely of conscripts except for the officers. With Russian training, the Afghan troops are more efficient than in 1985 and the total number is larger because of stricter draft regulations. However defection to the Resistance is a major problem.

Arms and equipment are entirely of Soviet or East European make. The 500 tanks are used in static positions to shell Mujahideen targets. The most important artillery weapons are the 120 mm and 82 mm mortars; field guns are virtually useless in the mountains.

Air Force: 5,000 men with 125 combat aircraft and 40 helicopter gunships; some of these, while carrying Afghan markings, could well be crewed by Russians. There are 5 helicopter transport squadrons.

Para-military forces: About 30,000 in all, comprising gendarmerie, border police, Afghan Communist Party Guards, village and youth militia and the *Sarandoy*, a Ministry of Interior armed force 6,000 strong. In addition, there are 35,000 members of KHAD, the security police. Many are students and relatively few of the entire force are militarily trained.

Soviet Forces in Afghanistan

Army: 120,000 at the end of 1986; those units withdrawn for propaganda purposes had been replaced. About 12,000 are members of the KGB and MVD. The force comprises 4 headquarters, 1 airborne division, 2 air assault brigades, 3 motor rifle divisions, several artillery brigades with heavy howitzers and mortars, and 1 armoured division.

Air Force: About 250 jet fighters and fighter-bombers and 350 helicopters, of which 150 are troop transports. As the Mujahideen have no aircraft the Soviet fighters are largely a show of strength to impress the Pakistanis.

Resistance

Possibly 150,000 (50,000 less than in 1985). About 30,000 are intermittently active, with perhaps 6,000-7,000 active on any one day. These 'regulars' are backed by what the Resistance calls 'reserves'—100,000 men, many of them refugees living in Pakistan. They are well supplied with personal small arms and in addition possess 76 mm guns, 122 mm howitzers, 107 mm and 122 mm multiple rocket launchers and a variety of mortars up to 82 mm.

The Resistance fighters have rocket-propelled grenades and a number of anti-tank weapons, together with anti-personnel mines. For air defence they are equipped with Blowpipe, Stinger and SA-7 SAM missiles, together with anti-aircraft guns of 12.7 mm, 14.5 mm and 20 mm calibre. Many of the weapons have been captured from the Soviet and Afghan armies.

The Mujahideen have 7 'official' fighting groups and 30 regional 'unofficial' groups, all under different leadership. All the base Headquarters are in Pakistan.

Proving Ground for Soviet Military

It became clear in 1987 that after seven years experience in Afghanistan the Soviet army is putting the lessons it has learned into practice in the Warsaw Pact forces opposing NATO. By mid-1987 more than 400,000 Soviet troops had rotated through Afghanistan, including 33,000 officers. A tour of duty in Afghanistan is regarded as a vital asset in an officer's career.

The appointment in 1986 of Army General Valery Belikov as commander of the Soviet Group of Armies in East Germany reflects Moscow's emphasis on bringing Afghanistan experience into European strategy. This particular Army Group is the spearhead for any surprise attack against the West. General Belikov is believed to be a specialist in deep penetration behind enemy lines, a tactic he developed in Afghanistan.

A significant change resulting from Afghan experience is the decentralisation of the Soviet command structure. Units in the field now have more responsibility over territory they operate in; commanders no longer need to refer every decision to headquarters. Counter-insurgency missions, involving small units of mixed Soviet and Afghan army troops operating in mountainous terrain, have prepared junior officers and platoon commanders to act more independently and take more risks.

Besides general combat experience, Soviet officers and NCOs have gained practical knowledge in counter-insurgency techniques and in co-operating with other branches, particularly air force tactical support. Combined missions of helicopters and fighter bombers against the guerrillas have seasoned the pilots in night operations. The Russians, impressed by the US tactical use of helicopters in the Vietnam War, have adapted many of the same tactics in Afghanistan. A very high percentage of Soviet helicopter pilots have served in Afghanistan, with up to 400 crews there at any one time.

The Afghan experience has led to the Russians placing greater emphasis on night-viewing equipment for infantry and on indirect fire weapons, such as grenade launchers and flamethrowers.

Despite the increasing experience of helicopter crews the guerrillas shot down two of them with British-made Blowpipe anti-aircraft missiles in May 1987. This first successful use of Blowpipes in Afghanistan occurred at Barikot, near the Pakistan border. The guerrillas concerned belong to the Islamic Party of Yunis Khalis, a fundamentalist group. Arms trade sources believe that the missiles may have been supplied to the Afghans via Nigeria.

References

1. Najib's personality is summed up in a British Foreign and Commonwealth Office briefing, October 1986.
2. Najib set out his policies in a speech in Kabul on 1 May 1986.
3. Colonel Matullah was interviewed by Richard Evans of Associated Press in Miram Shah, Pakistan, on 30 October 1986.
4. *Ibid.*
5. Senator Humphrey was writing for the *Washington Times* News Service, 29 June 1986.
6. Kurt Lohbeck, *Middle East Times*, 20 July 1986.
7. The documents were described and illustrated in *Jane's Defence Weekly*, London, 18 October 1986.
8. Report from Director-General, Pakistan Institute of Strategic Studies, Islamabad.
9. Some of this information comes from the Foreign and Commonwealth Office briefing, *op. cit.*
10. Yossef Bodansky, 2 August 1986.
11. From a Soviet Defence Ministry statement in Tass.
12. UNICEF figure.
13. Lieutenant General L. Perroots, director, Pentagon's Defence Intelligence Agency.
14. Afghanistan: Torture of Political Prisoners; Amnesty International, London.
15. Report from Muhammad Nader Shahalemi, president of Islamic Unity of Central Afghanistan, during a visit to the West. Independently verified from Teheran.

Angola Guerrilla (Civil) War

Guerrilla–Civil War in Angola

THE SPREADING STAIN OF CONFLICT

Background Summary

This war began before Angola's independence from Portugal in 1975 and became more violent after it. In the mid-1970s about 13,000 Cuban troops, using Soviet equipment, backed the Popular Liberation Movement of Angola (MPLA). This party formed the government. South Africa supported the National Union for the Total Liberation of Angola (UNITA). Fighters belonging to the South-West African People's Organisation (SWAPO) used southern Angola as a base for their war against South Africa, hence South Africa's involvement. The two superpowers were drawn into the struggle because of Angola's strategic position close to the oil tanker shipping lanes linking the Middle East to Europe and the United States. Throughout the war MPLA forces have held the larger portion of Angola, including the cities; UNITA, led by Dr. Jonas Savimbi, controls the more remote bush areas. UNITA sometimes changes from guerrilla tactics to conventional warfare with sustained attacks on MPLA fortifications.

Savimbi is a brilliant guerrilla leader but he made a serious miscalculation in 1985 when he predicted that the Angolan government's dry season offensive would take place in the country's eastern 'panhandle'. As he expected, during August and into September the fighting was intense there as Soviet T-62 tanks blasted UNITA's infantry. In the middle of this battle Savimbi heard that the government had

attacked on an even larger scale in the south. As the result of a clever enemy feint attack, his strongest units were 350 miles out of position. Savimbi needed a week to move reinforcements south by truck, and in this crisis he played his trump card: he called in South African military help. The result was the battle for Mavinga. Possession of the large airstrip there would give the Angolan government the springboard necessary to crush Savimbi, a southern air base from which fighters and bombers could destroy UNITA bases, including Jamba. Savimbi asked the South Africans to take 2,000 of his troops and put them outside Mavinga and to provide him with mortars, guns and ammunition. To fly these reinforcements and supplies the South African Air Force risked its C-130 Hercules transports but won the battle of Mavinga for Savimbi.

(For full details of the entire war see **WAR ANNUAL** 1.)

Summary of the War in 1985

The government (MPLA) forces' main objective in 1985 was to break UNITA's morale, largely by making the guerrillas believe that the military strength opposing them was invincible. The Angolan armed forces began 1985 with a strength of 45,000, plus 10,500 trained militia. They had nearly 650 tanks and 90 combat aircraft. The Angolan army had become more professional and depended less on Cuban and Soviet support—though this did not mean fewer Cuban and Russian troops in the country.

In August 1985 the MPLA forces failed in a massive attempt to capture Jamba, UNITA's main base. Nevertheless because government troops and their foreign allies had been able to approach Jamba, Savimbi's prestige suffered. The danger to UNITA brought South Africa's commitment to the guerrillas into the open. The Defence Minister stated that South Africa would intervene 'militarily and without limit' to save Savimbi.[1]

Savimbi showed that he was prepared for a long war when he announced in February 1986 that his strategy was to impose an unacceptable burden on the Cubans and Russians. 'When enough Cuban officers are returned home in coffins Castro will face the wrath of his own people,' Savimbi said. He disclosed that China, Arab nations, notably Morocco and Saudi Arabia, and black African countries were helping UNITA.

The War in 1986-87

Early in 1986, in an article in the US journal *Policy Review*,[2] Savimbi set out his operational objectives:

> Our strategy is to raise the costs of the foreign occupation of Angola until the Cubans and Russians can no longer bear the burden. A combination of rising military, financial and political costs will finally drive the imperialist forces from our shores. A central element of this strategy is to deny the colonial forces the revenues that finance their occupation. Today the Cubans and Russians exploit Angola with a rapacity unrivalled by the Portuguese. Soviet fishing fleets have swept our coastline and fish has disappeared from the Angolan diet. Our diamonds, minerals and oil from Cabinda Province are taken in payment for arms and support of Cuban troops. The MPLA pays Castro $1,000 a month for each Cuban soldier in Angola. These mercenaries can afford to stay in our nation only as long as they are paid. So UNITA attacks the diamond mines, sabotages the bridges and destroys the industries that support the Cuban occupation.

The essential difference of the war in 1986-87 period is that Savimbi widened UNITA's sphere of operations. In doing this he was challenging the government's frequently repeated statement that MPLA troops and their Soviet and Cuban allies were restricting UNITA's power of movement. It was true that much of UNITA was operating in the south-east but its activities were hardly restricted. Savimbi's men were operational on the central plateau, the *planalto*. A small group of Western journalists was able to confirm this when they flew into Huambo (in November 1986) as guests of the Luanda government.

Because of guerrilla activity, the rich farms outside Huambo had become a no-man's-land and 200,000 refugees had tripled the city's population. The airport is heavily guarded by anti-aircraft batteries, tanks and Cuban troops. Government spokesmen told the journalists that any attacks by UNITA were 'isolated' actions by bandits and that there was no threat to government control of the *planalto*. The propaganda backfired because the journalists, having eluded their guides and guards, found that government officials ventured into the countryside only in heavily armed convoys. Also, the International Red Cross, despite the need to help starving people, could not safely use the roads and depended on air supply.

From foreign relief workers the journalists also learned that frequent fighting was taking place in the nearby jungle, mostly as the result of UNITA ambushes of government forces.[3] Both sides planted thousands of land mines in abandoned cornfields and most victims were civilians. A Red Cross factory in Huambo makes artificial limbs at the rate of 60 a week but is still failing to keep pace with the highest *per capita* rate of amputees in the world. In the Huambo region 6,000 victims of the war are wearing artificial limbs.

The UN Office for Emergency Operations in Africa, which deals with financial, food, medical and security crises, includes Angola in its list of most severely affected countries and UNICEF reports that Angola has the world's highest child mortality rate.

American Aid: European Criticism

In March 1986 the Pentagon and CIA began shipping sophisticated American weapons, notably Stinger missiles, to Savimbi's guerrillas. In June a delegation of staff members from the Senate Select Committee on Intelligence slipped secretly into Angola to evaluate Savimbi's military organisation. Before they returned to Washington the group met CIA station chiefs in Kinshasa, Zaire, and Pretoria, South Africa.[4]

Savimbi built camouflaged tree-top platforms from which to fire his Stingers at Soviet-built fighters and bombers. In one two-month period UNITA claimed to have shot down 10 aircraft—jets, helicopter gunships and 1 Antonov 22 transport. During 1986 air power became a key factor in the war, as the government forces increasingly relied on Soviet anti-aircraft equipment and more aircraft.

Several leading Western newspapers criticised Savimbi during 1986-87 and none more trenchantly than *The Guardian*, London, in a editorial of 13 April 1986.

> Dr. Savimbi, once a Communist who studied guerrilla warfare in Mao's China, is no moral crusader against Soviet influence but just an African leader, who happens to be a brilliant self-publicist, on the make.

The Daily Telegraph, London, had a rather different view on 2 April 1986:

> Mr. Savimbi is more than a simple anti-Communist standard-bearer. His personal and nationalist credentials are substantially better than those of other leaders in Angola and in much of black Africa. His fatal handicap has been his military, political and economic liaison with South Africa.

In March 1986 UNITA has damaged its credibility by kidnapping 160 civilians at the north-eastern diamond-mining town of Andrada. The hostages were then force-marched across 800 miles of bush, 450 of which were through MPLA territory. It was the fifth mass kidnap which UNITA had carried out as part of its campaign of propaganda and economic sabotage against the Luanda government. The attack on Andrada was more than a hostage-taking operation. The guerrillas seized a large hoard of diamonds and then blew up machinery and vital installations in the town, destroying Angola's diamond industry for several months.

In August 1986 reports of massacres came out of Angola. UNITA guerrillas were said to have attacked the farming village of Camabatela (population 5,800) in north central Angola on 8 February. According to these accounts they destroyed government buildings, blew up water towers and petrol stations and then slaughtered 107 villagers. Later 13 of the 75 wounded died from wounds inflicted by bullets, machetes and knives.

UNITA spokesmen deny that their troops were involved in the massacre. The UNITA story is that about 90 UNITA fighters had driven out the government troops stationed there and during the fighting 40 soldiers and 11 guerrillas were killed. The UNITA force stayed for 3 days. A few days later government troops returned to avenge their defeat, the UNITA leaders said. They tortured civilians to intimidate the population and to get as much information as possible about UNITA.

Cambatela is largely peopled by the Kimbundi tribe, which strongly supports the Luanda government, but it also has many Bakongo people, who do not back Luanda. While either side could have committed the massacre it is difficult to see a motive for UNITA, which has a policy of trying to win the support of the bush people.

UNITA Operations in the North

In opening up a new area of activity 800 miles north of its traditional strongholds, UNITA had the help of the government in neighbouring Zaire. Zaire is supposedly neutral but has the tacit backing of the United States; the Americans see Zaire as another barrier to Soviet-Cuban expansionism.

By putting some of his best units into northern Angola, Savimbi threatened the oilfields in Cabinda province and around its capital city, Soyo. The oilfields make Angola the second largest oil producer in black Africa, with an output of 280,000 barrels a day. The government rushed troops to the region but they could not prevent a UNITA bomb from destroying Soyo airport's terminal building on 28 October 1986. The intensified guerrilla activity resulted in more Cuban forces being sent to Cabinda.

The Angolan army Chief-of-Staff, Colonel Antonio dos Santos Franca, claimed that the government troops killed 230 UNITA guerrillas in the northern sector during 1986. They were members of hit-and-run raiding parties, he said, and no major military activity was likely. However, UNITA's hit-and-run raids stretched the length of the eastern part of the country, from Zaire to Namibia, and forced the government troops to move only in large numbers. During 1986 UNITA's fighters had victories at the battles of Kangamba, Kuete, Munhango and Mazombo.

A UNITA assault team attacked 150 Angolan soldiers guarding a major dam at Gove on 14 November killed 12 of them and then damaged the dam with explosive charges. Foreign relief workers said that 17 civilians were killed. UNITA may have had casualties but left no wounded behind.

On 16 November a UNITA commando unit penetrated the defences of Vilinga to inflict great damage on the oil installations which supply the city of Huambo. Following this raid the MPLA news agency, ANGOP, published a report that South African troops had not only taken part but had led the operation. This brought a furious denial by UNITA's Chief-of-Staff, General Demostenes Amos Chilingutila,

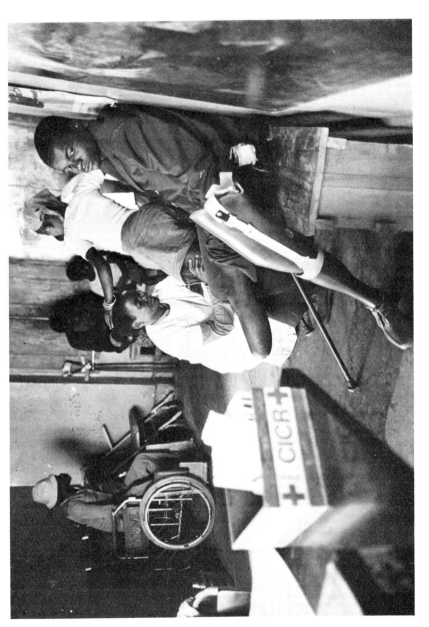

In Angola many wounds are caused by land-mines and booby traps. UNITA runs a factory making artificial limbs for soldiers and civilians (Courtesy Marcus Savambo.)

Soviet-made tanks and other armour captured by UNITA troops from Cuban forces in Angola. Using a regular army structure, UNITA fights a conventional war against the Angolan Army and its Cuban allies. (Courtesy Marcus Savambo.)

A battalion of UNITA infantry on parade at their main base at Jamba. That rebel troops could parade in this way is an indication of their confidence in their intelligence and defence systems. (Courtesy Marcus Savambo.)

Jonas Savimbi, leader of UNITA in Angola, with one of his senior staff officers. He is holding a military trophy. The conventional uniforms are an indication of UNITA's largely regular army. While guerrilla-harrying activities take place, the war in Angola is mainly fought on conventional lines.

who described ANGOP's report as a 'disinformation smoke-screen intended to confuse international public opinion about MPLA's military losses'.

UNITA certainly did not need South African help; its officers have had infinitely more experience than the South Africans.

By late 1986 UNITA military activities were so frequent and well organised that the Chief-of-Staff, from his office in Jamba, issued almost daily communiqués in the manner of a regular army at war. For instance, on 22 November 1986 he published communiqué No. 87/86:[5]

> **Zaire Province**—On 18 November, our forces attacked a motorised military convoy from Luanda to Banza-Congo carrying military supplies to units in Zaire province. The attack resulted in the destruction of 28 vehicles and the death of 16 MPLA troops in the incident. Our forces recovered a large quantity of arms.
>
> **Benguela Province**—On the 19 November, our forces attacked a military convoy moving from Benguela to Huambo, 12 km from Kaimbambo; 7 vehicles were destroyed and 19 MPLA troops died in the incident. Our forces recovered a large quantity of arms.
>
> **Moxico Province**—On the 18 November, our forces in the area of Simoje, twice attacked the MPLA's 30th Brigade in its attempt to supply the motorized 1st Brigade. The convoy lost 20 of its troops, 14 wounded and 14 vehicles that were destroyed in the action.
>
> During the above period, the balance of the operations is as follows:
>
> 136 MPLA troops killed
> 31 MPLA troops wounded
> 9 MPLA troops captured
> 87 MPLA troops joined our ranks
> 43 Vehicles destroyed
> 41 Weapons captured
> 78 Bombs captured

The struggle shall triumph;
United we shall win.
JAMBA, ANGOLA, 22 November 1986
The Chief of Staff
Demostenes Amos Chilingutila
–General–

Communique No. 89/86 was issued on 29 November, 1986.

> 1. In the continuation of our counter-offensive attacks, our Armed Forces carried out several attacks throughout the country, including the following:
> On the 25 November, our forces destroyed a supply convoy moving from Benguela to Huambo in the area between Babaeira and Quinjenje. The convoy was made up of 50 vehicles including heavy trucks and personnel carriers. After the attack, 30 vehicles were burnt and the rest were rendered useless including 3 BTR-60 armoured cars of the escort.
>
> 2. On the same day, 25 November, another convoy, this time of fuel supplies,

moving from Luanda to Moxico province, was ambushed and destroyed in the area between Ndalatando (formerly Salazar) and Malanga. The attack resulted in the burning of 80,000 litres of fuel.

3. On the 28 November, our forces attacked the township of Beca-Monteiro in Zaire province, which later fell to our hands after 6 hours of battle. The MPLA lost 35 men and our force captured many soldiers and a large quantity of bombs and 113 weapons. The population of the township, which was about 2,000, was freed from the yoke of slavery. During the same period our forces suffered 6 dead and 27 wounded.

The Angolan Government Press office confirmed that actions had taken place on the dates mentioned in the UNITA communiqués. It is impossible to verify the statistics but the degree of alarm in all Angolan cities indicates that UNITA activities are frequent and successful.

As one way of adding to his war chest Savimbi exports and sells thousands of tons of timber to a South African trading company. The valuable teak and other tropical hardwoods are felled by UNITA soldiers, who sometimes work under South African supervision. The wood is then floated down the Cuando river out of southern Angola to an assembly point in the Caprivi Strip, part of Namibia.

Organization[6]

The strike arm of UNITA is called Armed Forces for the Liberation of Angola (FALA). FALA's headquarters claim that it has a 'regular' army of 26,000 and a guerrilla force of 34,000. The regulars fight conventional operations on the borders of the liberated areas. They are organised in battalions of 900 to 1,500 men, 'mobile battalions' of 350-450 men and 'special forces' of 25-45. While the regulars have the most important tactical task, the guerrillas operate strategically—that is, they must keep up pressure against the enemy throughout Angola as well as win popular support. Nevertheless, they are formally organised into two types of unit—'compact columns' and 'independent columns'. The independent units prepare the ground for the compact ones. They build up a network of sympathisers, spread propaganda, intimidate when necessary and thus create the environment in which their comrades of the compact columns can operate.

Training

The basic three months' training is given mostly in Portuguese and sometimes by Portuguese mercenary instructors. Political indoctrination is part of the training. Recruits who impress their instructors may be marked down for specialist training in anti-aircraft warfare or demolitions. Their camps are set out in the manner of any Angolan village and are difficult to detect from the air, but they are as well organized as any Western army 'school'. The largest are in the Jamba area.

Weapons

Most versions of the AK-47 (Kalashnikov) are used—AKM and Hungarian AMD-65, Rumanian AKM and Chinese type 56. Many types of light machine-guns are used, including the Heckler and Koch HK21 and HK 21A1. The most common heavy machine-gun is the 12.7 mm DSh K38. The 40 mm grenade-launcher is standard equipment in the regular and guerrilla forces. That UNITA is not merely a guerrilla force is best shown by its artillery inventory. It includes 122 mm D-30 howitzers, 76 mm and 57 mm guns, 75 mm and 82 mm recoilless rifles, 122 mm and Grad surface-to-surface missiles, Sam-7 surface-to-air missiles and several types of double-barrelled and triple-barrelled anti-aircraft guns, believed to be Hispano-Suize HSS-804 type. So far not used in action are captured T-34 tanks, BRDM and other armoured personnel carriers.

Logistics

More than 6,000 men are believed to be employed in UNITA's supply system. Transport, much of which is captured, includes 80 Toyotas, 200 Mercedes trucks, 110 Unimog, 50 Russian Ural trucks, as well as Polish, East German and Soviet jeeps. The number of Land-Rovers, used by senior officers, is unknown. Supply convoys leave from Jamba almost daily for UNITA's distant posts. The monthly fuel consumption is reported to be 50,000 litres of petrol and 600,000 litres of diesel, virtually all of it from South Africa.

MPLA Forces[7]

For better control, the Angolan High Command has divided Angola into 10 military regions, all of which have some Cuban presence. Total strength of the MPLA military structure is 85,000, nearly all of the men being conscripts.

The Cuban Army has 15 regiments in Angola; a regiment at full strength has 2,000 men, a battalion 665 and a company 220. However, not all units are at full strength and the total number of troops is between 25,000 and 27,000 supported by 12,500 civilian workers. There are 1,600 Russians, all highly trained specialists, instructors and advisers. In close co-operation are 3,500 East Germans who control communications and railways and are much involved in Intelligence. About 4,000 Portuguese are under arms but are more under Cuban than Angolan command. SWAPO strength in Angola is 5,000 and 1,000 members of the African National Congress (ANC) are being trained in Angola.

South African Involvement

South African forces, notably the 32nd 'Buffalo' Battalion backed by artillery, attacked Angolan forces and shelled Cuito Cuanavale in Cuando Cubango province early in August 1986. Cuito Cuanavale is a strategic jumping-off point for Angolan government troop operations. Angola claimed that 40 South Africans were killed and four captured. A force of 3,000 UNITA and South African troops remains in a defensive position north-west of Mavinga to protect the approach to Savimbi's headquarters.

On 5 June 1986 a seaborne South African force attacked three Russian ships in the southern Angolan harbour of Namibe, sinking one of them. By attacking Russian ships the South Africans took a calculated risk. The Russians said that the ships were carrying food and threatened retribution, but if they were to step up their activities in Angola they would merely stiffen the Americans' resolve to keep Savimbi fighting.

The irony is that by keeping Savimbi militarily supplied the Americans are helping him to maintain his attacks on US-operated oil facilities in Cabinda province. UNITA and South African raiders have repeatedly tried to sabotage these installations. If successful, they would cripple Angola's economy. A crack Cuban unit is stationed there to defend the installations; it is another bizarre irony of the war that Cuban troops are defending American interests.

The South Africans justify their many incursions into Angola by asserting that the MPLA provides bases for SWAPO guerrillas. This is true but it is sometimes difficult to see the validity of some South African attacks, as on the Cabinda oil depots.

Propaganda War[8]

Both sides in the Angola war use radio commentaries as their main vehicle of propaganda. UNITA broadcasts a programme in Portuguese called 'Voice of the Resistance of the Black Cockerel'. The MPLA presents its point of view through speeches, often by the President, José Eduardo dos Santos, broadcast in Portuguese by Luanda domestic radio. Both are monitored by the BBC.

UNITA Broadcast

Extracts from a BBC-monitored commentary entitled 'Obscure tactics in a situation that is favourable to UNITA', 0330 GMT, 9 November 1986.

Undoubtedly the situation being experienced by UNITA both at home and abroad is extremely favourable. Militarily we have been able to stabilise the situation following the mighty attempt to annihilate UNITA by MPLA hordes under the leadership of Soviet experts. Although there are still large scale operations being launched against UNITA's armed forces and liberated areas, the dimension of last year's actions against us was not repeated this year. . . . Politically and militarily, UNITA has never been stronger. . . . The facts demonstrate that our enemies—the Soviets and Cubans and their associates—are in serious shape and are likely to resort to desperate actions to intimidate men of goodwill. Our immediate attention should be centred on the visit by Comrade Chairman Dr. Savimbi to Europe. We know that it will certainly mean yet another victory for UNITA and the Angolans who seek an end to the war in Angola. . . . The initiative is ours, diplomatically, politically and militarily. Now is the time to close ranks within Angola and among Angolans around the ideal of resistance and behind the indisputable leader, General Savimbi. The strengthening of our co-operation has become a dominant factor in the view of our friends in Africa and throughout the world. The enemy will yield, but the combat will be relentless for some time to come. . . .

MPLA Broadcast

Extracts from a speech by President dos Santos in Malanje to mark the 11th anniversary of national independence, 1200 GMT, 12 November, 1986.

> Our experience of struggle has demonstrated that our strength for the defence of independence lies in the national unity of all true patriots. The MPLA has wisely carried out this historical task by bringing together all Angolan citizens regardless of race, tribe, religion or political conviction, into a broad fighting movement. . . . However, the Portuguese colonialists and their allies were able to organise groups of Angolan traitors . . . some of these groups continue to receive massive assistance from outside and create enormous difficulties for our people. . . . They claim that they are fighting for independence and liberty against so-called Soviet-Cuban colonialism, while everybody knows that there is no true liberation struggle in the world that does not have the direct or indirect support of the USSR and Cuba. . . . The ringleader of the UNITA puppets has made several promises to his allies. Now he finds himself incapable of fulfilling them. His plans have failed in all areas and his survival is thanks only to the protection and direct intervention of the South African army in the south-west of Cuando Cubango. . . . It is no secret that a number of UNITA elements, exhausted and tired of suffering in the bush, surrendered to our armed forces. . . . They were treated humanely as will be all those who, deceived by their ringleaders, now regret their actions and present themselves to our authorities. . . .

The propaganda from both sides is generally at this rhetorical, proclamatory level; it is self-congratulatory and it denounces the enemy. A study of the language used shows neither finesse nor subtlety. Apparently the foreign backers of the two sides have had little influence in improving the presentation of information and none at all on propaganda. Savimbi has a 30ft-high reproduction of a photograph showing him with President Reagan, made on a hand-painted banner for use in political rallies.

In January 1987 the Angolan government scored a significant propaganda victory by winning to its cause a former prominent enemy. He is Daniel Chipenda, who was one of the leaders of the pro-American National Front for the Liberation of Angola (FNLA). This was the most implacably anti-Communist rebel organisation and closely supported Savimbi's UNITA. It lost some of its strength when Chipenda left to live in exile in Portugal in 1979. He has great publicity value for the government because he is from the Ovimbundo tribe, from which UNITA draws its strongest support.

UNITA's case has impressed the US organisation, 'Black Americans For a Free Angola'. It continually calls on the US government and Western Europe to support Savimbi 'before his resistance fighters are swallowed up by Russian-backed forces'.

President José dos Santos and his government are desperately anxious to be on good terms with the US and to supplant Savimbi and UNITA. The United States is alone among the major Western powers in refusing to recognise the avowedly Marxist-Leninist government. Most European governments believe that Angola would return to stability if all foreign forces moved out. Some Portuguese politicians with much experience of Angola believe that partitioning the country between MPLA and UNITA is the only alternative to decades of ruinous war.

American support is vital to *both* sides in the war. The United States is Angola's biggest trading partner and more than 50% of Angolan oil—which accounts for up to 90% of the country's foreign exchange—is exported to the US.

In 1987 the Angolan war was at a stalemate. The Luanda MPLA government could not be overthrown with the Soviet leadership so deeply committed to its preservation. Savimbi could not be beaten while the United States and South Africa were determined to keep UNITA in the field. In terms of territory held the war was also stalemated. Angola is two and a half times the size of France. Of this huge area Savimbi controlled, in 1987, an area twice the size of England. In such an area the war could go on for years—and probably will.

However, in mid-1987 Jonas Savimbi offered to allow the reopening of the Benguela railway in what he described as an attempt to end the war. In a statement issued through his Washington office, Savimbi said that he would permit the railway to function provided that the government did not use it for military purposes.

Such a reopening would help Zambia, Zaire and Zimbabwe, which have been increasingly relying on South Africa as a transit point for their exports. This reliance has prevented southern African nations from imposing economic sanctions on Pretoria in a bid to push South Africa towards ending its system of racial segregation.

Almost immediately after Savimbi's offer over the railway it became known that Soviet-supplied heavy equipment was pouring into Luanda. In an interview, the Soviet ambassador to Angola, Arnold Kalinin, said that policy decisions taken at the last Soviet Communist Party Congress 'could not be interpreted as moves towards disengagement in Angola so long as the US continues to give military backing to UNITA'. He said that by giving this military aid 'the US is taking its final stand in southern Africa'.

The ambassador's comments are taken to mean that Angola will also be the scene of the Soviet's last-ditch stand in southern Africa, and it will not be a situation like that in Afghanistan, where the Russians went through the motions of disengagement.

If Angola seems indissolubly linked to the Soviet Union and dependent on its military support, it is the result of several factors. They are: the US decision to increase the stakes by backing UNITA; the government's rejection of initiatives towards a negotiated solution; the Soviet Union's global strategy in which Angola is a major factor; the failure of arguments in Angolan ruling circles, particularly the air force, that Angola should look both to East and West for aid.

Soviet policy in Angola obviously has as much to do with the Soviet's global strategy as it has to do with Angola itself.

References

1. South African government statement.
2. *Policy Review*, January 1986.
3. *Newsweek*, December 1986; and other press sources.
4. US State Department briefing.
5. UNITA war communiqués distributed to reporters in Jamba.
6. This information comes from a Portuguese military source.
7. Diplomatic sources in Luanda.
8. Largely from BBC Monitoring Service; dates given in text.

Bangladesh Guerrilla War

MUSLIMS VERSUS BUDDHISTS

Background Summary

With the founding of Bangladesh in 1971 the Chakmas people of the Chittagong Hill Tracts came under attack by the Bangladeshi Army. The Chakmas, a Buddhist people without a martial tradition, were to be driven out of the Hill Tracts, an area of 13,000 sq. km. to make way for large numbers of Muslim Bengalis.

After brutal harassment and massacre, the Chakmas formed a self-defence force, the Shanti Bahini guerrillas. Armed by India and the Soviet Union, the Shanti Bahinis became a proficient and ruthless fighting 'army'. Its men raided Bengali settlements and ambushed Bangladeshi army units. In 1984 the Bangladeshi high command sent the crack 24th Division, the 'Bengal Tigers', into the Hill Tracts and its commander, Major General Noor Uddin Khan, was given a free hand to find a 'permanent solution to the Hill Tracts problem'. (*For details of the entire war see* **WAR ANNUAL** 1.)

Summary of the War in 1985

According to Survival International, London, more than 185,000 Chakmas had died in a campaign of genocide, as Bengali Muslims spread throughout the Tracts. Nevertheless, Bangladeshi soldiers were also being killed. The 6,000 Shanti Bahinis, indirectly helped by some dissident Indian tribes, were fighting 125,000 troops, police and para-military units. Unable to defeat the guerrillas, the government's forces destroyed villages which sheltered them and murdered their inhabitants.

The War in 1986-87

During this period the Bangladeshi troops were given special training in jungle warfare against guerrillas. Selected men were formed into 'independent companies' of the type which the Australian Army used in jungle campaigns in 1941-45. Self-contained and capable of operating for weeks at a time without re-supply, these companies sought to trap the Shanti Bahinis in their jungle hideouts. They have not been spectacularly successful, largely because the guerrillas operate in very small groups.

The army, still commanded in the Hill Tracts by General Uddin Khan, adopted a ruthless form of psychological warfare. The General told the Chakmas they could stay if they converted to Islam; he knew that most of the Buddhists would not do this and anticipated that many would become refugees. Tens of thousands did so and fled into India. The army also embarked on a deliberate campaign of rape to

35

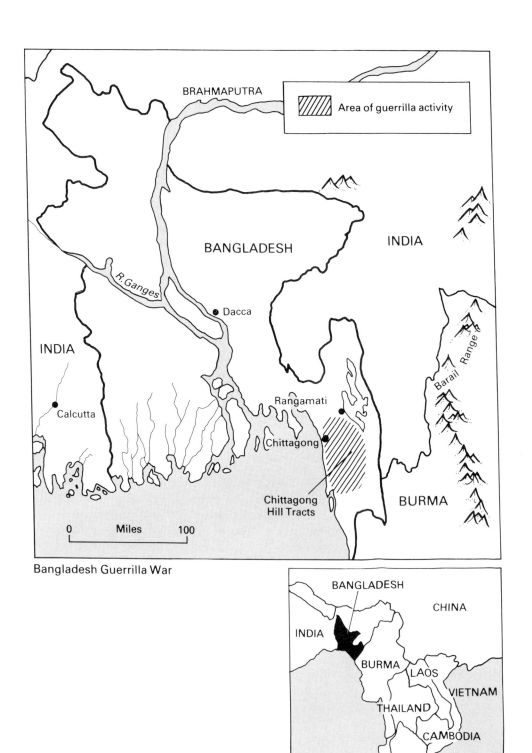

Bangladesh Guerrilla War

...es and thus free their land for the Muslim settlers. Many
...s nave been forcibly married to Bangladeshi Muslim soldiers.

In September 1986 the Shanti Bahini guerrillas proved that they were still not cowed. They raided a Bangladeshi Army camp at Ajodhyapur, near the Indian border. According to Bangladeshi sources, the attack was made from bases in India but the Indian authorities deny this. The guerrillas also attacked a major military outpost at Tabalshari. These actions are unusual for the Shanti Bahini, who had previously concentrated on attacking enemy troops in the jungle and on small posts.

The guerrillas come from at least 32 tribes but they exhibit a remarkable degree of co-operation. The Bangladeshi officers are impressed by the speed with which communication takes place from tribe to tribe. A large part of the guerrillas' foreign supply has been choked off but they capture enough army arms and equipment to keep going.

Survival International has appealed to the Indian Prime Minister, Rajiv Gandhi, to allow Chakma refugees to stay in India. The organisation believes that Indian officials try to send back the refugees while allowing no information to reach the outside world.

In 1987 there were reports, for the first time, that foreign military 'advisers' had arrived in the Hill Tracts. Their nationality could not be confirmed but they were believed to be Indian.

BOLIVIA

SOUTH
AMERICA

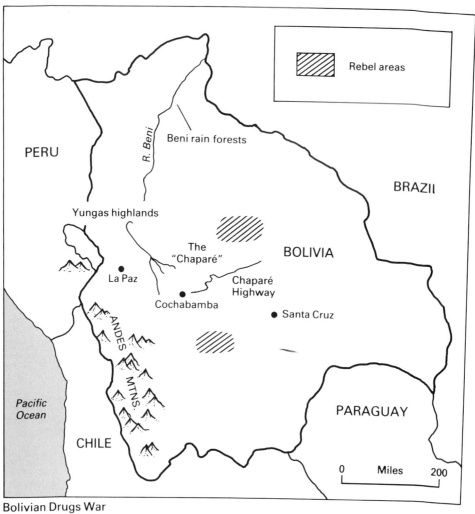

Rebel areas

PERU

R. Beni

Beni rain forests

BRAZIL

Yungas highlands

The
"Chaparé"

BOLIVIA

La Paz

Chaparé
Highway

Cochabamba

● Santa Cruz

ANDES MTNS.

Pacific
Ocean

PARAGUAY

CHILE

0   Miles   200

Bolivian Drugs War

drive out other families and thus free their land for the Muslim settlers. Many Chakma girls have been forcibly married to Bangladeshi Muslim soldiers.

In September 1986 the Shanti Bahini guerrillas proved that they were still not cowed. They raided a Bangladeshi Army camp at Ajodhyapur, near the Indian border. According to Bangladeshi sources, the attack was made from bases in India but the Indian authorities deny this. The guerrillas also attacked a major military outpost at Tabalshari. These actions are unusual for the Shanti Bahini, who had previously concentrated on attacking enemy troops in the jungle and on small posts.

The guerrillas come from at least 32 tribes but they exhibit a remarkable degree of co-operation. The Bangladeshi officers are impressed by the speed with which communication takes place from tribe to tribe. A large part of the guerrillas' foreign supply has been choked off but they capture enough army arms and equipment to keep going.

Survival International has appealed to the Indian Prime Minister, Rajiv Gandhi, to allow Chakma refugees to stay in India. The organisation believes that Indian officials try to send back the refugees while allowing no information to reach the outside world.

In 1987 there were reports, for the first time, that foreign military 'advisers' had arrived in the Hill Tracts. Their nationality could not be confirmed but they were believed to be Indian.

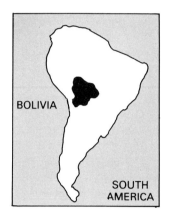

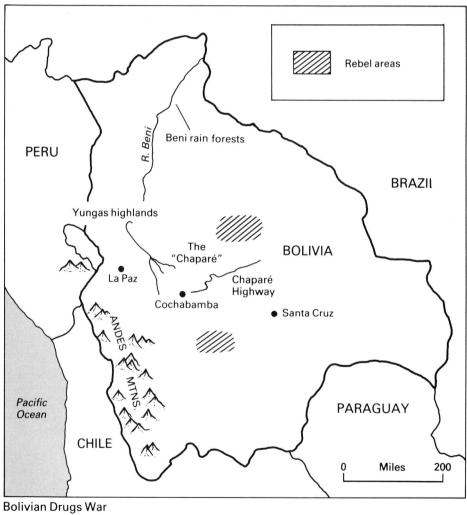

Bolivian Drugs War

Bolivian Drugs War

In July 1986 American troops were involved in a minor war over a major problem—the narcotics trade in Bolivia. Under conditions of strict secrecy, an American C-54 transport landed at the city of Santa Cruz and unloaded six Black Hawk military helicopters armed with .30 mm machine-guns.

About 160 American military personnel accompanied the aircraft but according to a White House spokesman none were combat troops other than the gunners on the helicopters. The others were described as 'various types of support forces'.[1]

Bolivia's President, Victor Paz Estenssoro, had asked for American help in dealing with the war being fought against the drug barons. Drugs, mostly cocaine, are produced with impunity by at least 25 organisations, each with its militia. The President said that his armed forces did not have the ability to transport anti-narcotics police to several places simultaneously and to defend them against attack. In fact, the Bolivian Air Force has a special operations group equipped with nine Hughes 500 combat helicopters. The real reason for the request for American military help was that senior Bolivian military officers were believed to be in partnership with the drug traffickers.

To obviate the inevitable criticism of American troops in a Latin American country, the operation was co-ordinated over a period of months by the White House, the State Department and President Estenssoro's most trusted aides.

The first 'co-operative raid' was carried out on 18 July. The Bolivian Information Minister went to great lengths to describe the American role as 'technical and logistical'.[2] It is known, however, that Black Hawk gunners did open fire on ground targets. Two more raids were made on 19 July.

In a sense the Bolivians were forced to ask for American military help because of their own inability to deal with the drugs problem and because US$7 million of American aid had been withheld to force the administration to take action against the most notorious traffickers.

The government already had a commando-type unit known as the 'Leopard Strike Force'. The Leopards had raided many jungle huts where the coca leaf is converted to paste. In these attacks men on both sides had been killed, notably in the Chaparé region which grows one quarter of the world's coca leaf.

Bolivia is the second poorest nation in the Western Hemisphere, after Haiti. Since 1983 cocaine has been the nation's leading export, bringing in US$500 million legally and US$600 million illegally.[3]

The US-Bolivian military operation was not as successful as it might have been because, despite the secrecy at the American end, the narcotics chiefs in Bolivia had several days' warning. In tactical terms the US operation is insignificant. As a strategical precedent it is important because it seems to imply that the United States will send troops, by local invitation, to take part in operations unrelated to conventional defence.

References

1.　Edward P. Djerejian, White House spokesman.
2.　Edgar Bernel, Economic Attache, Bolivian Embassy, Washington.
3.　Herman Antelo, Bolivian Minister for Information.

Burma Guerrilla War

CONFLICT AS A WAY OF LIFE

Background Summary

The war between the Burmese Army and the Karen people has been in progress since 1949. The Karen National Liberation Army (KNLA) of 4,500 is fighting for an independent homeland for the 4 million Karens. Loosely linked with KNLA are guerrillas from the Kachins, Shans, Arakanese, Mons, Kerreni and other tribes. Opposing them is an immensely larger Burmese regular army. For decades, the main battlefield has been the vast Irrawaddy Delta.

(*For full details of the entire conflict see* **WAR ANNUAL** 1.)

Summary of the War in 1985

Continually frustrated in its attempts to trap and wipe out the guerrillas, the Army High Command decided on a strategy of crushing one ethnic group after another, beginning with one of the weakest, the Kerreni people. Simultaneously, well-trained army officers were sent on lecture tours in the Delta villages to explain the merits of the Burmese Socialist Party and the 'destructive evil' of the Karen leaders. This propaganda warfare campaign was abortive as troops escorting the lecturers generally looted every village they visited and thus antagonised the inhabitants. General By Mya, commander of the KNLA, as well as president of the National Democratic Front alliance, retaliated against the government's peace offensive by attacking army posts in areas where the KNLA had never before operated.

The War in 1986-87

Taking advantage of the government forces' preoccupation with the Karens and others in the south, the armed forces of the anti-government Burmese Communist Party (BCP) went on the offensive in the north. The BCP had held fortress-like positions at Hsi Hsi Wan and Ta Pang and the town of Kyuhkok (also known as Pangsai) in the north-east near the China-Burma border. The area had been in BCP hands since 1970, and under the terms of a truce the government forces had not attacked.

In the latter half of 1986 the BCP, having made an alliance with rebel ethnic groups, attacked and overwhelmed government posts in an effort to widen the area of territory it held. The rebels were initially successful but the government sent in two light infantry divisions brought from the Delta. These men had been fighting at sea level; now, in the north-east, they were in conflict at an altitude of 1,200 metres in thick jungle. However, they killed 591 BCP fighters in their first counter-

Burma Guerrilla War

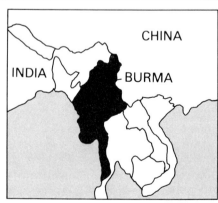

offensive, for a loss of 175 government troops. After a sustained campaign of two months the army regained all the territory held by BCP before the fighting began. The triumph was more of a consolation prize than a genuine victory for the government because the greater part of the BCP force of 20,000 evaded capture.

In the south the military position has deteriorated dramatically for the government because the rebels have become better organised, even if more fragmented. There are now 12 separate rebel fighting forces, the principal one still being the KNLA. The others are: Kachin Independence Army, 5,000; Kerreni Army, 600; Kawthoolei Muslim Liberation Front, (KMLF), 3,800; Kayan New Land Party, 250; Mons State Army, possibly 1,000; Palaung State Liberation Army, 600; Pa-O National Army, 500; Shan State Army, 3,600; Shan United Army, possibly 4,000; Shan United Revolutionary Army, 1,250; Wa National Army, 300.

Apart from the KNLA, the group which most worries the government and its army chiefs is the KMLF, which during 1986 expanded itself by taking over two smaller guerrilla groups, the Ommat Liberation Front and the Rohingya Patriotic Front. It is also closely linked with the KNLA. Apart from the KNLA, the KMLF is the best armed group. Because it is a Muslim organisation it has been able to get weapons and money from several Islamic states. The only two definitely identified are Libya and Pakistan; Saudi Arabia and Kuwait are suspected suppliers and financial backers.

Each of the many 'armies' is fighting for a separate state. If the government were to grant all demands the republic of Burma would cease to exist. The Burmese Army objective of picking off one guerrilla group after another did not work in 1986 because of counter-tactics evolved by General By Mya, one of the world's shrewdest guerrilla commanders of the past 50 years. By Mya induced a few of the smaller groups to act as decoys and position themselves in such a way as to invite attack by the army. He then ambushed the attackers with his well-trained and highly disciplined KNLA fighters.

In 1987 the Burmese Army became more successful and on 14 February attacked Klerdy, a stronghold of the KNLA and pushed about 1,000 Karen civilians across the Thailand border 6 miles away. Two days later it took the town of Huey Pong Lao from the Kayan rebels. An army attack on the Shan United Army's mountain camp at Doi Lanh was repulsed.

The Army's Strength

Burma has a population of nearly 41 million so the total armed forces of 187,000 does not appear excessive. There is a People's Militia of 35,000 and People's Police Force of 38,500. The army itself, at 170,000, did not increase in size during 1986-87 but the air force (9,000 men) and the navy (8,000) did. This was largely because the government is using more helicopters and river patrol boats in almost desperate efforts to discover the guerrillas' movements.

A significant change has taken place within the army; 25 of the 91 infantry battalions have been reconstituted as 'independent' battalions. On active service against guerrillas, the commanding officer of each of these battalions is permitted to make all decisions without reference to higher authority. In difficult country this independence is designed to give him greater flexibility and incisiveness. On a few occasions this appears to have worked and the army has had minor victories. It is, in fact, an army of high quality and has no conscripts.

The army's equipment, other than its 80 120 mm mortars, 120 76 mm and 80 105 mm howitzers, is of little use in jungle fighting. The 24 Comet tanks and 65 armoured fighting vehicles are rarely used in combat though the latter are of some use in supplying outlying posts.

For the High Command there is no obvious solution to defeating the guerrillas but a well-trained marine corps operating from gunboats and patrol craft could be used to drive guerrilla units into army nets.

In 1987 the government embarked on an all-out campaign to capture or kill General By Mya. Immense rewards are on offer to individuals and to entire communities. Rapid promotion is promised to any soldier who can account for By Mya. The guerrilla leader is astonishingly elusive but he is not popular with some of the other guerrilla chiefs and betrayal might well achieve what force of arms has failed to do. In the meantime the nation is US$4 billion in foreign debt, largely because of the unceasing conflict.

Attitude of China and Thailand

The rebels no longer enjoy the foreign support they had when China openly backed the Communist rebels and Thailand condoned the ethnic insurgencies along its border. Both these neighbours of Burma say that they are no longer helping the rebels. The Communists may have been getting help from Vietnam and Laos; Burmese troops discovered foreign bodies and equipment at Kyuhkok.

Narcotics Trade Involvement

Some rebel groups make so much money from the opium trade that they need little foreign support. Khun Sa, leader of the Shan United Army, made a profit of US$8 million in 1986. Burma received international aid—including US$5.5 million from the United States in 1986—to help it fight the drugs traffic. Poppy fields in Shan have been sprayed with an American herbicide similar to the 'Agent Orange' used in Vietnam.

Central America

(For particular wars see sections on El Salvador, Guatemala and Nicaragua)

The instability which plagues Central America is caused by long-standing social and economic problems, injustices and resentments. Until recently they were aggravated by the lack of social justice and opportunities for the expression of views. Outside forces with little interest in either democracy or economic and social development exploited these conditions. In the 1960s and 1970s Costa Rica was the only stable democracy. Nicaragua, Honduras, El Salvador and Guatemala were ruled by oppressive authoritarian regimes. Guerrillas were active in El Salvador and Guatemala.

In 1977-79 tension increased and became open warfare in Nicaragua when the Sandanistas overthrew the Somoza regime. In El Salvador the left-wing Faribunda Marti Liberation Front (or FMLN) guerrillas became stronger. In 1979 the Nicaraguan Sandinistas supported the FMLN but were themselves opposed by the Contras—Nicaraguans who opposed the Sandinistas. The United States supported the Contras. After 1980, tension increased still further when the Soviet bloc strongly backed the Nicaraguan regime and built up its armed forces.

With the threat of general war hanging over the whole of Central America and the danger that it might bring in Latin American countries as well as the super-powers, neighbouring nations became alarmed. In 1981 various governments proposed a regional settlement and in January 1983 the Foreign Ministers of Colombia, Mexico, Panama and Venezuela met on the Panamanian island of Contadora to discuss what might be done. The island gave its name to the Contadora Process, now known simply as Contadora.

Contadora attracted much international support and most nations regard it as the best means of negotiating a comprehensive settlement among the Central American states. Contadora put forward 21 objectives, which were accepted by all parties in September 1983. The process would, the Contadora planners hoped, bring an end to cross-border subversion, to the arms race and to foreign military bases and advisers. The traffic in arms would cease, full pluralist democracy would be established and human rights—so long ignored—would be respected.

The movement gathered momentum in August 1985 when the Foreign Ministers of Argentina, Brazil, Peru and Uruguay formed a Contadora Support Group. By 1987 the most energetic efforts by the Contadora countries had not brought about a binding agreement but they had reduced tensions through a series of 'development processes'. These were:

Process 1: January–July 1983; communiqués appealed to the Central

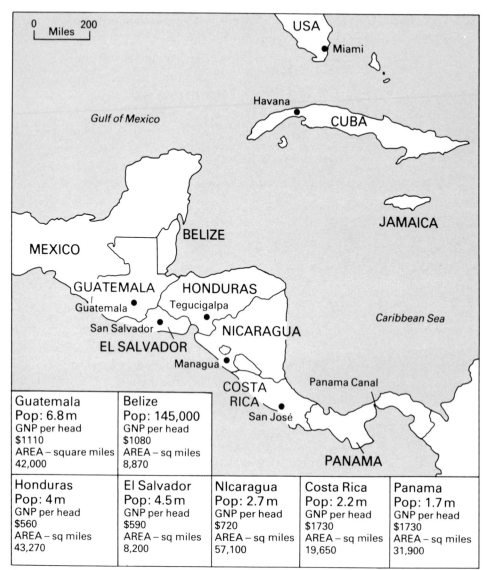

Guatemala Pop: 6.8 m GNP per head $1110 AREA – square miles 42,000	**Belize** Pop: 145,000 GNP per head $1080 AREA – sq miles 8,870			
Honduras Pop: 4 m GNP per head $560 AREA – sq miles 43,270	**El Salvador** Pop: 4.5 m GNP per head $590 AREA – sq miles 8,200	**Nicaragua** Pop: 2.7 m GNP per head $720 AREA – sq miles 57,100	**Costa Rica** Pop: 2.2 m GNP per head $1730 AREA – sq miles 19,650	**Panama** Pop: 1.7 m GNP per head $1730 AREA – sq miles 31,900

Central America

American countries to take part in internal and external dialogue to build some kind of framework for peaceful co-existence.

Process 2: September 1983; the Contadora countries and the 5 Central American states agreed on a Document of Objectives.

Process 3: January 1984; specific measures to be taken to fulfil the commitments of the Document of Objectives were agreed on.

Process 4: January 1984; drafting and negotiation of Contadora Act for Peace and Co-operation in Central America.[1]

Developments reached stalemate late in 1986, and early in 1987 a critical stage. The Secretary-Generals of the United Nations and the Organisation of American States (OAS), together with the Foreign Ministers of Contadora and the Contadora Support Group, made a five-nation tour of Central America. All feared the outbreak of general fighting, hence the need for the moral weight and authority of the UN Secretary-General, Xavier Perez de Cueller, and the Secretary-General of the OAS, Joao Baena Soares, in the mission.

A border clash between Nicaragua and Honduras reminded everyone how easily war can break out. Open Soviet and Cuban support for the Sandinistas, no less than that of the United States for the Contras and Honduras, repeatedly provokes tension. According to the US Assistant Secretary of State for Latin America, Elliot Abrams, Contadora is working on the false premise that the Sandinistas can be prevailed upon, through diplomacy, not to export their revolution. According to the US line the Sandinistas are not to be trusted and therefore a negotiated deal with them is not possible. Mr. Abrams says that democracy can only be achieved through military pressure, once the Sandinistas 'begin to feel pain'.[2]

'The Secret War in Central America'

The American Society of International Law in its quarterly *Journal* (January 1986, vol. 80, no. 1) published an 86-page article by John Norton Moore entitled 'The Secret War in Central America'. This article, the longest ever published by the *Journal*, deals largely with the concept of legality. It applies international law both to the Sandinista regime in Nicaragua and to American support for the Contra opposition. The essay begins with this statement:

> The core principle of modern world order is that aggressive attack is prohibited in international relations and that necessary and proportional force may be used in response to such an attack.

Mr. Moore's central finding is that the Sandinista regime is a product of aggressive attack masquerading as self-defence and that because of this it is the duty of the world community to assist those who are resisting the Sandinistas. Some of the key paragraphs would interest any student of war.

> The secret war in Central America illustrates the danger to world order—and to the legal order itself—posed by the assaults of radical regimes. . . . That war is conducted through assistance in organizing Marxist-Leninist controlled insurgencies; the financing of such insurgencies; the

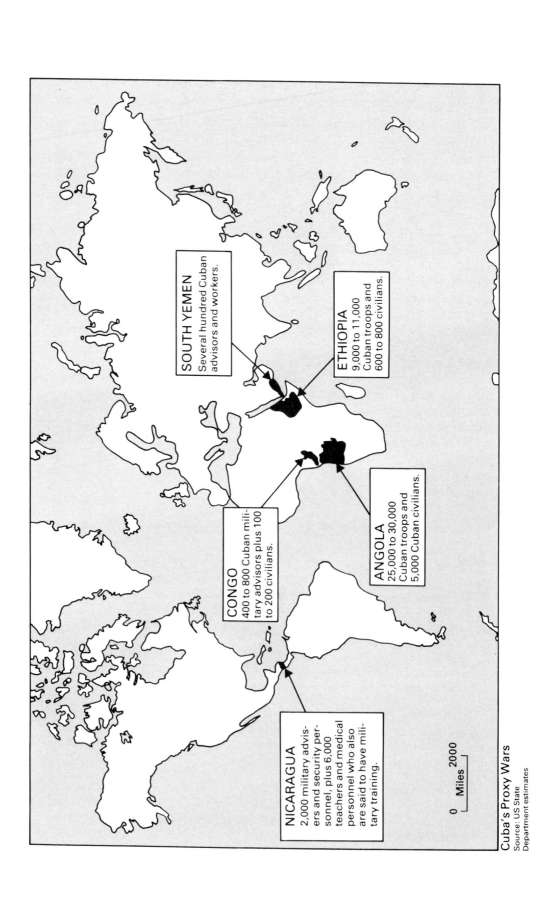

SOUTH YEMEN
Several hundred Cuban advisors and workers.

ETHIOPIA
9,000 to 11,000 Cuban troops and 600 to 800 civilians.

CONGO
400 to 800 Cuban military advisors plus 100 to 200 civilians.

ANGOLA
25,000 to 30,000 Cuban troops and 5,000 Cuban civilians.

NICARAGUA
2,000 military advisers and security personnel, plus 6,000 teachers and medical personnel who also are said to have military training.

0   Miles   2000

Cuba's Proxy Wars

Source: US State
Department estimates

provision and trans-shipment to them of arms and ammunition; training the insurgents; assistance in command and control, intelligence, military and logistics activities; the extensive political support. It also includes terrorist attacks and subversive activities preliminary to and supportive of an all-out covert attack.

Arrayed in support of this secret war is a diverse conglomeration of radical regimes and insurgent movements from the Soviet Union and Soviet bloc nations such as East Germany, Bulgaria, Czechoslovakia, Cuba, Vietnam, Ethiopia and North Korea, to Libya, Iraq, Iran and the PLO.

The strategy of covert and combined political-military attack that undergirds this secret war is a particularly grave threat to world order.

By denying the attack, the aggressors create doubts as to its existence; and by shielding the attack with a cloud of propaganda and misinformation, they focus world attention on alleged (and sometimes real) shortcomings of the victimised state and the permissibility of defensive response. The result is a politically 'invisible attack' that avoids the normal political and legal condemnation of aggressive attack and instead diverts that moral energy to condemning the defensive response. In a real sense, the international immune system against aggressive attack becomes misdirected instead to defensive response.

Aggressive attack—particularly in its more frequent contemporary manifestation of secret guerrilla war, terrorism and low intensity conflict—is a grave threat to world order wherever undertaken. That threat is intensified, however, when it is a form of cross-bloc attack in an area of traditional concern to an opposing alliance system. That is exactly the kind of threat presented by an activist Soviet-bloc intervention in the OAS area.

The remedy for strengthening world order is clear: return to the great vision of the founders of the UN and OAS Charters. Aggressive attack, whether covert or overt, is illegal and must be vigorously condemned by the world community, which must also join in assisting in defense against such attack. At a minimum, it must be understood that an attacked state and those acting on its behalf are entitled to a right of effective defense to end the attack promptly and protect self-determination.[3]

Refugee Problem

By mid-1987 Central America had more than 500,000 refugees. They include Guatemalans running away from endemic violence, Salvadoreans who since 1981 have been at the mercy of paramilitary groups or guerrilla movements or Nicaraguans now tired of their revolution. Many of these refugees are concentrated in Costa Rica and Honduras. For some years Nicaragua used to be a haven for Salvadorean refugees who have gradually become assimilated within farming co-operatives. Very few refugees are today arriving in Nicaragua. Costa Rica, which has no army and only 700 policemen, is worried that some groups of refugees might feel tempted to create a state within a state—or to take over Costa Rica.

References

1. This summary of 'Processes' from a briefing paper issued by the Foreign and Commonwealth Office, London.
2. Statements issued by the Assistant Secretary of State between 1 January and 18 January, 1987.
3. Source quoted in the text.

War in Chad

Background Summary

The immense country of Chad (700,000 square kilometres) has not known peace since it became independent from France in 1960, largely because of Colonel Gaddafi's interference in the country's affairs from the time of his own coup in Libya in 1969. Libya occupied the 60-mile wide Aozou Strip in 1973 and supported Hissène Habré and his *Forces Armées du Nord* (FAN). Soon after this Gaddafi backed Goukouni Oueddei and his *Forces Armées Populaires* (FAP) against Habré.

Oueddei formed the *Gouvernement d'Union Nationale de Transition* (GUNT). Gaddafi's switch of allegiance and sponsorship brought 15,000 Libyan troops into fighting against FAN, which was backed by Egypt, Sudan and the United States. FAN captured the capital, N'djamena, in June 1982, Oueddei fled the country and Habré formed a government. Libyan aggression continued and in May 1983 Libyan forces helped GUNT to capture Faya-Largeau and other places. France sent troops and aircraft to back Habré's FAN forces. *Operation Manta* was the code-name for the French campaign in Chad between August 1983 and September 1984.

(For full details of the entire war see **WAR ANNUAL** 1.)

Summary of the War in 1985

As Gaddafi consolidated the Libyan presence in Chad with six military bases the Organisation of African Unity (OAU) tried to negotiate an end to the war but the attempt was abortive. France and Libya signed an agreement to end their respective involvement in the war, Gaddafi did not keep to his promise. At the end of 1985 Habré held the Libyans in check in the north but in the south several rebel groups opposed him, notably *Codos Rouges*, commanded by Colonel Alphonse Kotiga. There were then three main armies operating in Chad, apart from the Libyans. In encounters at Oum Chalouba and Kouba Olanga, FAN troops defeated Libyan-backed Chadians. The French remained poised for a Libyan attack and continued to regard the 16th parallel as the limit south of which Libyan incursions would bring swift French retaliation. They now called their actions in Chad *Operation Epervier* (Sparrowhawk).

The War in 1986-87

Intermittent fighting continued throughout 1986 and it gradually became clear that, politically, the character of the war was changing. It had become less a war between Chadian factions than one between Chad and Libya, with other parties

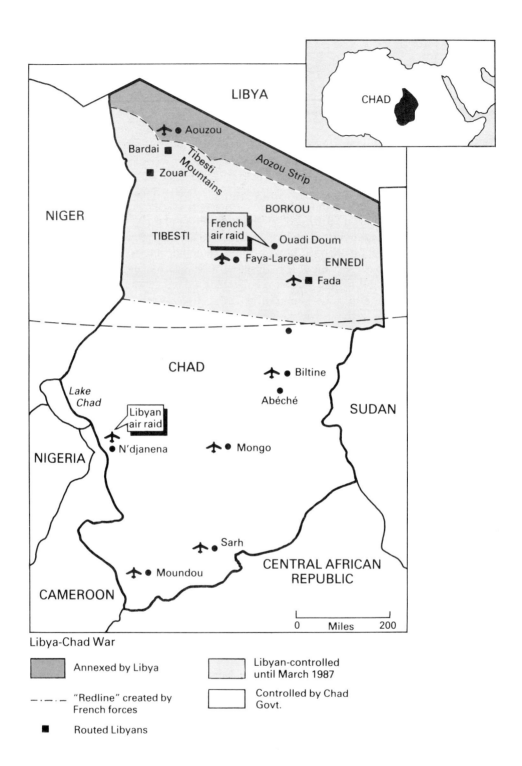

Libya-Chad War

playing supporting roles. During the second half of the year Habré commanded the new Chadian National Armed Forces (FANT), which included some soldiers formerly loyal to Oueddei.

The Franco-African conference—a meeting of Francophone countries chaired by France—held at Lomé in mid-November 1986 was dominated by discussion over the conflict in Chad. Only a few weeks later the war reached an even more critical stage with a Libyan offensive, beginning on 12 December to capture the strategic oasis towns of Fada and Zouar. A Chad military communiqué[1] alleged that the Libyans used napalm and toxic gases on the fourth day of fighting in the Tibesti region. According to the same communiqué the Chadian forces routed the Libyans at Bardai, killing 400 and capturing or destroying 20 tanks. During this battle French planes parachuted 12 tons of arms, fuel and food to the Chad troops. The French government gave its *de facto* approval to Habré's attempt to reconquer the territory occupied by the Libyans.

French-American co-operation concerning Chad now reached significant proportions. Three American Air Force C-5A Galaxy transport planes flew to Nantes to airlift American and French military equipment. Particularly important were French-made Acmat-type four-wheel drive trucks. In addition two Chadian battalions at the Kotakoli commando school in Zaire were made available to the FANT High Command.

The first few days of January 1987 were momentous. On 2 January the Chadian Army attacked the Libyan force at Fada. The fighting was unusually violent. About 700 Libyan troops were virtually exterminated and only a few dozen prisoners were taken. The Chadians seized 'considerable' quantities of military equipment, including heavy Soviet tanks, six Marchetti SF-260 planes, three of which were ready to fly, a substantial number of anti-aircraft and anti-radar missiles as well as a radar station in perfect working order. On the same day, a military column which had left N'djamena 10 days earlier reached Zouar in the Tibesti desert and recaptured it.

On 4 January four Libyan MiGs bombed Chadian positions at Arada, Oum Chalaba and Kalait, south of the 16th parallel. French troops were garrisoned at Kalait and though they suffered no casualties the government could not allow this provocative challenge to pass without retaliation. Three days after the bombing 14 French Mirage and Jaguar fighter-bombers, flying at dune level, made a pin-point raid on radar installations at Ouadi Doum, Libya's southernmost military installation in northern Chad.

The Jaguars hit the radar installations with electro-magnetically guided Martel AS-37 anti-radar missiles. Within three hours Gaddafi responded by bombing Chadian troops at Kouba Olanga. He was determined to demonstrate that the destruction of the Libyan base at Fada by Chadian troops did not deprive him of means of action and he was apparently determined to provoke French forces.

The French played down the incident. Prime Minister Chirac described the Libyan air raid as an 'insect bite' that deserved a 'serious call to order'.[2] Speaking on television[3] about the French air strike, the Defence Minister Giraud said, 'It was a precise, significant response, which does not amount to an escalation. We are anxious that the character of the conflict should not change.'

The Libyan troops captured at Fada were put on display in N'djamena. The exhibition took place in Independence Square before a crowd of 200,000, the largest the city had ever seen. The prisoners, some of them wounded, were displayed on the back of a huge German truck and it was instantly clear to the assembled Chadians that they were Libyans. They would have been stoned to death had not their guards quickly driven them to safety.[4]   Habré, a low-key politician, failed to capitalise on his troops' success. The French and others urged him to undertake a political and media drive to demonstrate that, confronted by the Libyan invader, Chad's legitimate government was able to recover its national territory. The idea was to force the hand of some sub-Saharan African leaders who privately storm against Gaddafi, but refrain from doing so in public, especially at meetings of the OAU. Some African countries, notably Algeria and Congo, had always been reluctant to accuse Gaddafi of direct involvement in the Chadian fighting. The Libyan offensive should have convinced them of this involvement. Nigeria condemned Libya's occupation of northern Chad and called for an emergency conference of other concerned African countries to 'preserve the peace, which is threatened by Gaddafi'.

After the fall of Fada, Gaddafi sent envoys to Harare, Algiers, Khartoum, Accra and Lagos to canvass support for his own 'peace conference'. In Lagos his envoy, Ali Treiki, signed an agreement committing Libya to withdraw its army of occupation as part of an overall peace settlement. However, such a settlement could take a long time because nobody trusts Gaddafi's motives. He has always regarded Chad as his base for the great Libyan advance into Africa and is unlikely to give it up. While calling for a peace conference Gaddafi called up large numbers of army reservists and sent 8,000 more troops into northern Chad. To counter this threat France airlifted 1,000 men to reinforce the 1,500 troops already in Chad. They were under orders not to engage the Libyans directly unless they crossed the 16th parallel. The reinforcing troops established a base at Abéché.

Meanwhile the Chad government-in-exile, which the Libyans had maintained in Tripoli for four years, disintegrated. Goukouni Oueddei, now no more than a puppet, was confined to his home in Tripoli. Oueddei had secretly asked Habré for a meeting to discuss unity. In October he tried to get away and was wounded in a shoot out with his Libyan guards. The Libyans quickly installed a new GUNT president, Acheikh Ibn Oumar. He could muster only a few hundred tribal followers and the rest of the GUNT forces joined with the Chad Army, which numbers about 12,000 effective men (out of a population estimated at 5 million). Virtually all Chad's military equipment is French-made. It has no military aircraft.

The arrival in N'djamena on 5 February of Hachim Daoud and Colonel Abdulkadir Kamougue, the former GUNT vice-president, virtually killed off GUNT as an effective force. Three days later, Gaddafi allowed Oueddei to move from Tripoli to Algiers. Foreign diplomats in North Africa saw this as a gamble by Gaddafi that Oueddei might yet contrive to wreck the new Chadian solidarity.

Three of the most influential men in Libya's military establishment, Colonel Abu Bakr Yunes, Colonel Mustafa Karubi and Major Lakhuildi Lahmidi want to end the war in Chad.

In a speech on 9 February[5] President Mitterrand stressed the contrast between a French military presence requested by Chad's government and Libya's 'army of occupation'. In particular he was addressing Congo's President Denis Sassou Nguesso, the OAU chairman for 1987. Habré, in his most important speech for years, told his people: 'Our objective is to preserve our territorial integrity and our success is only a matter of time.'

France has made several bombing reprisal raids but refuses to cover Habré's troops north of the 16th parallel. France's attitude concerning the 16th parallel is curious; Gaddafi always saw it as tacit French approval to the partition of Chad. In an interview on 6 January he claimed that according to the agreement between himself and Mitterrand 'if the French troops intervene north of the 16th parallel I am entitled to intervene south of it'.[6] His forces crossed the parallel twice on 4 January to bomb Oum Chalaba, Arada and Kalait.

The Chad troops soon showed that they could achieve major victories without direct foreign aid. In mid-March 1987 they made a fast, surprise attack on Ouadi Doum and its strategic airstrip. Using Toyota jeeps equipped with Milan and SAM missiles as their spearhead, the Chad force took all their objectives and killed more than 1,000 Libyan troops and allied mercenaries.

Habré had anticipated that he would have to fight for the vast oasis of Faya Largeau, situated on an open plain between the Tibesti Mountains and the Ennedi plateau. The loss of the airstrip and of much of Ouadi Doum influenced Libyan decisions about future plans, especially as Chad troops had already infiltrated the oasis. They were not in large numbers but the officers of the Islamic Pan-African Legion of 3,000, which formed the bulk of the garrison at Faya Largeau, lost their nerve. On 22 March they blew up their fuel and ammunition dumps and pulled out. Sandstorms slowed down their retreat but also checked the arrival of the Chad force. Ouadi Doum has the only hard-surface runway in the country, thus limiting the possibility of air cover and supply for the Libyan troops.

In December 1986 some commentators saw Gaddafi's Chad offensives not simply as battles for control over a piece of desert but once again over the political leadership of the Sahel and North African region. One observer assessed that 'Gaddafi's offensive against Chad is his revenge for the American raid against Tripoli on 15 April 1986'.[7] The ultimate failure of the offensives in the face of the Chad counter-offensives has damaged Gaddafi's status and credibility. This was shown by the arrival of President Mitterrand in Algiers for talks with President Chadli—within hours of the Libyan reverses.

The Chad government's successful campaign to drive Libyan troops from the north of the country isolated a Libyan force camped at the villages of El Tina and Kernoy, in western Sudan.

Libyan forces in Chad in March, before their reverses at Ouadi Doum and Faya Largeau, consisted of 14,000 troops, including 2 mechanised battalions, 2 tank battalions with T-55 tanks; 3,500 men of the Islamic Pan-African Legion; 100 mechanised infantry combat vehicles; 40-60 air defence guns; SAM missiles; 12 M1-24 Hind helicopters; and a variable number of MiG fighter-bombers.

Soviet Loss of Face

Because of the Chadian government's defeat of Libyan forces and the virtual dissolution of GUNT, the Soviet Union, which had backed Libya's policy, suffered an embarrassing loss of face in the rest of Africa. African diplomats in Moscow were also amused by the existence there of two separate Chadian missions, each claiming the sole right to speak for the divided country. The Russians had formally recognised Oueddei's GUNT 'Chief of Mission' though neither this man nor his movement had much following in Africa.

Soviet 'advisers' have been seen in the Aozou strip.[8] They are involved in two important projects. One is the building of a radio transmission station close to the Zuweyah military base which will intercept American and French military transmissions from the Sahel to Morocco and the Mediterranean. This station is linked with conventional radio and television networks designed to jam the local broadcasts of neighbouring countries, such as Niger, Mali and especially Tunisia. The second project involving the Russians is the completion of a 1,850 km Libyan coastal defence system aimed to prevent a military landing.[9] The Aozou Strip will be more difficult for Habre's Chad Army to recover than the Libyan bases in northern Chad.

References

1. Issued at N'djamena, 18 December 1986.
2. Press conference in Paris, 5 January 1987.
3. 8 January 1987.
4. James Wilde, *Time* Magazine, who was present in N'djamena.
5. At a dinner given for the Congo's President.
6. *Libération*, 6 January 1987.
7. Thierry Lalavée, *Executive Intelligence Review*, 16 January 1987.
8. By Italian geologists, who reported to their Foreign Ministry.
9. Diplomatic and Intelligence sources in Libya and Tunisia.

Conflict in Chile

WAR ON 'MARXIST TERROR'

An attack on the life of Chile's President Augusto Pinochet, on 6 September 1986, was attributed to the biggest of the armed organisations which oppose his dictatorial rule—the *Frenta Patriotica Manuel Rodriguez* (FPMR). This came as a shock to public opinion—which had never before taken FPMR seriously—and not least because it came so close to a successful assassination.

Since its formation in 1983, FPMR's actions had mostly been on power-lines and public buildings. During July and August 1986 there were 116 such attacks. The discovery in August of large caches of weapons—3,000 M-16 rifles, rockets and rocket launchers, munitions and explosives—caused widespread astonishment.

The Left was neither interested in, nor capable of, such a degree of military confrontation, most people believed. The assassination attempt changed this. Most Chilean observers consider that the assassination attempt, in view of the resources and the Intelligence required for organising it, could only have been mounted by the FPMR with the help of senior army officers. Some of these observers say that it was a 'perfectly planned botched assassination'.

The President reimposed an official 'state of siege', which gave him wide-ranging powers to detain and censor the opposition. In the longer term, however, it left unanswered the problem of how Chile's armed forces intended to defeat the Communists if they had failed to crush them after 13 years in power.

The FPMR operates as a self-contained military unit, estimated by some sources to be more than 10,000 strong. It has a national presence and is capable of disrupting life in Chile to a greater degree than the government had supposed before the Pinochet assassination attempt. A second, much smaller armed group, is the Revolutionary Left Movement (MIR). Since it was founded in 1965 it has had a political-military strategy and has claimed responsibility for many bomb attacks and most of the isolated killings of members of the armed forces since 1983.

By November 1986 Chilean Army Intelligence had given the General Staff information which led to the army's main anti-terrorist activities being concentrated in two areas—in the desolate north and 600 miles south of Santiago, where the terrain is ideal for guerrilla warfare. Here access to Argentina and therefore to supplies is relatively easy. The army posted two specialist anti-guerrilla warfare brigades to the region. Since then the Second Army Division, in Santiago, has been trained in guerrilla fighting. A former Foreign Minister, Hernan Cubillos, warned in a radio interview: 'We are facing a war, already declared, and unfortunately it is going to be a dirty war.'

Before the annual round of promotions, retirements and postings in 1986, President Pinochet, who is also Army Commander, demanded that the General Staff give him the power to decide the main postings, 'in view of the serious and

Conflict in Chile

deteriorating security situation'. He then carried out the biggest reshuffle in his 13 years of power. The result was to reinforce the importance of counter-insurgency and Intelligence specialists at the expense of conventional warfare experts. For instance, the army's representative in the ruling *Junta* of four was replaced by the head of the secret police, General Humberto Gordon.

By the end of 1986 Pinochet had exiled more than 7,000 political opponents. On 1 January the President announced that most of them would be allowed to return home within 90 days. This gesture of goodwill was timed to coincide with the Pope's first visit to Chile in April 1987.

With few Western journalists reporting from Chile and local journalists under strict censorship and threat of imprisonment or death—several have been murdered—guerrilla activities receive little mention in the world's Press. However, a ruthless if 'selective' war is being fought in mountains, valleys and forests as the freedom fighters—as they increasingly call themselves—ambush army patrols and attack isolated posts.

Various 'commando' groups have emerged, most of them with enigmatic titles such as 'Number Five' or 'September 11'. This label is taken to be the group's foundation day. The various militias maintained by opposition political parties raise barricades and try to create no-go areas for the military patrols.

Diplomatic sources say that if Pinochet remains as President and Chile is not returned to a democratic, civilian government the unseen war in Chile will not only become dirtier but much hotter.

Colombia Guerrilla and Narcotics War

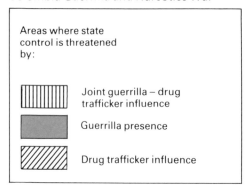

Areas where state
control is threatened
by:

Joint guerrilla – drug
trafficker influence

Guerrilla presence

Drug trafficker influence

Colombia Guerrilla War

LONGEST WAR IN LATIN AMERICA

Background Summary

A civil war began in 1948, basically between liberals and conservatives. It soon drew in the Colombian Revolutionary Armed Forces or *Fuerzas Armadas Revolucionarias Colombianes* (FARC), the military arm of the Colombian Communist Party. The pro-Cuban Army of National Liberation (ELN) and the Maoist People's Liberation Army (EPL) were formed in the 1960s. The most powerful of all was M-19, a Leftist-nationalist-Castroite group formed in 1973. In 1982 the Workers' Self-Defence, known in Colombia as ADO, joined the guerrilla war. In 1982 a new Conservative President, Belisario Betancur, secured a cease-fire, at least in principle, in the hope that the guerrillas were more interested in social reform than in their own group's power.

(*For full details of the war see* **WAR ANNUAL** 1.)

Summary of Events in 1985

The stronger guerrilla groups regarded Betancur's reforms as a sign of his weakness and M-19, EPL and ADO withdrew from the peace discussions. Any peace was illusory: 207 soldiers and police were killed and 900 wounded by guerrillas. Pitched battles took place between security forces and FARC and M-19, which was led by Alvaro Fayad Delgado. His close links with Colombia's drug barons became increasingly evident throughout the year.

The Colombian guerrillas are unlike those of most Latin American countries: they do not have popular support among the population of 29 million anywhere in the country. However, they ensure co-operation through threats and a range of punishments running from beatings to arson, kidnapping and murder. The only government victory in 1985 was the defection of Luis Alberto Rodriguez, a deputy commander of FARC. Up to the end of that year 20,000 people had died in the war. Foreign diplomats in the capital, Bogota, said that only the cutting off of Cuban and Soviet-bloc military aid could end the fighting.

The War in 1986-87

The Liberal Party leader, Virgilio Barco, became President in the national elections in April and promised, as other leaders had done before him, that peace would be restored. Less than four months after his accession Barco was facing political assassinations and criminal murders, disappearances, peasant massacres, daily guerrilla acts of sabotage and attacks on military posts, summary executions blamed on various paramilitary groups or hired guns working for big-time drugs traffickers.

Violence has become a basic, almost trivial fact of life accepted by everybody though routinely condemned by the authorities, the church and the intellectuals.

November 1986 was a black month for the second successive year. In 1985 M-19 had attacked the capital's court buildings and murdered 95 people, including 11 judges. The tally for November 1986 was worse still—at least 70 guerrillas and as many soldiers were killed in battle and over 200 policemen seriously wounded. Scores of small farmers caught up in the fighting were kidnapped or massacred. Damage, especially through sabotage to oil installations, was widespread and estimated to be US$50 million. A Liberal leader and former national President, Alfonso Lopez Michelsen announced that 'geographically speaking the country is in guerrilla hands'. The Catholic Church warned that 'Colombian democracy is again imperilled'.

M-19, having lost leaders, credibility and face in the botched November 1985 assault on the court buildings, was not the main front-line force in 1986. ELN, a tiny, poor group in 1984, had become the spearhead force. It has amassed a great deal of money through robberies and blackmail and has so broadened its operations that it now calls itself the National Guerrilla Co-ordination (CNG) and gives orders to M-19, EPL and other 'self-defence' groups.

ELN is thought to be led by a Catholic priest, Father Perez, who has split from his church. In November 1986 it carried out major raids in the provinces of Oriental, Arauca, Santander and Antioquia. Rumours about who is behind ELN's rapid rise to power—as well as numerical strength of 50,000—have abounded in Bogota. The Cubans are suspected. Even more strongly, several diplomats blame the Libyans as well as other Middle East Islamic fundamentalists. A European diplomat has said: 'The extremist Muslims are happy to bait, through the local guerrillas, a country in league with the Great Satan, the United States.' The Great Satan is the epithet applied to the US by the fanatical fundamentalist Ayatollah Khomeini.

In the short term the most disturbing aspect of Colombia's violence is the spate of murders and attacks on officials of the Patriotic Union, a Right-wing organisation of government officials and supporters. Between September and December 1986, 300 party members were killed, among them a score of municipal councillors, four members of departmental legislatures, one member of the House of Representatives and one Senator. Many representatives and senators have received death threats and nearly all have armed bodyguards.

FARC was still the most powerful guerrilla organisation in the country but observed an armed truce for much of 1986, largely through the impressive leadership of Manuel ('Sure-shot') Marulanda, the country's most renowned guerrilla leader. Marulanda tries to avoid head-on confrontations with the army and preys on landowners and businesses, especially oil companies and other multi-national concerns. Politically part of the Colombian Communist Party, Marulanda's FARC consists almost entirely of peasants and has 27 'fronts' spread through the country's mountains and jungles. With a staff of 200, he operates from a command post at La Caucha, in the mountains 80 miles south of Bogota. La Caucha is hidden in trees, often swathed in cloud and is three days on horseback from the nearest road. A network of collaborating peasants is spread for miles over the surrounding countryside. In the past the army tried to infiltrate patrols through to La Caucha; all disappeared. A major army offensive could take La Caucha but it would then be empty. Reports in 1986 that Marulanda, now 57, has retired are false.

According to Amnesty International reports, death squads are common and never caught. Some such squads are in uniform and others in civilian clothes; they travel in army vehicles or in unmarked cars without licence plates, pass freely through army roadblocks, park in police compounds and have been seen handing over prisoners at military bases and barracks.

Military War Against Drug Traffickers

In 1986 President Barco made the deliberate decision to use the armed services as the only force capable of opposing the immense power of the drug barons. In mid-December 1986 this military campaign began in earnest and within 6 weeks the army had achieved notable success. It captured Evaristo Porras Ardila, one of the country's top five drug traffickers, who controls a network linking several countries. Within days three major drug traffickers sought for extradition to the United States were seized, as well as another 15 from an army blacklist. The army carried out 1,500 anti-drug raids throughout the country, during which more than 500 suspects were arrested and large quantities of illegal weapons found. In addition, the army, with navy and air force co-operation, carried out a government directive to control the import and export of chemicals for use in making illegal narcotics. The three services enforced the licensing and inspection of aircraft, airports, ships and warehouses and placed 2,700 Colombian companies under direct surveillance to prevent the drug mafia from gaining access to the products produced or imported by those firms. It was a remarkable display of military planning and precision but its very success invites retaliation.

Colombian Armed Forces

In theory the Colombian armed forces should be able to master the guerrilla forces as it has the drug traffickers. The army itself has a strength of 53,000, including 24,000 conscripts, and some of its units are well-trained and thoroughly accustomed to jungle and mountain campaigning. The army is organised in brigades rather than divisions and most brigades have three infantry battalions, an artillery battalion, engineer group and a mechanised 'rapid deployment group'. Several brigades include conventional cavalry units for operations in country impassable to vehicles. More than 180 armoured personnel carriers are in use and 150 reconnaissance vehicles, mostly Cascavels. As might be expected, the army relies heavily on mortars as ordinary artillery is useless in most jungle fighting, as are tanks.

The air force has built up its helicopter gunship element and in 1987 had 45 gunships, together with other helicopters—16 Hughes 500-MG Defenders and 10 Hughes Cayuses—intended for counter-insurgency operations. The separate military transport command has a large number of aircraft to move troops and supplies to remote posts in the vast country of 650,000 square kilometres.

The National Police Force, really a paramilitary organisation, has a strength of 50,000 and there are another 38,000 *carabineros* organised according to provinces.

Despite their manpower, airpower and firepower the armed forces are virtually powerless against the guerrillas while they continue to operate guerrilla tactics. Only when they stand and fight has the army any success against them. Even after nearly 30 years the Colombian Army seems unable to train its soldiers for counter-insurgency warfare. A basic problem is that the army's Intelligence section has been penetrated by the guerrillas; they know in advance every move the army proposes to make. Occasionally a guerrilla group murders a senior army officer as a warning to others that professional zeal carries its own penalty in a lawless land.

References

Some of the information for this account comes from Marcel Niedergang, a correspondent for *Paris Match* who knows Colombia well. The rest comes from diplomatic and private sources in the country, none of whom, for their own safety, can be named.

East Timor Resistance War

THE WAR INDONESIA DENIES

Background Summary

In 1975 when the Portuguese abandoned East Timor, after 500 years of colonialism, several factions sought to control the former colony of 500,000 people, living in an area of 15,000 square kilometres. The rest of East Timor was Indonesian and the Dutch had controlled the western half.

Civil war broke out on 11 August 1975 when the *Unaio Democratica de Timor* (UDT) seized key installations in Dili and Baucau. However, the most powerful group, *Frente Revolucionara de Timor-Leste Independente* (Fretilin)—which was said to be Marxist—won the bloody civil war and declared independence on 3 November 1975. A week later Indonesia invaded East Timor and annexed it.

(For full details of the war see **WAR ANNUAL** 1.)

Summary of Activities in 1985

By 1985 more people had been massacred in the East Timor war—probably 200,000—than in any other contemporary war except that in Kampuchea. In August 1985 a Fretilin spokesman told the UN Special committee on Decolonisation that Indonesia had subjugated East Timor using French helicopters and tanks, British aircraft, American transport helicopters and counter-insurgency aircraft and West German and Dutch frigates and submarines. Indonesia claimed that guerrilla resistance was insignificant; nevertheless the army suffered more than 1,100 casualties in a year. The Indonesian Navy and Air Force virtually sealed off the island so that news about the campaign of genocide—which Roman Catholic priests on the island allege against Indonesia—could not reach the outside world.

The War in 1986-87

During 1986 several East Timorese people evaded the patrolling ships and planes to tell of the war going on in the jungle-clad island. Their accounts, studied by military analysts, are consistent and compelling. Malaysian security authorities exhaustively interrogated several escapees and reported that they believed their stories. Indonesia's blanket over information is understandable. A successful independent government in a small state in the midst of its far-flung island territory would set an example for parts of the country beset by secessionist agitation.

East Timor is strategically located. The United States has the right of passage for nuclear submarines through the Ombai-Wetar Strait, a deep-water passage from the Indian Ocean to the Pacific Ocean. It is one of the most vital naval waterways in the world.[1]

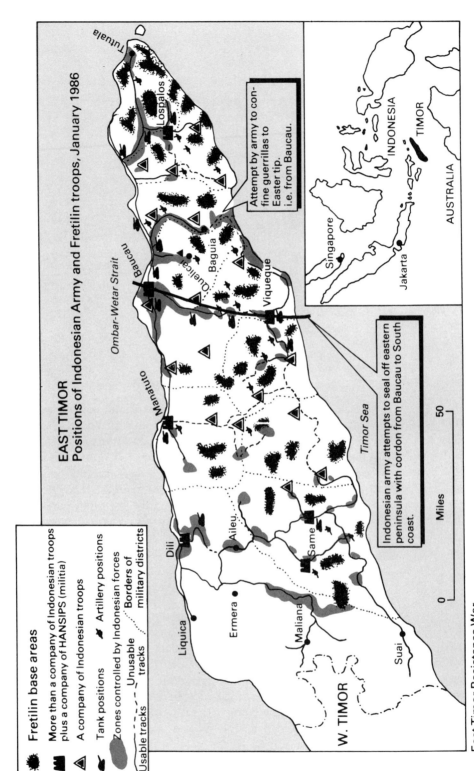

EAST TIMOR
Positions of Indonesian Army and Fretilin troops, January 1986

Fretilin base areas

🌲	More than a company of Indonesian troops plus a company of HANSIPS (militia)
◼	A company of Indonesian troops
△	Artillery positions
⚓	Tank positions
▨	Zones controlled by Indonesian forces
––––	Usable tracks
– – –	Unusable tracks
⋯⋯⋯	Borders of military districts

Attempt by army to confine guerrillas to Easter tip. i.e. from Baucau.

Indonesian army attempts to seal off eastern peninsula with cordon from Baucau to South coast.

W. TIMOR

Liquica
Ermera
Dili
Aileu
Maliana
Same
Suai
Manatuto
Baucau
Quelicai
Baguia
Viqueque
Lospalos
Tutuala

Ombar-Wetar Strait

Timor Sea

Miles
0   50

INDONESIA
TIMOR
Singapore
Jakarta
AUSTRALIA

East Timor Resistance War

Ragged guerrillas salute Fretilin President and military commander José Gusmão Sha Na Na in East Timor. He was returning from a patrol in the mountainous jungle. (Courtesy Catholic Institute for International Relations, London.)

Behind Fretilin lines: medical team, June 1983.

Indonesia denies that the East Timorese people are resisting strongly. However, photographs and tape recordings smuggled out by guerrillas indicate much activity. During 1986 it was revealed, for the first time, that in May 1983 a ceasefire was negotiated between the Fretilin commander, José Gusmao Xanana, and the Indonesian commander in Timor, Colonel Purwanto. Ceasefire negotiations are a clear indication that fighting has been heavy. The guerrillas also sent out a captured Indonesian counter-insurgency manual giving a detailed analysis of the Resistance's strength, which was far more extensive than Indonesia had publicly admitted. Instructions on the use of torture were included in the manual. This document was passed to Amnesty International which had it studied by experts. They declared it to be authentic.

In May 1986 another batch of documents reached Lisbon from the Fretilin Commander, Xanana. A map shows Fretilin's forces organised into companies operating in ten military zones in the central and eastern districts. An accompanying report states that most of the guerrillas high on the Indonesians' 'wanted' list are still fighting. The names of other leaders on this list but not previously mentioned in smuggled communiqués are known to former Portuguese administration officials. Some surrendered to the Indonesians in 1979 but, alarmed by Indonesian genocide, they rejoined the Resistance forces.[2]

The Indonesian Army appears to be concentrating its efforts in establishing a cordon across the island, south from Baucau, to contain the guerrillas in the eastern tip of the island or to drive them into more open country west of the cordon. The guerrillas can live off the land, but for weapons and ammunition they are heavily dependent on what they can capture from the army. During the latter half of 1986 they were without explosives but supplies arrived during 1987, apparently by submarine. The vessel was not identified but the explosives were believed to have come from Vietnam. This could indicate that it was a Soviet submarine, operating out of Cam Ranh naval base. Despite such aid it is not now believed that the Fretilin guerrilla command is as Marxist as had been thought. The Roman Catholic Church, which still has priests in East Timor, reports that Fretilin wants a democratic government in the country.[3]

In Indonesia itself there is at least one indication that the war in East Timor is far from over. Soldiers of all ranks consider the island a dangerous posting and dread being sent there. Fretilin guerrillas kill soldiers in their barracks beds. Others disappear while on patrol along jungle trails. Those who molest Timorese women are mutilated. An Indonesian army officer posted as an attaché to a European embassy said: 'Some Timorese people work for us but we have not a single friend on the island and in such a place it is impossible to defeat the guerrillas completely.'[4]

References

1. Paper published by the International Institute of Strategic Studies, London.
2. British Campaign for the Defence of Political Prisoners and Human Rights in Indonesia, London.
3. Monseigneur Carlos Ximenes Belo in a report to the Vatican.
4. Diplomatic source.

The Ecuador Affair

Ecuador Embarrassed by War

STORM IN A COFFEE-CUP

Most of Latin America's generals have relinquished power to elected governments but a rebellious one in Ecuador showed, in March 1986, that coups are not yet things of the past. On 7 March Ecuador's President, Leon Febres Cordero, dismissed the Air Force chief, General Frank Vargas for 'disloyalty'. The General hastened to the air base at Manta, 250 miles south of Quito, where he blockaded himself in with 600 rebels.

President Cordero sent an emissary who persuaded Vargas to surrender and return to the main air base near Quito. In exchange, the President agreed to ask for the resignation of the Defence Minister and the Army chief, two of the senior officials whom Vargas had accused of corruption.

On 13 March, Vargas again raised the standard of rebellion, telling the air force units at the base that the government has failed to keep its side of the surrender bargain. Next day 2,000 government troops, led by a general, marched on the base with artillery and tanks. A brisk 90-minute battle took place. According to an Army communiqué, its soldiers had wanted to avoid bloodshed and fired into the air. Vargas' air force troops aimed at the soldiers, who then roughly put down the rebellion. General Vargas, found hiding in the canteen, was again arrested.

In his home province of Manabi, Vargas had much political support and the President declared a state of emergency there. This was lifted on 18 March and the brief rebellion ended. The government announced that General Vargas was suffering from physical and mental exhaustion 'which had affected his ability to reason'.

Having become a popular figure who articulated the grievances of many ordinary Ecuadorians, Vargas still campaigned against the government. In this he was aided by his brother, a retired general who is a leading member of *Democracia Popular*, a group of radical Christian Democrats with much support among the peasants. In January Vargas kidnapped President Cordero and briefly held him to demonstrate his own power, while at the same time publicising further government corruption.

Still only 52, Vargas is now a hero and, according to diplomats in Quito, is likely to become a leading figure in Latin American politics.

While Ecuador's army totals 35,000 compared to the air force's strength of 3,000 a confrontation could well result in victory for the air force. It is much more devoted to General Vargas than the army is to President Cordero. Even the Presidential Guards' loyalty is suspect; it may have connived at the President's kidnapping. The air force has great prestige among the 10 million Ecuadorians and in its paratroop squadron it possesses one of the best units in Ecuador's entire armed forces.

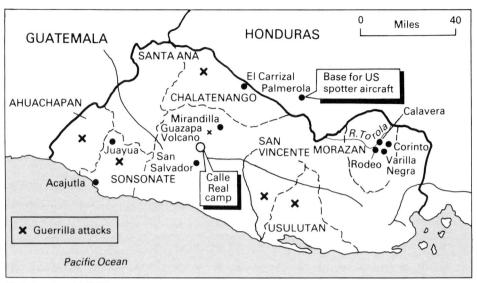

El Salvador Civil War

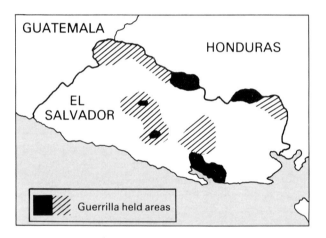

El Salvador Civil War

Background Summary

This conflict, which began in 1980, is commonly called a civil war but from the beginning it was more of a guerrilla war, with several organisations fighting the army. The guerrillas, all avowed communists of one type or another, opposed the Right-wing government of José Napoleon Duarte, whom many foreign observers describe as a fascist. The army could not effectively use its superiority in numbers and weaponry because much of El Salvador's 210,000 square kilometres area is mountainous, jungle-covered and sprinkled with villages where the guerrillas find shelter. After much urging by Fidel Castro of Cuba the many anti-government groups amalgamated into three bodies. They were:

(1) The Democratic Revolutionary Front (FDR), an amalgam of revolutionaries and representatives of Left-wing parties.
(2) The Unified Revolutionary Directorate (URD), a 15-member war council of top guerrilla leaders or *commandantes*.
(3) The Farabundo Marti National Liberation Front (FMLN), a co-ordinating, organisational body for the groups.

Following the murder of Salvador Cayatabo Carpio in 1983, Josquin Villalobos became the key guerrilla leader but there were three other prominent FMLN members. One, Shafik Jorge Handal, was general secretary of the Salvadorean Communist Party. Another, Eduardo Sancho Cantaneda, also known as Ferman Cienfeugos, led the armed Forces of National Resistance (FARN). The third was Roberto Roca, of the Central American Workers' Revolutionary Party.

To reduce support for the guerrillas President Duarte used death squads and between 1978 and 1984 14,629 peasants, 2,255 industrial workers, 1,783 students and 25,789 others were murdered. It seemed that the Salvadorean Army of 46,000 was steadily overcoming FMLN resistance, but the army suffered a severe reverse when it lost Colonel Domingo Monterrosa, a ruthless but brilliant officer, in a helicopter crash.

(For full details of the entire war see **WAR ANNUAL** 1.)

Summary of the War in 1985

This was another violent year. Various political leaders were murdered and the guerrillas waged a war of urban terrorism in response to the army's penetration of rebel-held countryside. Sometimes the guerrillas attempted large-scale operations, such as their attack on a government communications outpost on the slopes of San Salvador volcano. Nevertheless, the guerrillas wilted under 18 months of constant army pressure. With American financial help—US$454 million in 1985—the army increased in strength to 50,000 and the air force was strongly re-equipped. Villalobos stepped up the guerrilla campaign of economic sabotage, for instance destroying the electric power network. The fighting men on both sides suffered many casualties but civilians suffered even more.

Late in 1985 there were real fears that the Salvadorean war might spill over into Honduras after Honduran soldiers raided a Salvadorean refugee camp in Honduras. The FMLN threatened reprisals. American instructors with the Salvadoreans urged the army command to use many small self-sufficient commando-like groups to keep the guerrillas on the move. Simultaneously the Duarte regime waged a propaganda war to induce guerrillas to give themselves up on a promise of no punishment. While Duarte's army appeared to be slowly winning the war at the end of 1985 the FMLN was still the most potent insurgent army in Latin America.

The War in 1986-87

The El Salvador guerrilla commanders responded to the new army tactics by themselves forming small units of ten to 15 men. In January 1986 they could point to few territorial gains and controlled perhaps 10% of the country and 70,000 of El Salvador's 5.4 million people. But they were still capable of major destruction, as they proved in mid-January when Villalobos's People's Revolutionary Army (ERP) launched a midnight strike at Juayua, a government-controlled town in Western Sonsonate province. A large area was left in ruins. ERP's future tactics, as explained by a senior official in Morozan, would be blunt and brutal: urban warfare including kidnappings, economic sabotage including destruction of water supply, and the murder of American officials and advisers. 'In the long run killing Yankees is a form of undermining Reagan's policies', the ERP man said.[1]

The guerrillas plant many mines and booby traps, often in tin cans and bottles stuffed with fertiliser chemicals. They are said to account for 80% of army casualties; between 50 and 60 soldiers each month have limbs blown off and probably 10 to 12 peasants suffer in the same way.

The army has an insatiable appetite for manpower and by the end of 1986 and well into 1987 it was using press-gangs to increase its numbers. Few young men volunteer for the army and the period of conscription is only 2 years so there is a constant need to replace discharged men. Each barracks conducts its own round-ups, generally four times a year and usually in poor communities. The sons of the rich are tacitly exempt and should a 'mistake' occur and a young man of wealthy family be forcibly recruited his father will soon have him discharged.

In the face of public criticism, Duarte proposed, on 2 October 1986, a new law of obligatory military service for all men and women over the age of 18. The Roman Catholic church said that, while it wanted a peaceful solution to the war, the burden should be shared equally while the war continued. But it criticized the drafting of women. The wealthy got around the law by arranging for their sons and daughters to leave the country. Some guerrilla leaders had earlier forcibly recruited young men as fighters but found them 'inadequately motivated' and abandoned the practice.

There are more than 100 US military advisers in El Salvador, twice the official limit of 55 which the administration had promised to observe.[2] US-directed counter-insurgency strategy changed the nature of the conflict in 1986-87. American reconnaissance planes based at Palmerola in Honduras fly almost continuous surveillance missions over El Salvador to locate concentrations of people in guerrilla-held territory. This information is radioed to the Salvadorean air force and field commanders and the consequent bombing and strafing disperses, wears down and drives out civilians. According to one reliable estimate the civilian population of all guerrilla-held zones may be no more than 25,000. Colonel Sigifredo Ochoa, regarded as El Salvador's most effective combat commander, has established 12 free-fire zones in Chalatenango, where anyone found is regarded as a guerrilla fighter. In the free-fire zones troops destroy all human habitation, burn crops and kill animals.

At the same time Colonel Ochoa has refused to permit the International Red Cross to provide humanitarian or medical aid in any part of Chalatenango.[3] Colonel Ochoa has said: 'Without a civilian base of support the guerrillas are nothing but outlaws; without civilians the rebels have no food and cannot maintain their army. We are conducting clearance exercises.'[4] Operation Phoenix was one such 'clearance exercise' to get rid of suspected guerrilla sympathisers or *masas*. Beginning on 9 January 1986, it was an attempt to drive all civilians from the Guazapa volcano area. More than 4,000 soldiers took part in the sweep and aircraft bombed and strafed every sign of settlement.

US technology has made the operations of the Salvadorean air force more deadly. Its 300lb and 500lb bombs have been converted into fragmentation bombs; they explode about four feet above the ground and hurl steel fragments at chest height over a side area. The air force transport helicopter fleet of 65 ferries troops into guerrilla-held areas for rapid attacks. In 1986 the air force acquired three more AC-47 planes, with .50 calibre machine guns firing 1,500 rounds a minute, as well as four more Hughes 500 helicopter gunships.[5] These tactics have changed the nature of the war.

On 10 October 1986 an earthquake struck El Salvador. It killed at least 2,000 people, injured 10,000 more and left about 200,000 homeless. After the earthquake the guerrilla movements declared a unilateral truce, though this was probably less a humanitarian act than a recognition that Salvadoreans could not face more war at that time. This disaster-induced pause in the fighting did not become permanent and the destruction of thousands of houses in San Salvador has left a fertile ground for the spread of radical and revolutionary ideas.

Criticism of the US policy of support for the Duarte regime is tacitly shown by more than 200 Christian congregations and several Jewish synagogues which have formed a Sanctuary Movement in the United States, offering the traditional right of sanctuary in a church to Salvadorean refugees. The American government describes the refugees as economic migrants and therefore illegal immigrants, and deports them to El Salvador, where they face persecution and the risk of being killed by death squads or the security forces.

Only two cases among the tens of thousands of alleged human rights violations have been brought to trial throughout the war and in both the victims were US citizens. In 1984 five National Guard soldiers were found guilty of the rape and murder of four American women missionaries on 2 December 1980. In February 1986 two National Guard corporals were convicted of the murder, in January

The military presence in El Salvador is apparent in every town and village. The army rule is to regard everybody as a possible 'terrorist' and many thousands of innocent people have been murdered. (Courtesy El Salvador and Guatemala Committee for Human Rights.)

Soldiers of the El Salvador Army evacuate civilians from a war-ravaged part of the country. Helicopters provide the only safe form of transport in many regions. (Courtesy El Salvador and Guatemala Committee for Human Rights.)

1981, of two US agrarian reform advisers and the head of the Salvadorean agrarian reform agency.[6]

The most reliable statistics about the war, especially in human terms, come from *Tutela Legal* and *Socorro Juridico*. *Tutela Legal* is the Catholic Church's respected human rights office and *Socorro Juridico* (Juridical Help) is also connected with the Catholic Church. These organisations have recorded details of scores of thousands of individual cases and they report that the war has displaced about 550,000 Salvadorans and another 500,000 have sought refuge in neighbouring countries.

In some cases, since late in 1986, peasants have returned to their homes in the remote mountain hamlets of Morazan Province and have resisted army pressure to leave. Such courage is an indication of their desperation. Local army commanders suspect that the return of the villagers will help guerrillas who operate north of the Torola River. The army is concerned that the villagers may give aid to the guerrillas. But many villagers are tired of living in refugee camps or in garrison towns where they have to pay for everything—even firewood.

On one occasion residents from several hamlets around Varilla Negra were ordered to report the following day to the army commander in the nearby garrison town of Corinto. There they were told they would have to leave immediately and that the army would not be responsible for what happened if they stayed. One young man, Doroteo Amaya, started collecting signatures from the villagers asking the International Red Cross to intercede to allow them to stay. According to reliable sources, he was found dead the next moring with his ears and two fingers from each hand cut off. Most villagers believe the army killed him.

The men from the village of Calavera were also ordered to report to the military commander in Corinto, whom they call Lieutenant 'Long Knife'. The men said they, too, were told to leave and to spread the word to other hamlets. Two days later the men brought their families to Corinto. They said they would not leave. Faced with the large crowd, the officer backed down. But according to the villagers, he left them with this message: 'Go back to your lands and die.'

Lieutenant Colonel Mauricio Vargas, army commander of Morazan Province, said the orders to leave Calavera had been a mistake and that he had reversed them. Nevertheless, he refused to let people live in one area—Varilla Negra. 'What is going on is that the guerrillas are trying to put people in there,' said Colonel Vargas. 'Putting in people would generate conflict.' This does not keep some displaced people from trying to move back to their homes. Development workers say refugees are moving back into even the most dangerous zones. They have planted their fields and rebuilt the houses that were destroyed.[7]

A report in January 1987 by the US State Department claimed that humanitarian aid by private American citizens had been diverted to the guerrillas.[8] According to the report, which was based in part on captured documents and interviews with defectors, the US embassy in San Salvador ascertained that four recent fund-raising efforts were co-ordinated by the Committee in Solidarity with the People of El Salvador, known as CISPES. The report alleges that CISPES openly supports the FMLN and its political ally, FDR.

There can be no doubt that US involvement in the war has intensified. American specialists have trained and equipped units of the El Salvador National Police, which has a strength of 6,000, and the National Guard, which is 3,600-strong, to combat urban terrorism. This programme cost US$5 million.[9]

In 1986-87 two attempts at dialogue between the FDR-FMLN and the government ended inconclusively. The FDR-FMLN is committed to negotiations and they offer the only hope of achieving peace. Neither side is completely united and negotiations, which imply compromise and concessions, are a contentious issue. The negotiations for the release of the President's daughter, Ines, kidnapped by rebels in September 1985, were successful but they weakened Duarte's position. The political Right and sections of the army were contemptuous of what they saw as surrender to rebel demands. So as to secure army agreement to the exchange of prisoners which won his daughter's release, Duarte gave the military greater authority in the running of the war.

In mid-1987 it was clear that the power of El Salvador's land-owning and industrial élite remains intact, despite the government's promise of reform. Political dialogue is more and more subordinated to the counter-insurgency strategy. With American help, the army becomes stronger and stronger in terms of *materiel* and its tactics become more ruthless. The guerrillas, supplied by Cuba, may be down to 8,000 effective fighters but they are operating in 12 of El Salvador's 14 provinces. Thus the war is in a state of 'dynamic equilibrium', in which each side adapts to the advances of the other but in which neither side can win. Yet both are confident of victory in the long run.

References

1. In an interview with Ricardo Chavira, *Time* Magazine, 20 January 1986.
2. *Comment–El Salvador*, a publication of the Catholic Institute for International Relations, London, February 1986.
3. International Red Cross information.
4. Interview with foreign journalists, including correspondents of *Le Monde* and *La Prensa*, 2 January 1986.
5. Diplomatic sources in San Salvador.
6. US Embassy, San Salvador.
7. Report by Chris Norton, *Christian Science Monitor*, 4 August 1986.
8. US State Department Report, 17 January 1986.
9. US Embassy, San Salvador.

Ethiopia–Eritrea War

WAR FOR THE RED SEA

Background Summary

Ethiopia has been involved in a particularly barbarous conflict against the independence fighters of its province of Eritrea for 26 years. The war grew out of Eritrea's longtime conception of itself as a country separate from Ethiopia, which the Eritreans regarded as an imperialist interloper. Much of Eritrea's identity as a nation was imposed by the Italians, who ruled the area from 1880 until 1941. They imposed their language and welded Eritrea's diverse Christian, Muslim and animist peoples and its eight major nationalities into a political entity. After the British threw out the Italians in the Second World War and after a long UN debate, Eritrea was supposed to be guaranteed a measure of independence as an autonomous territory federated with Ethiopia. Despite UN Resolution 390A, that autonomy never existed in Eritrea.

The predominantly Muslim Eritreans claim that, as they are ethnically and religiously different from the Christian southerners who comprise most of Ethiopia's population, they should have a separate state. When Ethiopia annexed Eritrea in 1961 the Eritrean Liberation Front (ELF) fought for independence. In 1974 Colonel Mengistu became dictator of Ethiopia and launched his army of 80,000 men against the rebels, who numbered 40,000. Nevertheless, by 1977 the ELF was winning and only the city of Asmara remained to be captured. The Soviet Union which had been arming neighbouring Somalia, now changed sides and backed Ethiopia. With considerable help from the Russians the Ethiopians pushed the guerrillas from the main towns, but suffered 22,000 dead and 50,000 wounded.

At the same time, the Tigrayan People's Liberation Army (TPLF) was fighting for autonomy, while in the south the Ogaden tribes fought to unite with their countrymen in Somalia. Involved in so much fighting, the Ethiopian army expanded to 306,000, by far the largest in black Africa. EPLF, having superseded ELF as the main guerrilla force, inflicted some serious defeats on the Ethiopians.

(*For full details of the war see* **WAR ANNUAL** 1.)

Summary of the War in 1985

During the year the Ethiopian government spent half its budget in efforts to crush the guerrillas, who had six separate 'armies'. They were:

ELF: Eritrean Liberation Front: 6,000.
ELF-PLF: A union of the ELF and People's Liberation Forces: 10,000.
PLFRG: People's Liberation Front Revolutionary Guard: 5,000.

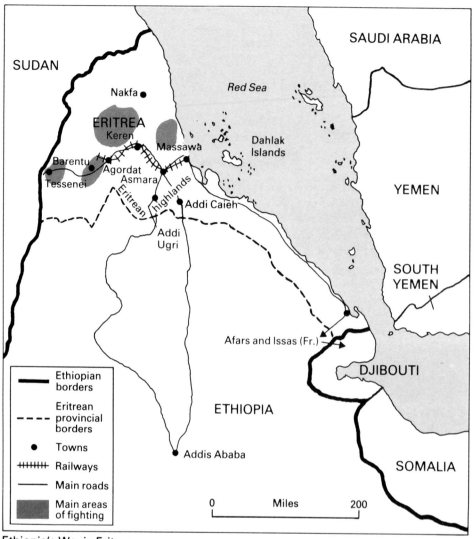

SUDAN

Nakfa ●

ERITREA

Keren

Barentu ●

Agordat

Tessenei ●

Asmara

Eritrean highlands

Addi Caieh ●

Addi Ugri ●

Red Sea

Massawa

Dahlak Islands

SAUDI ARABIA

YEMEN

SOUTH YEMEN

Afars and Issas (Fr.)

DJIBOUTI

ETHIOPIA

Addis Ababa ●

SOMALIA

▬▬▬	Ethiopian borders
╴╴╴	Eritrean provincial borders
●	Towns
┼┼┼┼┼	Railways
───	Main roads
▓	Main areas of fighting

0   Miles   200

Ethiopia's War in Eritrea

Eritrea

Ethiopia

EPLF: Eritrean People's Liberation Front: 12,000.
TPLF: Tigrayan People's Liberation Front: 5,000.
WSLF: Western Somalia Liberation Front: 4,000.

Despite the help of 1,600 Soviet, 3,500 Cuban and 300 East German advisers and specialists, the Ethiopians made little progress. EPLF controlled northern Eritrea from the Red Sea to the Sudanese border, with a 400 km, line of trenches. During 1985 the EPLF claimed to have killed, captured or wounded 29,500 Ethiopian soldiers; this figure was confirmed by international relief workers. In addition they captured 18 tanks, 138 vehicles, 5 armoured personnel carriers and 39 heavy guns.

The guerrillas' arms and equipment consisted largely of captured Soviet-made material but they also received supplies from Kuwait, Somalia and United Arab Emirates. These weapons had been made in the United States, France, Britain, Italy and West Germany. The Soviet commitment appeared to be as strong as ever because the Soviet leaders need Red Sea and Horn of Africa bases to fulfil their strategy of dominating the western Indian Ocean and the Gulf oil shipping routes.

To counter Soviet influence, the Americans back Somalia, which in 1985 had an army of 62,000 out of a population of 6 million. Apart from the dangers of a Soviet-directed Ethiopian attack, the Somalia regime of Siad Barre faced attacks by internal guerrilla groups, notably the Somali Democratic Salvation Front and the Somali National Movement.

The War in 1986-87

Throughout 1986 and 1987 Colonel Mengistu and the Military Council, the Dergue, held the country together through fear; 13 government bodies have the power of arrest and their prisoners are often the result of party in-fighting. Nobody knows how many people are in prison but at week-ends, when relatives are allowed to take food to prisoners, people line up four abreast in a queue that stretches for half-a-mile outside Addis Ababa gaol.

Many university professors and other professionals have fled the country. At least 6,000 students, sent to universities in the Eastern bloc, have fled to the United States, West Germany and Italy. Several ambassadors have sought political asylum. On 27 October 1986 Ethiopia's foreign minister, Goshu Wolde, during a visit to the United Nations in New York, defected to the United States.

Much of Mengistu's policy revolves around a vast collectivisation programme designed to promote, at the expense of the subsistence farmers, the production of cash crops to earn the regime the hard currency it needs to continue its wars against the various liberation movements. This process, known as villagisation,[1] is happening on a scale that recalls the actions of Stalin in the 1930s. By the end of 1986, 3 million peasants had been forced to move; the relocation of another 20 million is planned. The homes of those who refuse to move are burned, sometimes with the people inside. In the new villages the peasants are forced to work so hard on State coffee farms or on private land owned by officials or militiamen that they have only two days a week for their own land. The catalogue of abuses is horrifying. Mengistu rules brutally. At one time during 1986 he convened a meeting of the standing committee of the military council and walked out in the middle of the

The Eritrean People's Liberation Front holds more than 11,000 Ethiopian prisoners of war. It would be easy enough for them to break out but they dare not return home; the Mengistu regime refuses to admit that any Ethiopians have been captured and kills those who escape and return. (Courtesy John Gunston.)

Eritrean soldiers with a captured Ethiopian gun of Soviet manufacture. The Eritreans often raid Ethiopian depots to acquire ammunition for such guns, which they use against their enemy. (Courtesy John Gunston.)

A soldier of the Eritrean People's Liberation Front on reconnaissance patrol in the harsh mountain country of northern Ethiopia. The men and women of this force call themselves freedom fighters but they are members of a conventionally structured fighting organization. (Courtesy John Gunston.)

discussion. His soldiers then went in and massacred the 14 members.[2] He sometimes takes direct command of the fighting in Eritrea and has officers shot when he considers their units inefficient or ineffective.[3]

Unlike rebels fighting in Nicaragua, Kampuchea, Afghanistan or Angola, the Eritreans—with 24,000 fighting men in 1986—are fighting a conventional war, with set-piece battles. The army's eighth general offensive against them took place early in 1986 and was the most successful. The Ethiopian advance northwards was devastating. Many of the soldiers in the Ethiopian army are conscripts from southern areas, speaking different languages and coming from different cultures. These government soldiers treat northern civilians caught up in the war as they would foreign soldiers. Advancing soldiers burnt crops and houses, stole livestock and raped women.

Backed by Soviet weapons and equipment worth nearly a billion dollars, the drive seized more territory than any other campaign. Supported on the ground by Soviet T54 and T55 tanks, covered in the air by MiG 23 fighter-bombers, the Ethiopian troops overran scores of rebel-held villages. In a combined land, sea and air operation they recaptured the towns of Barentu and Tessenei in Western Eritrea. They took the rebels' key agricultural area in the Baraka Valley and established sea supply lines by capturing the Red Sea coastal plain.[4]

The EPLF fighters retreated deep into the hillside of Nakfa, their mountain fortress, and seeded the surrounding lowlands with land-mines. When the Ethiopian infantry and tanks advanced they suffered 1,200 dead and 8,000 wounded.[5] The Ethiopians made repeated air attacks with napalm and cluster bombs but could not dislodge the guerrillas.

The EPLF holds more than 10,000 Ethiopian prisoners in a massive camp spread out across several narrow valleys in the northernmost mountains of Eritrea. Living in groups of 2,000-3,000, the prisoners run the camps themselves, growing vegetables, and breeding rabbits, chickens, goats and ducks for food. Many of them have been in captivity for 10 years. For Ethiopia, these captives do not officially exist and Ethiopian planes have strafed their camps. The EPLF says that the prisoners will be released when an agreement can be reached. The Ethiopian government will not accept repatriation of its nationals because this would be *de facto* acknowledgement of the fighting and of the EPLF's successes. Early in 1987, after long negotiations, the International Red Cross resumed aid to the prisoners.

EPLF is one of the most self-sufficient and politically coherent of all national liberation movements but it cannot be defined as a 'democratic' resistance. All the guerrilla groups are Marxist struggling against a Marxist government; they have the same basic party line. Covert American operations, no matter how efficient, could never create a genuine democratic resistance in Ethiopia and over the years the US has tried to neutralise the Eritrean movement, usually through regional allies in the Middle East and North Africa. The rebels have crippled themselves by internecine squabbles.

Because of the EPLF's socialist character, the West sees it as a more serious long-term threat to its regional interests than the ruling Ethiopian Dergue. The use of satellites has reduced Eritrea's function as a communications centre but its control of 620 miles of Red Sea coast is still important. For the present the West is willing to allow the Soviet Union to pay for Ethiopia's military operations in Eritrea. Western leaders are confident that, once victory is achieved, Ethiopia will quickly turn back to the West. Meanwhile, it is indirectly helping the Ethiopian war effort by ensuring that all other avenues of support to the EPLF are cut off. Moscow is anxious that its most important ally in the region should not be faced with defeat at the hands of the separatist movement. As a result, it continues to prop up a military regime which it knows is looking for a way back to the West, while its military might is being used against a movement which stubbornly refuses to ally itself to the West.

According to many foreign relief workers and some government officials in Addis Ababa, the Soviet Union is helping the Eritreans as well as the Ethiopians. The apparent purpose of Soviet support for both sides is to ensure Ethiopia's continued dependence on Soviet military support. EPLF has such a large quantity of Soviet arms and equipment that it is difficult to believe that all of it has been captured from the Ethiopian army. Some of it, relief workers say, must have come direct from the Russians.

The TPLF appears to have won the 12-year war against the Ethiopians for the hearts and minds of the Tigrayan people; the organisation claims support in 80% of the countryside. During 1986-87 TPLF organised the return of perhaps 100,000 refugee Tigrayans from Sudan. It is re-establishing its political organisations as refugees return to their villages but it has come under the influence of the Marxist-Leninist League of Tigray (MLLT). Set up in July 1986, the MLLT wants to get rid of 'feudal and foreign' forces.

The Somali government watches the war with profound anxiety. They reason that if the Soviet Union cannot acquire Red Sea and Horn of Africa bases through Ethiopia-Eritrea it will try to reach the coast by breaking through Somalia.

The Aid Connection

The relationship of foreign humanitarian aid to continuing war has often been raised but never more vigorously than in the British government's aid programme to Ethiopia. When the British Minister of State at the Foreign and Commonwealth Office, Mrs. Lynda Chalker, visited Ethiopia in April 1987, opponents of aid argued that this was an appropriate time to withdraw Britain's support for a highly unpopular regime in Addis Ababa. They called for all government aid other than famine relief to be stopped and diplomatic links kept to a bare minimum; Britain should identify and support non-Marxist opposition groups.

The argument hinges on the apparent truth that foreign aid indirectly contributes to abuses of human rights on a vast scale, since it frees resources to pay for the resettlement of 5 million Ethiopians. The opponents of British aid also say that it buys no political influence.

There has always been disagreement among opponents of aid as to whether separatist movements in Eritrea should receive British backing and, if so, which of the many factions? Some experts argue that none of them deserves British sympathy. Voluntary aid workers, who are on the spot, strongly disagree, saying that any cut in aid would increase Ethiopia's vast human tragedy without influencing its Marxist regime. They advocate linking aid to policy concessions by the Dergue. The British Government has been advised by academics that, however unpleasant the Addis Ababa regime might be, it is efficiently in control and, although it depends on Soviet support, it dislikes the Russians and their allies.

References

1. Dr. Jason Clay, Director of Research at Cultural Survival, Harvard University, has studied this process.
2. Dr. Dawit Wolde, former Foreign Minister of Ethiopia, in a lecture to East-West Round Table Discussion Group, New York, October 1986.
3. Diplomatic sources in Addis Ababa and Djibouti.
4. A senior relief official on the spot.
5. Paul B. Henze, specialist on Ethiopia, Rand Corporation, Santa Monica, California.

Guerrilla War in Guatemala

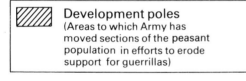

Development poles
(Areas to which Army has
moved sections of the peasant
population in efforts to erode
support for guerrillas)

Guerrilla War in Guatemala

NEW TACTICS ON BOTH SIDES

Background Summary

Successive military governments in Guatemala since 1954 have used violence and terrorism to suppress all opposition, even that of the moderate Christian Democratic Party (CDP). Guatemala's problems were at their worst in the period 1982-83, during the regime of 'born-again' Christian, President Rios Montt. The army conscripted 350,000 men, from a population of 8.2 million, into 'defence patrols', ostensibly to protect towns and villages from Leftist guerrilla attack. During Montt's regime the army massacred 10,000 unarmed civilians; Amnesty International estimates that since 1960 more than 100,000 people have been killed in the terror campaign. Under Montt the regular army numbered only 18,000, its artillery was largely confined to grenade-throwers and its small tanks were useless in the difficult terrain. The guerrillas, 9,000-strong, were equipped with Soviet-made RPG-7 grenade-launchers, Israeli-made Uzi machine-guns and American M-16 rifles. In February 1982 a US Embassy press handout in Guatemala estimated that eight out of ten guerrillas were Indians.

Summary of the War in 1985

Yet another general, Mejia Victores, ruled Guatemala in 1985 and continued the oppression of his predecessors. Labour leaders, Roman Catholic priests, academics and journalists were once again the traditional army targets. Victores forcibly resettled tens of thousands of villagers in areas under army control. The four guerrilla groups formed a coalition known as the Guatemalan National Revolutionary Unity. The total number of men and women may have dropped to no more than 3,000 but they were well led and armed. The strongest group, the Organisation of the People in Arms (ORPA), was led by Rodrigo Asturias. In 1985 Asturias changed his tactics from ambushes to attacks on army bases, outposts and supply depots. The army, now 33,000 strong, responded by increased death squad activity.

The War in 1986-87

In 1986 Vinicio Cerezo became the first civilian President for 32 years but General Victores remained as head of the armed forces. Encouraged by the presence of a civilian leader, the Mutual Support Group of the Relatives of the Disappeared (GAM) led by Nineth de Garcia, stepped up demands for human rights abuses to be investigated but Cerezo has been slow to respond.

The army's strategy against the guerrillas is built around the 'model villages', barracks-style settlements which carry large signs proclaiming AN IDEOLOGICALLY ANTI-SUBVERSIVE COMMUNITY. Built on the model of the 'strategic hamlet' system in Vietnam, the villages are clustered in what the army calls 'development poles' and are part of the counter-insurgency campaign against guerrillas in the rebels' former strongholds. The people of each village carry out a daily military ritual. As dusk falls they line up on parade before the flagpole. Their faces impassive, their voices flat, they chant the national anthem, the army hymn and the Guatemalan oath of allegiance. Overlooking each settlement is an army outpost in a fortified building; its job is as much to watch the residents as to look out for guerrillas.

The army believes that the peasants—60% of Guatemala's population are of pure Indian blood—if left in their original hamlets could easily become guerrilla supporters, either by choice or coercion. Their new villages are attractive and they have houses with running water and electricity, schools, health clinics and roads. These benefits were, however, bestowed on the army's terms. The peasants' original homes were burned, their crops and livestock destroyed. 'If they wanted to live they had to come in', a senior officer has said.

The villagers have been indoctrinated to believe that they owe their lives to the army. To repay this debt, the men are required to take part in the civil defence patrols, which operate in every village and small town in Guatemala. In 1986 service was obligatory for all males between the ages of 16 and 50. In 1987 this was extended to cover boys of 15 and men of 55. An estimated 1 million men, armed with carbines and shotguns, take their 24-hour shift as often as the local army commander tells them to. The Guatemala Episcopal Conference repeatedly asks for the patrols to be disbanded but the army is proud of its counter-insurgency campaign, and believes that the patrols are a key part of it. They work on a psychological principle as well as on military practice; by arming the villagers and giving them something worth defending they can be induced to believe that the guerrillas are their enemies.

Monseigneur José Pablo Urizer, Bishop of Quiché Province, considers the system immoral. 'For the indigenous Indian, land is part of his being,' he maintains. 'Their traditions have been stolen from them.' Since 1980 about 250,000 Guatemalans have fled to Mexico, Belize, Honduras and the United States; 100,000 live in camps in southern Mexico alone.

Guatemala has an area of 108,889 square kilometres, much of it mountainous and jungle-clad with deep river valleys, and the army's strategy has not put the guerrillas out of business: they are effective out of all proportion to their numbers and small groups continue to attack military bases. In 1987 it seemed that Rodrigo Asturias and his ORPA had found a way of countering the army's 'development poles' technique. His men do one of the few things open to them—they attack the army posts at the model villages. With grenades and explosive charges, they damage the strongpoints from which the soldiers keep watch on a village and then kill the garrison. Such an attack takes only a few minutes so that by the time an army helicopter gunship arrives the guerrillas have disappeared.

The guerrillas try not to compromise the villagers by asking for food—they steal it. It is known that they have some refuges in the jungles of British-protected Belize, to which the Guatemalan government lays claim. The presence of 1,800

This soldier of the Guatemalan Army is watching the dispersal of a demonstration by landless labourers following their five-day march from the Pacific coast. While there are signs of a return to democracy in Guatemala, it will be on the army's terms. (Courtesy Paul Harley.)

British troops there acts as a deterrent to invasion. The guerrilla bands are not short of arms, mostly Soviet-made equipment, which reaches them from El Salvador, Honduras and Mexico.

Unlike guerrillas in many other countries, the ORPA fighters often attack at night. Such small parties are involved that control in the dark is not a problem. The murder of a single senior army officer in his bed or the burning down of an army depot is considered a major triumph. Few guerrillas are killed or captured and some diplomatic observers say that this is why the frustrated army attacks innocent civilians.

Early in 1987 guerrilla raiders sank a Zodiac-type patrol boat at Puerto Quetzal naval base and at an air force station near Coban they destroyed a Bell helicopter. On paper the air force has 22 Bells but as only three are operational the loss was severe.

The periodic military sweeps of Guatemala in search of guerrillas involve practically the entire army of 12 infantry battalions, the armoured battalion, four reconnaissance squadrons and the two-battalion brigade of 'special forces', a commando-type formation. However, these sweeps are never fruitful because of the considerable and obvious preparation which goes on beforehand. Foreign diplomats say that they know three weeks in advance of a sweep.

The high hopes of peace which came in with President Cerezo have not been justified. In an interview with foreign Press correspondents, Cerezo said that he holds 30% of the power and the army 70%. Between 1980 and 1987 more than 200 massacres were reported to Amnesty International, together with countless individual killings and disappearances. Army patrols crossed the border into Mexico in 1986 and 1987, attacking people in refugee camps. There are 32 Guatemalan refugee camps in Mexico.

Given the high professionalism of ORPA guerrillas and the implacable army hostility to negotiating with them, peace seems unattainable. What has been called 'the dirtiest war' is a long way from over.

Foreign Assessments

Several international organizations have investigated violations of human rights by the military in Guatemala. This is a selection of extracts from their reports.

'For many years there have been denunciations against the systematic violations of human rights against the Guatemalan population. This situation is one of the most serious in all America, in which the Indians have been the victims of massacres, tortures, detention on a massive scale, the destruction of homes, crops and harvests.' The International Indian Treaty Council, in a paper to the UN Human Rights Commission, August 1983.

'Guatemala could be considered the worst violator of human rights in Latin America, even when compared to El Salvador.' A delegation of European Catholic agencies, leader Bishop Eamonn Case of Ireland, in a report, August 1983.

'The Guatemalan Army has been principally responsible for the most grievous violations of human rights, including destruction, burning and sacking of entire towns and the deaths of both combatant and non-combatant populations in these towns.' From *The Situation of Human Rights in Guatemala*, prepared by the Inter-American Commission of Human Rights, October 1983.

Holy War–Jihad

Background Summary

Jihad is not an alternative war or a substitute for war—it *is* war. It is fought openly and conventionally as in the Iran-Iraq war, covertly by assassination, and in terrorist form through kidnappings and suicide bombings. *Jihad* has been ceaseless since the founding of Islam in the 7th century; Ayatollah Khomeini 'declared' the present phase of the conflict in November 1979. The present campaign is largely in the hands of the Shi'a Muslims of Iran, together with the more extremist of the Sunni Muslims, such as Colonel Gaddafi of Libya.

Jihad is not merely Islam's war against the Christian West and against the Jews; it is also aimed at all Muslim monarchs, as monarchies are anathema to strict Shi'a Muslims. Kuwait is a major target because the government refuses to release from prison 17 Shi'a terrorists imprisoned for a series of bombings in 1983.

Other enemies are 'reactionary' regimes, such as that of Egypt, and those which Muslims accuse of having betrayed Islam, such as Morocco. Gaddafi, who regards himself as the Mahdi—the 'expected one' of Islam—regards his opponents as enemies to be destroyed in Holy War.

Many acts of Holy War were committed in the period 1979-85 including the truck bomb attack on the US Marine Headquarters in Beirut, on 23 October 1983. Throughout this period *Islamic Jihad* set up a system of strategic commands to cover the world. Various wars are jihadic to some extent. They include: the Iran-Iraq war; the Bangladesh-Shanti Bahini war; the Afghanistan war; the Indonesia-East Timor war; the war in Lebanon; and the Philippine war against Muslim insurgents.

(For a full description of the phenomenon of Holy War and activities since 1979 see **WAR ANNUAL** 1.)

Holy War During 1986-87

During 1986 it was learned that *Islamic Jihad* had decided to make kamikaze attacks on American warships and certain US installations, such as embassies, in the Middle East.[1] 'Martyrs', mostly Shi'a Muslim Iranians, were being trained as pilots of light aircraft. Packed with explosives, the planes would be deliberately crashed on to the selected targets. That no such attacks had taken place up to mid-1987 had more to do with efficient Intelligence and counter-measures than any change of policy by the *Islamic Jihad* command.

Much terrorism carried out by Iranian and Arab agents during 1986-87 was part of the holy war campaign and its targets were mostly European and American. Attacks were planned and co-ordinated within the Iranian embassies in London, Rome, Vienna and Paris. A party of eight Iranian terrorists was arrested in Paris on

22 March 1987 and identified as being directly under the control of the Speaker of the Iranian parliament, Hojateleslam Rafsanjani.

It was noticeable during 1986-87 that several previously unknown holy war/terrorist groups appeared. They include the Revolutionary Justice Organisation, the Organisation of the Oppressed of the Earth, *Islamic Jihad* for the Liberation of Palestine and Arab Fedayeen Cells. Some appear to be offshoots of the Lebanese Shi'a holy war organisation *Hezbollah* ('Party of God') but Intelligence reports suggests that they are sometimes *Hezbollah* itself acting under different names. *Islamic Jihad* deliberately creates confusion over the identity and sponsorship of groups. However, all are linked, at least at liaison level. Similarly, the Syrian and Libyan regimes are linked to *Islamic Jihad*; both countries supply high-ranking representatives to the policy-making and strategy-forming councils of the controlling organization.

Despite this degree of co-operation, some groups feel greater allegiance to one country or one leader than to others. For instance, in 1986 a new name came to light in the waging of holy war—that of Imad Murniyah. Connected with the Palestine Liberation Organisation (PLO) before 1982, he led a group of men which broke away from the PLO after its withdrawal from Beirut and his activities are now financed and directed from Teheran.

The unusually well-informed columnist of the *Washington Post*, Jack Anderson, reported that the Iranian ambassador to the Vatican, Ayatollah Khosrow-Shahi, 'is believed to direct a network of operations in Spain, Italy, West Germany, Britain and France. The notches on his gun include a former Iranian general and the United Arab Emirates ambassador to France—both assassinated.'[2]

Khosrow-Shahi discredited himself by an absurd claim to have converted the Pope to Shi'a Muslim faith and was replaced in 1987. Muhammad Moghaddam is now the highest religious-political Shi'a Muslim in Europe.

Khosrow-Shahi was certainly important in the *Islamic Jihad* command in Europe but his embassy in the Vatican was not the major operations centre. For several months this was the Iranian embassy in West Germany, from which 22 terrorist networks were controlled. This statement was made by Massood Rajavi, leader of an Iranian underground anti-Khomeini group known as the People's Mujahideen Organisation, itself committed to holy war but in this case against Khomeini. Rajavi alleged that a mosque in Hamburg was a 'vital link' in the *Islamic Jihad* structure.[3]

Early in September 1986 the Egyptian Security Police arrested 35 men on charges of plotting to overthrow the Mubarak regime. When the case came to court in December, the Prosecutor General explained that the group had stolen firearms, explosives and ammuniton from army depots 'in order to launch *jihad* to destroy the nation's ruling system'. The accused men include five military officers and several individuals implicated in the assassination of President Anwar Sadat in 1981.[4]

The officers are Major Fahki Abdel Badie, Major Ebdel Samir Dessouki, Captain Muhammad Abdel Waheb, Abdel Rahman and Lieutenant Muhammad Abou Muhammad Ali.

One objective of *Islamic Jihad* is to purge the Middle East of Western influence. To this end the famous American University of Beirut (AUB) became a major target in 1986-87. For decades AUB was the symbol of liberal values in the Middle East. it was modern, cosmopolitan, tolerant and secular. It prized knowledge and freedom, opposed backwardness and ignorance and was the embodiment of what the United States represented to a hopeful generation of Arabs. Nineteen of the signatories to the United Nations Charter in 1945 were graduates of the AUB.

Like America itself, the AUB was vulnerable to attack. For these reasons—its power and its vulnerability—it became a special target for attack by Islamic zealots. This is why several American professors on the staff of the university were kidnapped. AUB President, Malcolm Kerr, was murdered by a gunman on the doorstep of his office.

Ninety foreigners were kidnapped in Lebanon in the period 1985-87; to mid-1987 ten were known to have been killed.

France fears renewed holy war. The fear stems from the decision to order trials for the Lebanese terrorist Georges Ibrahim Abdallah and three members of the French terrorist group *Action Direct*—and their subsequent conviction. French anti-terrorist policy centres on intricate Middle East diplomacy. French officials say that they do not negotiate with terrorist groups but they do acknowledge attempts to woo Iran and Syria. To satisfy Teheran, the French expelled activists hostile to Khomeini in France and paid back US$300 million of a billion dollar loan taken out from the former Shah of Iran's government. The French government has sold arms to Iran. To satisfy Damascus, the French refused to follow the example of the British and break diplomatic relations after Syria's complicity in the attempted destruction of an El Al aircraft in April 1986.

Colonel Gaddafi, throughout the 1986-87 period, had a triple approach to *jihad*. At one level he was involved in international terrorism through the financing, training and encouragement of terrorism. There was, however, nothing new in this. Secondly, he openly preached *jihad* in African states. 'Africa must be Muslim,' Gaddafi said in a speech in Kigali, capital of Rwanda.[5] 'Christians are intruders in Africa and agents of colonialism; we must wage a holy war so that Islam will spread in Africa.'

The occasion for his attack on Christianity was the opening of a mosque and an Islamic centre, worth US$5 million, which Libya had largely financed. 'You are hoisting the banner of Islam below the Equator, in the messiah of Allah,' he announced. Attacking President Mobutu of Zaire, who is Christian, Gaddafi went on: 'Killing Mobutu and his aides is the duty of every Muslim. You must incite Muslims in Zaire and urge them to engage in *jihad* so that Mobutu may be toppled . . . .'

Gaddafi's third approach to *jihad* is conventional warfare. Throughout 1986 Libyan missions in several countries recruited mercenaries for Gaddafi's Islamic Legion, or its branch, the Pan-African Islamic Legion. Maltese newspapers, among others, carried full-age advertisements in English seeking recruits. Part of the advertisement read: 'The Great International Revolutionary, Muammar Gaddafi, has announced that the doors are open for volunteers . . . to work in technical and installation fields of all types of weapons, the naval, air force and land ones as well as air defence . . . .'

For his Pan-African Legion, Gaddafi also wanted fighting soldiers and he managed to induce Mauritanians, Rwandans, Nigerians, Sudanese and others to flock to his banner as 'warriors for *jihad* . . . soldiers for Allah'. These men fought in Chad. (See the account of the Chad-Libya war, pp. 48–53).

References

1. Intelligence and diplomatic sources.
2. *Washington Post* 20 January 86.
3. West German police confirmed this. They arrested 46 Iranians who had earlier been expelled from West Germany but had illegally returned.
4. *Al Ahram*, the leading Cairo daily newspaper, 14 December 1986.
5. Broadcast over "The Voice of the Greater Arab Homeland" for Tripoli: 17 May 1986; 2015 GMT.

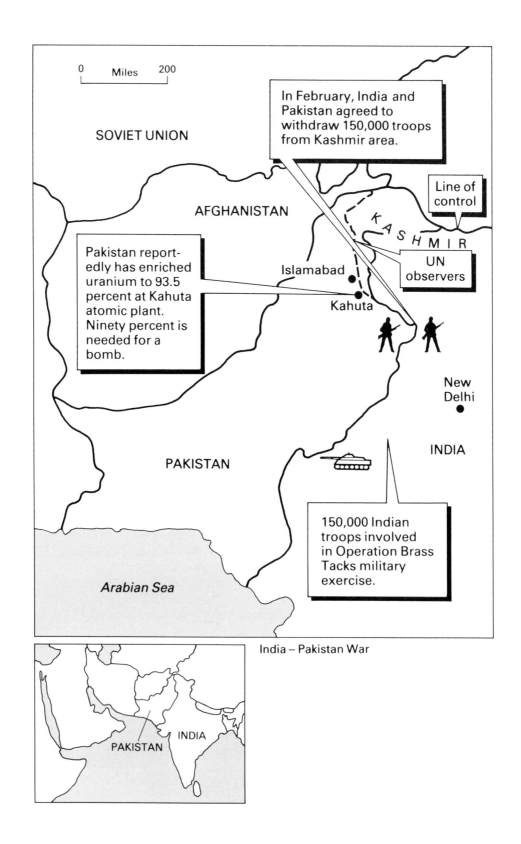

0 Miles 200

SOVIET UNION

AFGHANISTAN

In February, India and Pakistan agreed to withdraw 150,000 troops from Kashmir area.

Line of control

K A S H M I R

UN observers

Pakistan reportedly has enriched uranium to 93.5 percent at Kahuta atomic plant. Ninety percent is needed for a bomb.

Islamabad

Kahuta

New Delhi

PAKISTAN

INDIA

150,000 Indian troops involved in Operation Brass Tacks military exercise.

Arabian Sea

India – Pakistan War

PAKISTAN

INDIA

India–Pakistan War

Background Summary

India and Pakistan share a 2,000-mile border that stretches from the Arabian Sea and the deserts of Sind and Rajasthan to the giant snow-covered mountains of the Karakoram Range. In Kashmir the Indian and Pakistan armies have been in a state of tense conflict and low-key war since 1947. Divided by a UN ceasefire line, India holds two-thirds of Kashmir and Pakistan the other third. Pakistan's claim to the whole territory is that the population is two-thirds Muslim. The argument is also over water; the headwaters of the rivers that flow through Pakistani Kashmir originate in India. In addition, Pakistan is worried that India holds the Siachin glacier which overlooks the strategic 800-mile Kakakorah highway which links Pakistan with Peking. Pakistan and China are allies.

(*For full details of the entire war see* **WAR ANNUAL** 1.)

Summary of the War in 1985

Early in the year small-scale but fierce fighting took place, the Pakistanis suffering 50 casualties and the Indians 30. In June Pakistani aircraft bombed Indian positions on the glacier and in a series of dogfights India claimed to have shot down two Pakistani aircraft. UN observers, who are permanently stationed in the region, reported that casualties ran into hundreds. Pakistan claimed that India was contemplating a full-scale invasion.

Operations in 1986-87

The danger facing the Indian government in Kashmir is the emergence of a Muslim fundamentalist party, the Muslim United Front (MUF). The MUF worries both the local Indian political parties—the Congress Party and the National Convention party. All the MUF candidates profess loyalty to the Indian constitution but the largest faction of MUF, *Jamiat-i-Islami*, has long supported the secession of Kashmir to Pakistan. In an election campaign the Indian Prime Minister, Rajiv Gandhi, told predominantly Hindu crowds in Jammu that the election campaign was 'a war against anti-national forces' and accused *Jamiat* of being part of a well-planned foreign conspiracy. The MUF spokesman, Abdul Ghani, did not help the cause of peace when he referred to the Hindus as 'a creedless people with no religious philosophy'. The Indians are convinced that Pakistani agents are behind the troubles in the Punjab and that Pakistan is arming and training Sikh militants.

During 1986 both sides concentrated troops in the Jammu section of the border.

The Pakistani Army dug a 30-foot deep, anti-tank canal along the border, with a mixture of heavy and light tanks protecting it. Tension was so great that 100,000 people fled the area. In February 1987 India and Pakistan reached an agreement to prevent border clashes from erupting into large-scale conflict. Pakistan withdrew an infantry division and an armoured division which had straddled the 'chicken neck' area of Khemkaran, linking Jammu and Kashmir with the rest of India, while India pulled back one division. In the past ferocious fighting has taken place over the 'chicken neck'. In the meantime India carried out an enormous army exercise involving 150,000 troops known as 'Brass Tacks' in the Rajasthan Desert. The Pakistanis called this 'provocative'.

This allegation was based on the scenario for Brass Tacks, which was divided into four parts—first, an exercise on the assumption that Pakistan had seized some Indian territory; second, a defensive exercise, and third, an offensive exercise. It was the fourth element which most worried Pakistan—a simulated Indian thrust into the Sind area of Pakistan to capture Hyderabad and an attack on the Pakistani coast near Karachi. 'The scenario is too uncomfortably close to what a real attack would be,' one authority has said.[1] 'Add to this the fact that the Indian army has been transformed in the past 5 or 6 years into a heavy mechanised force.' India found the Pakistani manoeuvres equally menacing.

India is under increasing pressure to enter a nuclear arms race with Pakistan, following reports that Pakistan is close to, or has already achieved, a nuclear weapons capability. The US is also selling sophisticated military equipment to Pakistan. This equipment, worth US$4.02 billion, includes radar and early-warning systems. Pakistan is the United States's one ally in the region. In 1981 the US waived the 'Symington amendment', which prohibits US aid to countries possessing unsafeguarded nuclear equipment and technology, to allow aid to Pakistan after the Soviet invasion of Afghanistan.

The stated purpose for so much additional military strength is that it will help to check border attacks from Soviet-occupied Afghanistan. However, India considers that Pakistan is more likely to use its now considerable military power against India. In any case, some Indian sources claim, Pakistan is already a nuclear power.[2]

The presence of 65 UN observers in Kashmir—increased from 40 in 1986—is probably responsible for keeping the conflict within the definition of a 'border war'.

References

1. Prem Shanker Jha, editor of a leading Indian daily newspaper, *The Hindustan Times*.
2. Commodore Jasjit Singh of the Indian government-sponsored Institute for Defence Studies and Analyses.

India's Sikh–Hindu War

TERRORISM IN PUNJAB

Background Summary

The Sikhs of the Punjab chose to remain part of India at the time of partition in 1947. They understood that they would be given a Punjabi-speaking state which they would call Khalistan, that Chandigargh would be the capital and that the new state would get its share of water and electric power. These simple requirements grew to a list of 45 political, religious and economic demands. In 1980 the Sikhs embarked on a civil war against the central government. Jarnail Singh Bhindran-wale became leader of the nationalist *Akali Dal* party, preached an implacable religious fundamentalism and turned the Golden Temple of Amritsar into a great fortress. It became the scene of a pitched battle in June 1984 when the Indian Prime Minister, Mrs. Gandhi, ordered Indian commandos to capture the temple and defeat the terrorist extremists. In the battle, code-named Blue Star, 60 Indian soldiers were killed and 600 Sikhs, including Bhindrinwale, who was aged only 36. Sikh members of Mrs. Gandhi's bodyguard assassinated her on 31 October 1984.

(*For a description of the entire war see* **WAR ANNUAL** 1.)

Summary of the War in 1985

The Sikhs replaced all their own moderate leaders with extremists and began a terrorist campaign against Hindus. Joginder Singh, Bhindrinwale's aged father and the new leader, declared a 'holy war' to gain more political and religious autonomy. Rajiv Gandhi, having succeeded his mother as Prime Minister, tried to reach a settlement with Sikh moderates but negotiations became impossible when they were attacked and murdered by extremists. Sikh strategy broadened in 1985 and underground groups, such as the *Dal Khalsa*, the *Babbar Khalsa* and the *Dashmesh* Regiment, established bases in Europe—notably in Britain—Canada and the United States. An operational headquarters was set up in Britain and its leaders found ways of giving instructions to Sikhs in India. Pakistani agents set up training camps for Sikh rebels in Daska and Sialkot in Jammu State.[1] Terrorist acts proliferated; a group based in Canada is believed to have planted the bomb which blew up an Air India Boeing 747. Prime Minister Gandhi predicted a lengthy 'terrorist war'.

The War in 1986-87

Sikhs make up less than 2% of India's 760 million population. In Punjab they constitute a 52% majority. Historically, they have had a greater influence over India's economy, politics and army than their numbers suggest. The *Akali Dal* party

India's Sikh-Hindu War

maintains that the Sikhs' role in the army has gradually declined, but there seems little evidence to support this. Their participation in the army of 1 million has stayed at 10%-12% for a decade. Sikh leaders also say that they are concerned that Sikhs in the armed forces are denied promotions because of lingering suspicions that they are unreliable. Operation Blue Star, which triggered the defection of about 5,000 Sikh soldiers, certainly brought profound changes to the image of Sikhs in the Indian army.

As the Sikhs' war for a separate state of Khalistan intensified, the number of Sikh extremists and their supporters multiplied. Violence increased and terrified Hindus migrated from Punjab to other states while Sikhs outside Punjab moved back. In the week following Mrs. Gandhi's assassination more than 2,150 Sikhs were slaughtered in New Delhi, besides another 617 in other places. Sikh terrorists quickly began to even the score.[2]

Supporters of the All-India Sikh Students Federation (AISSF), the youth wing of the *Akali Dal*, occupied the Golden Temple on 26 January 1986 and on 30 April, from the Temple, they declared the independence of Khalistan. To retain his credibility as Chief Minister of Punjab, Surjit Singh Barnala had no recourse other than to sanction the police to clear the Temple. This was successfully done, although only at the price of exploitation by Barnala's political rivals within the *Akali-Dal* party; they withdrew their support in the face of such 'sacrilege'. In this second raid on the Golden Temple the authorities employed a new national security formation of police commandos who, because of their black uniform, have acquired the name the 'Black Cats'. They used stun grenades in their operation.

On 10 August 1986 India's former army chief, General Arun Vaidya, who ordered the assault on the Golden Temple was assassinated by Sikh gunmen and in October that year there was an attempt on Gandhi's life. Besides Hindus, the terrorists gun down moderate Sikh political figures, civil servants and policemen. As a result, members of the security forces avoid confrontation; several have been identified as being in league with the terrorists. In October 1986 two policemen were among a terrorist gang that attempted to assassinate Punjab police chief Julio Ribeiro. Sikh policemen are known to reveal police radio frequencies to terrorists.

Tension has erupted into violence on many occasions. In New Delhi on 2 December 1986 Hindus fought sword-swinging Sikhs, as police tried to control 16,000 rioters. On 4 March 1987 an off-duty Sikh policeman from near Amritsar made a visit to the Golden Temple. When he entered a residential area to seek accommodation for the night he mentioned that he was a policeman. He was seized and taken to the Temple, where he was tortured. His screams of pain were heard by a nearby guard who summoned a rescue party of 26 unarmed policemen. They were fired on with pistols and beaten with clubs before a 10-man army patrol rescued the relief group and the tortured man.

While the great majority of the 14 million Sikhs are content to live in peace with Hindus in Punjab, which is India's most prosperous state, the existence of such terrorist groups as the Khalistan Liberation Army and the Khalistan Commandos threatens that peace.[3] Mrs. Gandhi said that India will not again be divided. Her son Rajiv has reaffirmed that promise. Already the 1.4 million Gurkhas in West Bengal demand a state of their own. Various Muslim groups among the 100 million Muslims in India also want independent homelands. The Indian government knows that to surrender to Sikh demands would result in violent dismemberment of the country.[4]

References

1. Report from UN observer force in Jammu-Kashmir.
2. The figures are those of the Indian Government; several reports indicate that they are much higher but kept secret so as to prevent an even bloodier Sikh revenge.
3. The Sikhs are in several ways comparable to the Protestants of Ulster. This indicates the intractable difficulties of finding any kind of ultimate solution.
4. In private conversation Indian government ministers refer to the 'Sikh War'.

Iran–Iraq (Gulf) War

CONFLICT IN MARSHES, MOUNTAINS AND DESERTS

Background Summary

The Gulf War began on 17 September 1980 when the Iraqi President, Saddam Hussein, ordered his army to capture Iranian territory which he claimed belonged to Iraq. The main bone of contention was the Shatt-al-Arab waterway, Iraq's only outlet to the Arabian Gulf and through which it exports much of its oil. As the once powerful Iranian army disintegrated during the early rule of the Ayatollah Khomeini, the time seemed to be ripe for invasion to regain the whole of the Shatt-al-Arab. Saddan Hussein had other objectives, the chief of which were:

> To make Baghdad the power centre of the Middle East. To replace non-Arab Iran as the dominant Gulf nation. To undercut any effort by revolutionary Shi'a Islam to subvert Iraq through its large Shi'a Muslim community.

The Iraqis had powerful armed forces while the Iranians, most of their best Generals executed by the religious zealots, were led by *mullahs* with little military experience. The Iranian air force had relatively few operational aircraft but an Iraqi pre-emptive assault hit 10 major Iranian air bases on 22 September 1980. As the Iranian Phantoms were in protective hangars few were lost.

The Iraqi infantry assault invasion achieved tactical surprise. Military analysts, politicians and journalists predicted that Iraq would win the war in a matter of weeks; the Iraqi attack was likened to a blitz and to 'an Israeli-type' attack. But the Iranian lines did not break and the leadership did not accept defeat and propose peace.

For the first year the conflict was limited to artillery duels and patrol actions. In 1981, as more pro-Shah Iranian commanders were allowed to return to their posts, the Iranian army stopped the Iraqis on the Kharun River and a counter-attack drove the invaders beyond their borders. By now Egypt, Saudi Arabia and Jordan were backing Iraq while Syria and Libya supported Iran. In July 1982 Iran launched *Operational Ramadan*, a massive assault by wave after wave of Revolutionary Guards (*Pasdaran*). Their casualties were immense but in places they recovered some territory.

On 6 February 1983 the Iranians attacked with 200,000 troops on a front of 25 miles south-east of Baghdad. The thrust broke through but Iraq's air strength killed 6,000 Iranians that day and Iran's final gain was small. Iran struck again in April 1983 but the assault beat itself out against the Iraqi defences. By the end of the year Iran had lost 120,000 men killed and 30,000 taken prisoner. Meanwhile Iraq had acquired enormous quantities of Soviet arms and equipment and had built up a fortification system. In all, 40 nations were selling armaments to the two combatant countries.

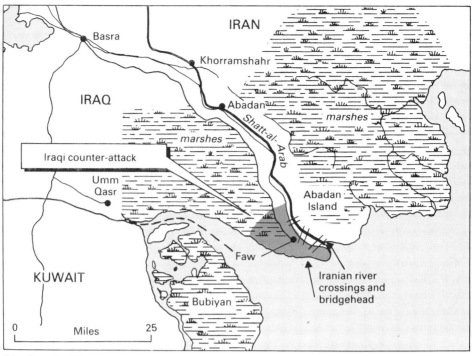

The Faw Battle

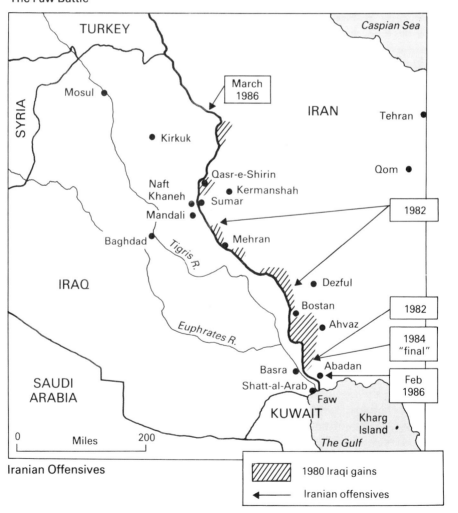

Iranian Offensives

//// 1980 Iraqi gains

← Iranian offensives

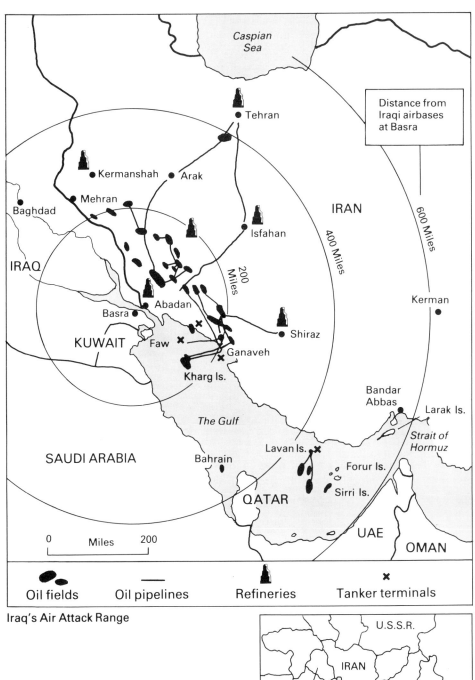

Distance from Iraqi airbases at Basra

Caspian Sea

Tehran

Kermanshah • Arak

Mehran

Baghdad

IRAN

Isfahan

600 Miles

400 Miles

200 Miles

IRAQ

Kerman

Basra

Abadan

KUWAIT   Faw   Ganaveh

Shiraz

Kharg Is.

Bandar Abbas

Larak Is.

The Gulf

Strait of Hormuz

SAUDI ARABIA

Bahrain

Lavan Is.

Forur Is.

Sirri Is.

QATAR

UAE   OMAN

0   Miles   200

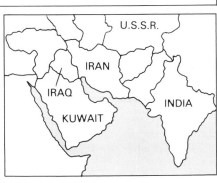

● ● Oil fields   — Oil pipelines   ▮ Refineries   ✕ Tanker terminals

Iraq's Air Attack Range

U.S.S.R.

IRAN

IRAQ

INDIA

KUWAIT

Great set-piece battles continued into 1984. *Operation Daw 5*, which began on 27 February, was one of the most important, with 500,000 Iranians engaged. Some actions of this battle took place in marshlands, north of Basra. Another phase was fought out in flat desert, north-east of Basra; yet another in the reed-filled Hawizah Marshes, near the confluence of the Tigris and Euphrates rivers. In a period of four weeks the Iraqis killed 40,000 Iranians and lost 9,000 of their own men. The Iraqis used mustard gas on the southern front and caused 1,000 Iranian deaths. When Iran threatened to use chemical weapons in retaliation the Iraqis stopped their gas attacks. Yet another Iranian offensive took place on 18 October 1984 in hills overlooking the Tigris plain. Some ground was gained but two days later an Iraqi counter-attack pushed the Iranians back.

At the end of the year General Qassemali Zahir Nejad was largely responsible for a new Iranian strategy. Its aims were:

> To threaten Iraq in the south.
> To make major repeated attacks in the north directly west towards Baghdad, 150 miles away.
> To wage a general war of attrition, in the belief that time and numbers were on Iran's side.

Foreign observers were now convinced that neither side could lose the war and that any end would be brought about by the overthrow of Saddam Hussein within Iraq or by political moves. Iraq made repeated requests for peace negotiations but all were rejected by the Iranian leadership.

(*For a full description of the entire war, including details of the combatant nations' military strength, see* **WAR ANNUAL** 1.)

Summary of Operations in 1985

Both sides refrained from making massive frontal attacks and devoted the greater part of their military energy to improving their defences. Iraq completed a great lake—known as Fish Lake—and a network of canals to defend Basra, at a cost of at least 1 billion dollars. Meanwhile the Iranians dug long and deep tank traps and built heavily-defended gun positions to stop any tanks which might got through.

The Iraqis' principal targets for 1985 were the oil installations of Iran's Kharg Island and tankers using its facilities. In this way the Iraqis hoped to cripple Iran's economy. Wanting an 'honourable' peace, the Iraqis hoped to bring about a settlement imposed by the great powers. At the end of 1985, after more than five years of fighting, Iraq held 270 square miles of Iranian territory while Iran claimed to have captured 368 sq. miles of Iraqi territory. Iranian dead totalled at least 170,000 and possibly as many as 250,000; the Iraqis held 41,000 Iranian prisoners. About 66,000 Iraqis had died and 11,000 were prisoners. The great danger was that the war would spill over into Kuwait and Saudi Arabia, both of which have large Shi'a minorities who consider Ayatollah Khomeini as their spiritual leader.

The propaganda war was fiercely fought in 1985, both sides justifying the war on religious grounds. Teheran Radio presented the conflict as 'a war between Islam and heresy'; that is, between Khomeini's fiery type of Shi'a Islam and the rule of Iraq's secular Saddam Hussein. Khomeini called Hussein 'the epitome of atheist filth'. In Iraq the war against Iran was described as the continuation of the battle of Kadisiya in 637 when the Arabs destroyed the Persian Empire. Iraq, the world was told, was fighting for the Arab race against 'the vile Persian aggressors'.

The War in 1986-87

Iran's *Operation Dawn 8* began on 9 February 1986. Five divisions of troops crossed the Shatt-al-Arab at several points south-east of Basra and captured the coastal town of Faw on Fao peninsula. Iraqi resistance stiffened and contained the assault but again casualties were heavy. The Iraqis claimed to have killed 25,000 Iranians; the Iranians claimed 12,000 Iraqi dead. The offensive was so spirited that the Iranians approached the Kuwaiti border and Kuwait and Saudi Arabia put their forces on high alert. Major-General Shawkat Ata, commander at Fao when the Iranians attacked, was called to Baghdad to explain—and disappeared.

Dawn 8 was followed by *Dawn 9* on 24-25 February, more than 500 miles further north. In line with the strategy of forcing the Iraqis to guess about the next major attack, the Iranians struck north-east of Sulaimaniya, about 60 miles east of the vital Kirkuk oil centre. The attack was largely designed to encourage the pro-Iranian Kurdish guerrillas but it also captured 200 sq. miles of territory and 60 deserted Kurdish villages. Iraq again used mustard gas, as well as the nerve gas tabun and cyanide-based poison. The Iranian High Command claimed that 8,500 of its soldiers had been affected. The Iraqis denied using chemical weapons but a United Nations specialist medical team of doctors from Spain, Australia, Sweden and Switzerland reported that gas had killed or seriously wounded at least 700 Iranian soldiers.

At the end of *Dawn 8* and *Dawn 9* the Iranians could claim some victories. On the central front their troops in the Maimak Hills were less than 70 miles from Baghdad; in the Hawizah Marshes Iranian soldiers were within sight of the Baghdad-Basra railway; on the Fao peninsula they held their positions. But with Iraqi aircraft dominating all the battlefronts a significant Iranian breakthrough seemed unlikely.

The battle of Faw was of high strategic importance. The Faco peninsula itself does not mean much but the fighting at Faw says much about the competence of Iraq's soldiers and Iraq's will to go on fighting. Iraq had six times as many aircraft as Iran, yet the Iranians, mostly at night, sneaked over on pontoons, on floating walkways and on a fleet of small boats, which they hid by day. The Iranian High Command went on reinforcing its 30,000 troops in the bridgehead and kept open the lines of communication even though the Shatt is half-a-mile wide and the tide rises and falls 10 feet a day. Some of Iraq's best units, such as the armoured brigade of the Presidential Guard, were thrown into the battle under the command of some of the best generals. Yet in March 1986 the Iraqi counter-attack became bogged down against an Iranian defensive arc in flat, wet country five miles from the wrecked remains of the town of Faw. To get the Iranians out of their well-entrenched positions the generals would have to use infantry but they shrank from the casualties this would cause, despite their President's exhortation that the Iranian bridgehead had to be eliminated 'at all costs'.

By March 1986 Iraq had 1 million men under arms in 30 divisions; half were in regular units, half in militias. The High Command achieved this massive total by

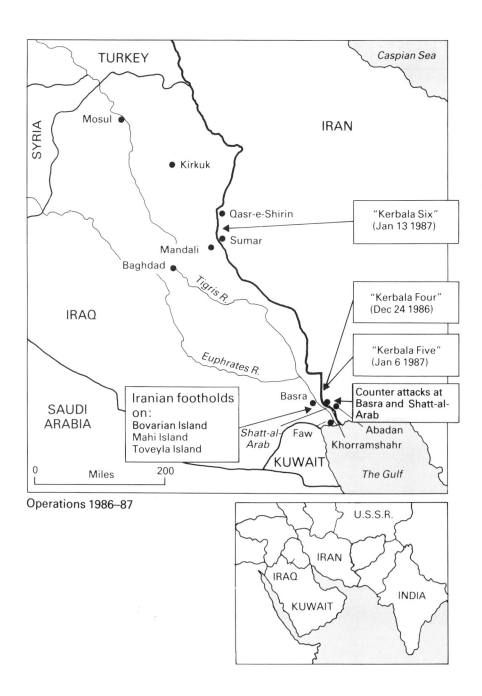

TURKEY

Caspian Sea

SYRIA

Mosul

IRAN

Kirkuk

Qasr-e-Shirin

"Kerbala Six"
(Jan 13 1987)

Sumar

Mandali

Baghdad

Tigris R.

IRAQ

"Kerbala Four"
(Dec 24 1986)

Euphrates R.

"Kerbala Five"
(Jan 6 1987)

Counter attacks at
Basra and Shatt-al-
Arab

Basra

Iranian footholds
on:
Bovarian Island
Mahi Island
Toveyla Island

SAUDI
ARABIA

Abadan

Shatt-al-
Arab

Faw

Khorramshahr

0   Miles   200

KUWAIT

The Gulf

Operations 1986–87

U.S.S.R.

IRAN

IRAQ

INDIA

KUWAIT

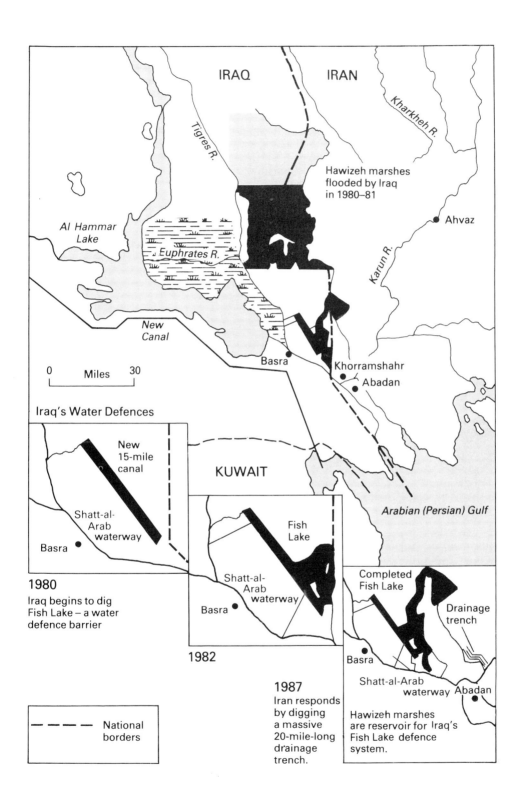

IRAQ   IRAN

Kharkheh R.

Tigres R.

Hawizeh marshes
flooded by Iraq
in 1980–81

● Ahvaz

Al Hammar
Lake

Euphrates R.

Karun R.

New
Canal

0   Miles   30

Basra ●   Khorramshahr ●
            Abadan ●

Iraq's Water Defences

New
15-mile
canal

KUWAIT

Shatt-al-
Arab
waterway

Basra ●

1980
Iraq begins to dig
Fish Lake – a water
defence barrier

Fish
Lake

Shatt-al-
Arab
waterway

Basra ●

1982

Arabian (Persian) Gulf

Completed
Fish Lake

Drainage
trench

Basra ●

Shatt-al-Arab
        waterway   Abadan ●

1987
Iran responds
by digging
a massive
20-mile-long
drainage
trench.

Hawizeh marshes
are reservoir for Iraq's
Fish Lake defence
system.

– – – – – National
           borders

recruiting every young and middle-aged man for an indefinite period. The conscripted Iraqi males were replaced in town and country by 1.5 million foreign workers, mostly Egyptians and Sudanese, and by Iraqi women. The participation of the female population strengthened the war effort. According to reliable sources 10,000 North Yemeni troops are fighting with the Iraq Army. Large numbers of Egyptians are actually in the ranks and Jordan has several hundred 'advisers' in Iraq.

The immense amount of money needed to run the war was still not a problem, largely because of oil revenues. In 1986 Iraq was able to increase its oil exports through Turkish and Saudi pipelines and was sending out 1.6 million barrels a day. In 1987, thanks to another pipeline to Turkey, its export capacity increased by 500,000 barrels a day. Soon after the Iranian attack on Faw, Kuwait and Saudi Arabia had renewed the 3-year-old agreement under which they jointly sell 350,000 barrels a day on Iraq's account.

The Disaster at Mehran

For Iraq, the most disheartening experience of the entire war was the battle of Mehran, an encounter that might well appear in the training manuals of international military colleges as an object lesson in mismanagement. In mid-May 1986, 25,000 members of the 2nd Iraqi Army Corps rolled up to the border near Mehran, a town just inside Iran. Under the Poshkuh Mountains, 160 km east of Baghdad, it had long since been reduced to rubble by fighting and shelling. It held no strategic value but an Iranian garrison of 5,000 defended it.

On orders from Baghdad the two divisions, assisted by artillery, closed in on the defences in a pincer movement. They encountered little resistance from the defenders and quickly took the area, together with 400 prisoners. This was the first step of an 'active defence' strategy—to strike across the border and bring the Iranians to the spot. The second stage was supposed to be a withdrawal from that zone and hit another undefended, more vulnerable objective. A military analyst in Baghdad explains it in this way: 'You make the first position a magnet but you get out when the battle heats up.'

Baghdad now decided to exploit Mehran for propaganda value and Iraq's publicists announced that the 'great victory' was a turning-point. Iraq would continue to hold the city but would consider swapping it for the Fao peninsula. This was a futile offer considering that the Iranian defences in Fao had been built up to 40,000 men and, despite almost continuous shelling, they stayed put. The Iraqi divisions did little more than camp at Mehran. For reasons which no Iraqi leader has been able to explain, the commander sent reconnaissance patrols only 12 miles to the first ridge line of the Poshkuh Mountains. Had they gone further they would have found Iranian reinforcements assembling in the mountains all around the Iraqis, and above them as well. The Iranians attacked and the battle became fierce.

At its height the Iraqi army called urgently for air support. But direct contact is impossible in the Iraqi army because of the tortuous line of communications and because the political leaders will not permit one branch of the army to contact another branch in case they are planning a coup. All requests must pass through Baghdad politicians and sometimes the reply arrives a day later. Air support needs to arrive within minutes. Because of the bottleneck, on 1 July the army flew 33 helicopter sorties when it should have flown 533 and on the same day the air force flew only a few missions.

The Iranians broke through the Iraqi lines and overran their headquarters, killing 500 Iraqis, including a brigadier, Khidr Ali, wounding another 2,500 and taking 1,100 men prisoner. Major-General Adin Tawfiq, who had led the first attack into Mehran, was blamed for the disaster and recalled to Baghdad. He has not been heard of since.

New Offensives

The Iraqi General Staff were confident that they could check an Iranian assault on Basra with their remarkable water defences and a type of Maginot Line belt of fortifications 10 miles deep and running right up to Amarah. The impressive defences had been laid out as a huge killing ground on to which Iran's packed infantry would be lured and then wiped out. Iraqi Intelligence appears to have been faulty. The Iranians were no longer, in late 1986 and into 1987, depending on sheer weight of numbers. Iraqi communiqués continued to emphasize Iran's huge losses—which indeed there were—but Iran was repeatedly talking of limited attacks.

The Iraqi generals appear not to have noticed that Iran was able to hit harder and with fewer troops, partly because the troops are better trained than in the past and because they are better equipped. The Revolutionary Guards had been given much practice in amphibious assault, small-scale operations and infiltration.

On the night of 24 December 1986 Iran launched yet another offensive, code-named *Kerbala 4*, using 60,000 men on an exceptionally wide front of 25 miles, from Abu al-Khasib, not far south of Basra, to the island of Umm al Rassas, near Abadan. The Iranians crossed the Shatt-al-Arab on a slow-flowing stretch about 500 yards wide and tried to dig in on the Iraqi side. After 48 hours of heavy fighting they were thrown back. It was a significant reverse because the force consisted entirely of Revolutionary Guards, without the usual leavening of regular soldiers. The regular army has always advised against set-piece attacks against well-prepared Iraqi positions. The Iraqis stopped the offensive but they lost 10,000 dead in doing it.

Quickly regrouping, the Iranians used Ahwaz as rear headquarters and began *Operation Kerbala 5* on 8 January 1987. The leading troops established a bridgehead across the Jasim River, really an irrigation canal joining Fish Lake to Shatt-al-Arab, near Basra. This was a clear military success and another demonstration of the Iranian capacity to overrun any fortified Iraqi position along the 800-mile border. Being only 6 miles from Basra, the Iranian guns could easily shell the city. The battle went on well into February. In Erbil province of northern Iraq an Iranian attack killed or wounded 1,500 Iraqi soldiers. The Iranians destroyed Iraq's Fifth Army Corps HQ in the Diana region.

In a pronounced change of tactics, the Iraqi army used massed infantry from two of its most illustrious and seasoned corps—the 3rd and the 7th—supported by armour, to push back the Iranian forces from their salient. Iraq had until then relied primarily on its artillery and aircraft and avoided ground combat in attacks. Defence Minister General Adnan Kheirullah, who is also Deputy Commander-in-

Chief, is credited with having stopped the Iranian offensive and with the success of the counter-offensive which destroyed the Iranians' bridgehead. Nevertheless, Iran still held about 35 sq. miles of Iraqi territory.

Kerbala 5 had come to a halt but it was not a defeat for Iran and it left the Iraqi government shaken. Diplomatic sources estimate that 20,000 Iraqis and 45,000 Iranians died in the battle. Given the relative size of the two countries' populations (Iran–45 million, Iraq–15 million) a casualty ratio lower than 1 to 3 counts as a victory for Iran. In addition, Iraq could not transfer reinforcements from the north where another Iranian Army was stationed ready to take advantage of any such step. Several leading Iranians, including the Speaker of the Iranian Parliament, Hojatoleslam Rafsanjani, said the aim of *Kerbala 5* was not to capture Basra but to wear down the Iraqi war machine. By late March 1987, with the Tigris and the Euphrates flooding from the thawing mountain snow-water, the terrain east of Basra was impassable, thus making this part of the front relatively safe for Iraq.

According to one report, in February 1987, the Iraqi leadership had become so obsessed with minimizing casualties, that for political purposes it had ordered the freezing of soldiers' bodies killed in conflict so that they could be released in batches to families. In Iran, with its emphasis on martyrdom, casualties are glorified rather than hidden. Harrowing pictures of war-wounded, their limbs smashed by shell-bursts, decorate the lobbies of hotels. Children are taught in the classroom that martyrdom is everyone's sacred duty.

With such indoctrination Iranian society in itself is still a formidable war machine with virtually limitless manpower; 25 million of the population of 45 million are under the age of 25. The clerics of Iran—the ayatollahs, the hojatoleslams, the mullahs—justify the theological rule of Iran by the holy war which the nation is fighting. They have, therefore, nothing to gain by reaching a peaceful solution at this point.

Iraq's Problems

The Iraqis have only been able to counter the Iranians' reckless daring with their superior technology, their access to virtually unlimited weapon supplies and their hope that the Iranians will bleed themselves to defeat. But the Iranians can always pull back, as they did in the early days of the war; the Iraqis cannot afford to withdraw anywhere. The Iranians, by gnawing away at the Iraqis' Soviet-style static defences may eventually produce a hole through which their hordes can pour. Iran needs a vast influx of new weaponry, at the very least a sustained supply of spares to mobilize its air force, artillery and armour. Despite huge amounts spent on the international arms black market, and what has been squeezed out of President Reagan in clandestine shipments, Iran still has not been able to amass sufficient new hardware to exploit its tactical superiority.

At times Iraq's forces, certainly the most seasoned in the Arab world, demonstrate fitness and bravery, yet they can follow this with indecision and hesitancy. They need to be willing to take risks and suffer short-term consequences and casualties for longer-range victories—but they have rarely done this.

If Iran succeeded in breaking through to Basra the implications would be serious for the Iraqi government. The loss of Basra, with its 1 million people, mostly Shi'as,

An Iraqi militia unit being trained in 'aggressive forward movement' at Camp Al Nohrowan near Baghdad. These soldiers are members of a volunteer infantry brigade.

would be a severe blow to the Iraqi people and to the army's morale, already suffering after the defeats at Faw and Mehran. The breakthrough troops could link up with those on Fao peninsula. It might then be possible for an Iranian force to push north on the Baghdad road, west to the port of Umm Qaar and north-east towards Kerbala and Najaf, the holy cities which have long been a target of Iranian ambitions. The Khomeini regime would have several options, one of them being the establishment of an 'Islamic Republic of Southern Iraq'. This would alarm Kuwait, Saudi Arabia and Jordan.

Iraqi Air Power

Iraq has about 1,000 pilots but only 50 are considered good enough to fly dangerous and difficult missions. These include low-level attacks on Kharg Island and the long-range mission to destroy Iran's oil terminal on Sirri Island in the southern part of the Gulf on 12 August 1986. Many air missions are flown at 20,000 feet and the bombing is done blindly, using map co-ordinates, a much less effective method than visually sighting the target and bombing it from low altitude.

In November 1986 Iraq made rare use of its superior air power to inflict devastating damage on military, oil and other industrial targets. In a single day 54 planes were used to attack targets in south-west Iran. At the same time Mirages flashed down the Gulf to carry out the first strike on Iran's oil-loading terminals at Larak Island, in Hormuz Strait. This was a 600-mile trip each way, further than the Iraqis had ever ranged in their efforts to disrupt Iranian oil. Five tankers were hit. The Iranians use a fleet of shuttle tankers to ferry their oil down the 400-mile 'Exocet Alley' to Larak. During 1986 24 neutral ships were destroyed and more than 90 crippled—these attacks making a total of more than 500 in the Gulf since 1982. At various times during 1986-87 both sides made air raids on each other's capitals and sometimes fired long-range missiles. The Iranians fired a Soviet Scud-B missile at Baghdad in November 1986, killing 53 people in a residential area.

By mid-1987 the Soviet Union had replaced Iraq's losses in *Kerbala 5*. The replacements include MiG 27 fighters. Iraqi officials admitted that their air force lost 40-50 combat aircraft but the real figure was certainly higher; the loss indicates increased efficiency in Iran's air defences. In addition, the Soviet Union has supplied MiG 29 interceptors and electronic equipment to counter Iran's missiles.

Iraq owes Moscow an estimated US$10 billion for arms and another US$5 billion in trade and other aid. On a visit to Moscow, Defence Minister Adnan Kheirallah and Foreign Minister Tariq Aziz managed to induce the Russians to reschedule the debts 'on easy terms'.

Iran's Arms from Abroad

The clandestine shipments of US arms to Iran played a large part in the battles of late 1986 and early 1987. The Americans say that Iranians got 2,008 TOW anti-tank missiles and spares kits for 235 Hawk surface-to-air missiles in the secret shipments. But much bigger shipments reached Iran in 1985 and 1986. Foreign reports from the battlefield east of Basra reveal the existence of heavier Iranian firepower than for some time. The Iranian command claims that 80 Iraqi aircraft and seven helicopter gunships were shot down during the *Kerbala 5* battles.

Diplomatic sources say that another 20 were brought down in February, 1987. These could be exaggerations but US Congressman Robert Torricelli testified before a House Foreign Affairs Committee; after returning from Baghdad, that the Iraqi Air Force had admitted to him that it had lost up to 50 aircraft during the Basra fighting. The Iraqis also told Torricelli that they had lost many tanks; no number was given. The Iranians claimed that by the end of *Kerbala 5* they had destroyed 700 Iraqi tanks, but this is assumed to be an exaggeration.

The Iranians used AH-1 Cobra helicopter gunships during fighting in the marshlands. This was unusual so it is reasonable to assume that spares for the gunships among the US shipments made the helicopter fleet airworthy once again. The Iranians have also received spares—the source is unknown—for the APQ-120 fire-control radars for their depleted force of F-4 Phantoms. They were thus able to use their US-made AIM-7 air-to-air missiles.

The Iraqis themselves reported daily attacks on Iranian Hawk batteries. Foreign analysts believe that most of Iraq's battlefield losses were more likely inflicted by shoulder-fired SAMs and anti-aircraft guns than by Hawks. The Iraqi high command admits that the American shipments gave Iran 'greater aggressive capacity' but claims that the superiority was 'temporary and not decisive'.

The Chinese Connection

The Iranian capacity to attack Iraq increased sharply during 1986-87 because of help from China, especially in the development and use of surface-to-surface missiles. Two types of missile have been identified. One is a Chinese version of the Frog, which has a range of 40 miles. The Iranians have already fired it at Basra, with devastating effect on buildings and on civilian morale.

Another type of missile, similar to the Soviet Army's Scud B, has a range of 180 miles. It should be ready for the battlefield in October 1987. The Iranians can reach Baghdad with this missile. The most alarming development, from the Iraqi and international point of view, is the HY-2 Silkworm, a Chinese mobile anti-ship missile with a range of 60 miles. It carries 1000 lb of explosives, and is the most destructive weapon in the Iranian armoury for use in the Gulf. The Silkworm is radar-guided and can sink a supertanker. Two tankers sunk in the narrower part of Hormuz Straits could cut off oil supplies.

Under an oil-barter deal with China, Iran has about 240 Silkworm missiles. None had been used in the earlier part of 1987 but satellite photographs showed three launching sites—at Henqam, Qeshm and Hormuz. In response to the new threat to Gulf oil shipping, the US Navy moved an aircraft carrier and 17 other warships into the Straits of Hormuz and the British Navy increased its flotilla to four.

The *USS Stark* Affair

On 17 May 1987 the American destroyer *Stark* was on patrol in the Gulf when an Iraqi F-1 fighter fired an Exocet missile at it. The ship was badly damaged and 37 sailors lost their lives. The incident was investigated by a team under Rear Admiral David Rogers, Director for Current Operations for the Joint Chiefs of Staff. His brief was to analyse the sequence of events not to 'learn who took what actions aboard Stark, nor to assign responsibility'.

USS *Stark* was in Readiness Condition 111, all air and surface sensors operating and all weapons systems operational. The ship was taking part in a two-way computer data exchange with two other navy vessels and a USAF AWACS. At about 5 pm AWACS reported a single aircraft evaluated as unidentified, assumed friendly, assumed Iraqi, flying south down the Gulf. At 5.58 *Stark* had radar contact on the Iraqi aircraft, at a range of 70 nautical miles.

At 6.06 pm the *Stark* detected a radar signal assessed as a search mode airborne fire control radar and three minutes later AWACS heard *Stark* issue warnings by voice radio over a military air distress network to the Iraqi aircraft. In the first warning *Stark* identified herself as a US Navy warship and in the second gave her position as 11 nautical miles from the aircraft. No reply to either warning was received.

AWACS observed a sharp right turn and speed increase by the aircraft, indicating possible completion of a missile launch. In fact, the pilot had fired at 5,000 feet and the Exocet was travelling at 500 mph. At 6.09 *Stark* reported having detected a fire-control lock-on from the airborne radar signal. At the same time, *Stark*'s port side lookout reported visual contact, evaluated as an inbound missile by the bridge watch. General Quarters was sounded and five seconds later the missile hit but did not explode. About 25 seconds later a second missile struck the ship and detonated in the crew's compartment.

This was the first assault on an American warship since the war began. It came only a few hours after a Soviet oil tanker, *Marshal Chukyov*, ran into a mine on the way to Kuwait. The two events highlight the new perils which now confront both the superpowers over this essentially secondary aspect of the war.

The Iraqi government officially "regretted" the incident and said that an inexperienced flier had fired the missile. It seems strange that an inexperienced pilot should be flying alone in a war zone, however.

The US government accepted the Iraqi explanation that the firing was a mistake.

With both superpowers protecting Kuwaiti tankers, the Iranian government threatened action against them, particularly against the Americans, who had agreed to permit Kuwaiti tankers to fly the American flag. In mid-1987 the Iranians were strengthening their naval bases along the Gulf. It was believed that they were training crews of small, fast patrol boats to mount suicide raids against foreign vessels. Also, with the "success" of the unintended Iraqi attack on an American warship, the Iranians believed that they could repeat such an attack.

During the same period Chinese Silkworm surface-to-sea missiles were being installed at seven points on the Iranian coast. They are Khawr Abd Allh, near the Khorramshahr naval base; Qeshm, near Bandar Abbas naval base; on Hormuz Island and Henqam island. The three latter sites are in the Straits of Hormuz.

The Silkworm, or HY-2, carries 1,100lb of explosive up to 50 miles. It is based on the 1950s Styx, which the Chinese obtained from the Russians, who were then allies of China.

In June 1985—it is now known—Iran and China struck a deal for 200 Silkworms, worth $500 million. Total Chinese arms sales to Iran in the period 1985-87 amount to $2 billion. About 70 Iranian naval officers, 30 pilots and other personnel have been given missile training in Iran.

Kampuchea–Vietnam's War against Guerrillas

Background Summary

Vietnam invaded Kampuchea (formerly Cambodia) in December 1978 'to protect the south-western flank from hostile influence'. This was a reference to China, which Vietnam considers its greatest enemy. From the beginning the Chinese supported those Kampuchean groups that resisted the Vietnamese occupation which was backed by the Soviet Union. The government of Kampuchea was no more than an unstable coalition between the Khmer People's National Liberation Front (KPNLF) and the Khmer Rouge, led by the infamous Pol Pot, whose men committed some of the worst massacres of the century against their own people; probably 2 million people were killed. Heng Samrin became Prime Minister of Kampuchea and collaborated with the Vietnamese invaders; he placed the Kampuchean Army at their disposal. The other groups took to the jungle. The Chinese mismanaged an invasion against the occupying Vietnamese in 1979 and in that year the conflict became a Resistance war. For some years it was not a genuine guerrilla war because the Kampuchean fighters established fixed lines of defence and bases. These defences were generally destroyed by the Vietnamese during the dry season and rebuilt by the Kampucheans in the wet season.

(For full details of the entire war see **WAR ANNUAL** 1.)

Summary of the War in 1985

With 160,000 troops in Kampuchea the Vietnamese High Command captured one Resistance base after another, with artillery barrages closely followed by conventional infantry attack. The Khmer Rouge lost their mountain stronghold, Phnom Malai, and the KPNLF lost all its bases. Finally the Vietnamese captured Tatum, the stronghold of Prince Sihanouk's force. Many thousands of Kampuchean fighters retreated to Thailand where they established bases—as well as refugee camps for their civilians. The Vietnamese fought them vigorously, planting tens of thousands of mines and booby traps on jungle trails and using helicopter gunships.

Late in 1985 it seemed that the Kampuchean Resistance was becoming more professional and disciplined. Foreign observers noted that the KPNLF was able to mount attacks against Vietnamese posts. These missions were successful largely because the civil population supported the Resistance. This indicated that by the end of 1985 the Vietnamese had not succeeded in winning the Kampucheans'

Opening Doors to Kampuchean Refugees

KACHIN

CHINA

BURMA

Hanoi

LAOS

THAILAND

Khao I Dang
refugee camp

ARAKAN

Bangkok

KAMPUCHEA

VIETNAM

Phnom
Penh

Ho Chi Minh City

0   100
Miles

Gulf of Thailand

Sites of refugee camps

BHUTAN

INDIA

CHINA

BURMA

VIETNAM

LAOS

THAILAND

Bay of
Bengal

KAMPUCHEA

Only six countries
resettled more than 1,000
Cambodians each from
Thailand between 1975 and
'86. Thailand says this
is inadequate.

US	136,349
France	32,431
Australia	12,922
Canada	12,760
New Zealand	2,695
Switzerland	1,412

sympathy, although hundreds of thousands of Vietnamese had moved into Kampuchea as permanent settlers.

The War in 1986-87

Vietnam's operations in Kampuchea are planned and managed by one of Hanoi's most secretive organisations, 'B68'. Located in Ho Chi Minh City, 'B68' has a big branch office in Phnom Penh, Kampuchea. The director is Ngo Dien, who is Hanoi's ambassador to Kampuchea.

For 1986 and again in 1987 'B68' decided not to carry out the usual offensives against the guerrilla and refugee camps across the Kampuchean border in Thailand. Such offensives had not succeeded in capturing or killing many guerrillas. The 140,000 people of Site Two, the biggest of the refugee camps, for the first time settled down to regular work, even to farming. However, Thailand closed the Khao 1 Dang refugee camp in March 1987; the 26,000 inhabitants were sent closer to the Thai-Kampuchean border, where they were more vulnerable to the fighting. The total number of refugees grew to 250,000—out of a population of 7 million.

The war was carried on inside Kampuchea. The Vietnamese laid more than one million mines along the 450-mile border in an effort to seal it off. This failed but one Kampuchean in every 100 is said to have been badly maimed in explosions from wood-covered mines, which cannot be located by conventional detectors.

In the earlier part of 1986—up to May—the Vietnamese moved in strength into the diamond-shaped wedge of eastern Thailand that cuts into Kampuchea; many guerrilla trails begin here and the Vietnamese tactic was to prevent guerrillas from entering or leaving Kampuchea. Where they suspect the existence of a concentration of guerrillas they use Soviet-supplied helicopter gunships, mostly Mi-6, Mi-8, Mi-24 and Kamov Ka-25. They frequently drop cluster bombs on scrublands but cause many more civilian than military casualties.

At the beginning of 1986 the Vietnamese Army of occupation numbered at least 180,000 and was under the command of General Le Duc Anh, who is regarded as the army's most enterprising general. His force was made up of two 'Front Headquarters', 14 army divisions—a Vietnamese division consists of 7,500 men—support troops, a naval base, helicopter gunships and fighter aircraft, including Mig-21s, used in a ground-attack role.[1] An army of 180,000 on foreign service in a small neighbouring country might seem to be immense but Vietnam has an army of 1 million men and total armed forces of 1,155,000—one of the largest in the world. Allied to the Vietnamese is the 40,000-strong army of Heng Samrin.

The guerrilla force opposing them in 1987 totalled about 66,000 in three main groups. They are:

Khmer Rouge: 35,000 men, nominally organized in divisions and regiments but more for administration than for combat.

KPNLF: 16,000 trained and armed men, plus 4,000 men trained but poorly armed or not armed at all. Prince Sihanouk's force, *Armée Nationale Sihanoukienne* (ANS) of 10,000 men.

Apart from personal arms, the guerrillas' best weapons are 12.7 mm machine-

Wounded guerrilla fighters of the Khmer People's National Liberation Front (KPNLF) are evacuated by ox-cart from Siemreap province to the Kampuchea–Thai border. The KPNLF has hospitals in Thailand. (Courtesy B. Chea.)

After nearly 10 years of fighting, the Kampuchean Resistance groups have become highly skilled in jungle fighting and most of their victories are achieved by surprise. They move through country which is so difficult—as seen here—that regular troops avoid it.

The KPNLF opposes Vietnam occupation of Kampuchea and its men operate as true guerrillas, using little known jungle trails and living off the land. These men were setting off to ambush a Vietnamese force. (Courtesy B. Chea.)

guns, RPG-7 RL and 60 mm and 82 mm mortars. They appear to have an inexhaustible supply of Chinese-supplied explosives.

From Thailand the guerrillas get into Kampuchea along four main paths (*see map*). The Khmers Rouges inflict heavy casualties on the Vietnamese in the mountainous regions of western Kampuchea. In the open country to the north Khmers Rouges and men of Son Sann's KPNLF army get across the border despite the Vietnamese barriers and carry out raids around Battambang. In April 1986, in the first joint raid by all three major Resistance groups, the Battambang airfield and fuel storage tanks were damaged. Strong raiding parties also attacked army posts near Angkor Wat and in the marshland around Tonle Sap. The Khmers Rouges specialise in blowing up trains and are said by diplomats in Phnom Penh to have wrecked ten during 1986.

The Vietnamese Army is well entrenched at the base of the low escarpment that runs along Kampuchea's northern border. Nevertheless the guerrillas—especially those from Prince Sihanouk's forces—consistently get through to carry out raids behind the Vietnamese lines. Just as consistently they slip across the border into Thailand for leave periods. The guerrilla leadership has come to realise that the men fight better if they can spend time with their families. The Thais only stipulation is that when they return to Thailand the guerrillas must not be in uniform, a fiction enabling the Thai government to claim that it does not have a military alliance with the guerrillas.

Further east the Khmers Rouges use a trail that runs inside neighbouring Laos and alongside Vietnam's border with Kampuchea. These fighters have penetrated deeply into the country to hit targets near the capital, Phnom Penh. So effective were the guerrillas during 1986 and 1987 that their activities have sapped the morale of the Kampuchean army of Heng Samrin. They avoid combat with the guerrillas or leave them alone. Several hundred troops are known to have defected to the guerrillas; in March 1986 an entire unit of 200 men went over. The Vietnamese Army distrusts the Kampuchean army and keeps it behind the lines on guard duties. About 1,000 men are sent each year to Vietnam and to the Soviet Union for training to become officers or non-commissioned officers. Despite this, reports of mutinies by Heng Samrin's soldiers are commonplace.

It is likely that in 1986 7,000 Vietnamese troops were killed or wounded, compared with the guerrillas' 5,000 casualties. The disproportionate number is significant, for it is generally accepted in military circles that a defending army needs a 10-1 advantage in manpower to defeat insurgents. In Kampuchea it is no more than 3-1, possibly 4-1 at certain times.

Vietnamese soldiers have a bad name in Kampuchea for looting, arson, rape and murder. In any war all such reports must be treated with caution but KPNLF bulletins of Vietnamese actions against the populace have the stamp of truth. Here are two examples:[2]

29 October 1986, 8.45 am: Vietnamese troops installed in Kaup Tauch village, Serei Sophon district, Battambang Province, fired with M.80 mm mortar on the Kuth Tasath village which caused two women killed. Mrs. Bin Hin and her daughter are victims of the shelling.

3 November 1986: Six Vietnamese soldiers looted and robbed the Phum Svay population, Thmar Pourk district, Battambang Province, of goods and belongings

Guerrilla routes into Kampuchea

viz 14,000 oriels, 1 cassette recorder, 1 sewing-machine, 1 electric amplifier and 600 *bahts*.

KPNLF combat communiqués are remarkably detailed and the names of Kampuchean regular soldiers who desert to KPNLF are published.

In an unusual action on 17 September 1986, KPNLF forces ambushed a convoy of 13 river boats carrying 572 Vietnamese troops moving from Chroy Changvar, near Phnom Penh, to Chnock Troo. After a 30-minute battle the KPNLF sank all 13 craft and inflicted many casualties. On 15 October KPNLF claimed to have sunk 16 boats in a similar ambush in Battambang province.[3]

The increasing strength of the Resistance worries the Vietnamese High Command so much that in 1987 frequent crisis meetings were held.[4] The casualty rate is not the major factor; the army is professional and has been fighting for four decades and accepts casualties. However, after such a long time the government would like to concentrate its stretched financial resources on economic development rather than the Kampuchean war. Government leaders repeatedly say they will withdraw from Kampuchea by 1990. The rebel Kampucheans do not believe the Vietnamese statements.

Soviet Involvement

The Soviet Union pays Vietnam US$3 million a day in 'general aid', and only a little less to finance the war in Kampuchea. In return the Russians not only have the Cam Ranh naval base but the immense Da Nang army base. In addition, the Vietnamese tie down a large part of China's army on the border. If relations between the Soviet and China were to improve then the Kremlin's interest in keeping Chinese forces occupied on the Vietnam border would decrease.

China's Involvement

Throughout 1986 and 1987 the Chinese considered themselves to be in a state of war with Vietnam, though hostilities rarely took the form of cross-border raids. During the dry season the Chinese heavily shell all Vietnamese Army posts within range. This tactic is an attempt to cut down the number of Vietnamese soldiers available to attack the Kampuchean guerrillas. When their allies, the guerrillas, attack the Vietnamese troops during the rainy season the Chinese greatly reduce their shelling. They increased the flow of weapons to the guerrillas in 1987.

The Resistance Peace Plan

Collectively, the guerrilla groups call themselves the Coalition Government of Democratic Kampuchea. They have collaborated on an eight-point peace plan, which calls for a Vietnamese withdrawal in two stages. After the first stage a four-party government would be set up, with representatives from the three Resistance organisations and Heng Samrin's party. Prince Sihanouk would become President and Son Sann the Prime Minister. The United Nations would then supervise democratic elections, after which Vietnam would pull out completely. Not surprisingly, the Vietnamese have objections; they want Heng Samrin to be Prime

Minister and they will not accept the Khmers Rouges in the government. The trouble is that the Khmers Rouges are by far the strongest Resistance force.

The Vietnamese fear that the Khmers Rouges would take over Kampuchea as the last Vietnamese soldier withdrew. While a moderate, Khieu Samphan, appears to be the voice of the Khmer Rouge, it is widely believed throughout South-east Asia that Pol Pot is still the force behind the scene. Pol Pot is said to be researching military strategy at an organization called the Institute of National Defence. China and Thailand say that they could force Pol Pot to honour a deal after a Vietnamese withdrawal. If the Khmers Rouges again became an army of brutal oppression and aggression, the Thais and Chinese say that they would give them no more support. The Vietnamese have yet to be convinced and say openly that the Khmers Rouges can only prove their good intentions by killing Pol Pot and his closest aides.

Foreign Support for the Guerrillas

The KPNLF has made a special plea to Britain for help. During 1986 the British Government contributed £850,000 to the international relief effort and a further £100,000 in humanitarian assistance to the group led by Prince Sihanouk and Son Sann. In an interview with the author, April 1987, the KPNLF Head of Bureau in London, Mr. B. Chea, said: 'It is felt that Britain should give more aid to Cambodia to end the Soviet-aided Vietnam aggression. The non-Communist nationalist fronts badly need modern arms to carry out guerrilla warfare in their liberation struggle; these arms should be of the same quality as those given by the Soviet Union to Vietnam. The United States has given a token arms aid of 5 million dollars to help the non-Communist fronts. It is felt that Britain should follow suit.'

References

Much of the information about the war in Kampuchea comes from Thai government officials; they are the most reliable source. The UN High Commissioner for Refugees has precise figures for the number of Kampucheans who have fled into Thailand.

1) Soviet Intelligence source.
2) KPNLF communiqué No. 49.
3) KPNLF communiqué No. 54.
4) Diplomatic sources in Hanoi.

The KPNLF maintains an efficient information/propaganda service abroad, notably in Paris and London. The information disseminated, tested against Thai sources and foreign diplomats in Phnom Penh, is generally accurate and reliable.

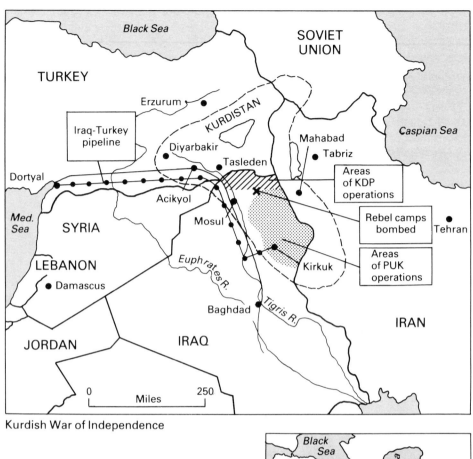

Kurdish War of Independence

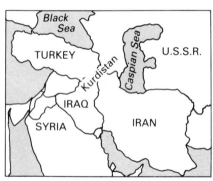

Kurdish War of Independence

CONFLICT ON FOUR FRONTS

Background Summary

The Kurds of Iraq, Iran, Turkey, Syria and the Soviet Union have been fighting for a homeland since the middle of the 19th century. Not one of the countries which surround the Kurdish heartland has any sympathy with their nationalism, which has been bloodily repressed. The Turks were particularly brutal in the 1920s and 1930s and in more recent years the Iranians and Iraqis have been equally repressive.

The Kurds have not always been fortunate in their alliances. For instance, in the early 1970s Mustafa Barzani, leader of the Iraqi Kurdistan Democratic Party (KDP) allied himself to the Shah of Iran and fought against the Iranian Kurds. When the Shah withdrew his support in 1975—in return for territorial concessions offered by Baghdad—the KDP was caught between the Iranian and Iraqi Armies. The Iraqis destroyed all Kurdish villages within 20 km, of the Turkish border and forced their people to move to southern Iraq. In 1983, with the Gulf War at its height, the KDP helped Iranian troops to cross into Iraq. The rival Patriotic Union of Kurdistan (PUK) led by Jalal Talabani helped to train Iranian Kurds to fight Khomeini's troops.

The Kurdish Workers Party (PKK), a nationalist and Marxist-Leninist organization, has had great influence in Turkey. In 1978 a university student turned terrorist, 'Apo' Abdullah Ocalan, formed the PKK, whose militants are known as Apoists. After the army coup in 1980 several of them were arrested. Ocalan found refuge in Syria, where he has his headquarters. Some Apoists have joined Palestinian camps in Syria and Lebanon. Some were given political asylum in Sweden, where they are alleged to have used violence. The murder of the Swedish Prime Minister Olof Palme is believed to be the work of Apoists. The Apoists reappeared in south-eastern Turkey in August 1984. Trained in Syria the exiled militants crossed into Iran and Iraq and used hit-and-run tactics against targets in Turkey. Their strategy then was to attack military targets and kill soldiers.

Summary of the War in 1985

The KDP, now led by Idris Barzani, elder son of the famous Mustafa Barzani, had about 15,000 fighting men in commands of 1,500 each. Despite the apparently conventional structure, they fought as guerrillas with hit-and-run raids. Their tactics were well known to their Iraqi enemies but they could not prevent Kurdish penetration of Iraqi cities. The oil installations at Kirkuk and the nearby pipelines were among their targets throughout 1985 but occasionally they mounted attacks against strong army posts. The Kurds' part in the war was more important than their limited military actions might indicate. They tied down many thousands of Iraqi troops in Kurdistan when Saddam Hussein and his general staff needed every available soldier in action against the Iranian forces. The various Kurdish factions show few real signs of becoming united. Apart from the KDP and PUK, the Socialist Party of Kurdistan (Pasok), the Iraqi Dawe Party (a Shi'a Muslim group) and the Turkish Workers Party of Kurdistan had fighting groups. All were nominally members of the National Democratic Front but unity was more in principle than in practice.

The War in 1986-87

Early in the year a supposedly secret Iraqi military report showed that the KDP had tripled the area of Iraq under its control.[1] It is an area 200 km long and 25 km wide along the Turkish border stretching from Syria to near Barzan. While not a vast region, it is big enough to hold camouflaged bases and at least 17,000 guerrillas, an army report has assessed. They are holding down 160,000 Iraqi soldiers. The Kurds' supply of weapons has improved, a significant fact considering that they were already well armed with Kalashnikovs, rocket-propelled grenade launchers, mines and explosives. This report warns that the Kurds are more confident and that their strategy is becoming 'broader'. This has proved to be the case, so it is necessary to look at the Kurds 'war of independence' on several fronts.

Iraq Front

Iranian offensives against the Iraqi north-east front early in 1987 were at least partly aimed at supporting and encouraging the Kurds. Cooperation between the two is now so great the Kurds and Iranians fight together in commando units behind the Iraqi lines. Even more significant is the Iranian influence in persuading Talabani's PUK and Barzani's KDP to work together more effectively against Iraq. Together they have 25,000 fighters. At the same time the KDP and PUK are closer to the Kurdish Workers' Party, PKK, which is Syrian-backed. More arms reached the Kurds during 1986 and 1987, notably Soviet-made anti-aircraft missiles and US-built artillery and mortars, supplied—sometimes in tortuous deals—by Iran, Libya and Syria.

In October 1986 the Kurds embarked on a rare conventional battle. About 2,500 men, using Soviet Katyusha rockets and heavy artillery, attacked formidable Iraqi positions at Kirkuk, while a company of Iranian commandos carried out sabotage raids. The Kurds have also increased their raids against transport on the vital road from Kirkuk to Turkey and have frequently cut the road. Should the Kurds gain control of the pipeline and the highway, the main trading artery between Turkey and Iraq, they could crucially affect the Gulf War by reducing Iraq's oil exports.

In ever bolder operations they are besieging garrisons and even towns. In February the combined Kurdish-Iranian commandos either destroyed or badly damaged the big power stations at Dukan and Dahok. Kurdish fighting strength is growing as the result of Kurdish soldiers deserting from Iraqi Army units. The Kurdish war against Iraq is having a strategic impact on the Gulf War itself because

A Kurdish freedom fighter on patrol in the mountainous country of Iranian Kurdistan. The Kurds, who are masters of ambush and of fighting in difficult terrain, have many enemies—Iranians, Iraqis, Turks and Syrians. (Courtesy HAZHIR TEIMOURIAN.)

the Kurds have, in effect, created a second front against the Iraqis, whose strength is dangerously stretched along a 650-mile border.

On 31 January 1987 Idris Barzani died of a heart attack—at the age of 42—and leadership passed to his brother, Mossood. Very much a leader from the front, Mossood Barzani is trying to build on the success of the policy of close relations with the regime in Teheran. Some observers believe that he has a better chance than his father or brother of uniting many of the Kurd factions.

Turkey Front

Although in the early 1970s one Turkish Prime Minister, Ferit Melen, was a Kurd, few Kurds hold top jobs in the administration and none at all in the army. The Kurdish language is banned under the Constitution and Kurdish literature is ruthlessly suppressed. With such grievances, nationalism breeds among the 10 million ethnic Kurds. The Kurds' immediate demands include the release of thousands of Kurdish militants from Turkish prisons and the disarming of the 'village guards'. These are ordinary peasants living in small and remote communities where usually there are no policemen. They are hired by the authorities to protect people from terrorist attacks. In 1987 the guards and their families became the chief target of the attackers.

Kurdish terrorists, operating from within Iraq, frequently attack Turkish villages just across the border. In one such attack, on 22 February 1987, a group of Kurds masquerading as Turkish soldiers, murdered 24 people, most of them women and children, in the village of Tasleden. In the three years to the end of March 1987, the Apoists had taken part in a total of 433 attacks, killing 211 people, 133 of them servicemen. The security forces in the same period killed 242 terrorists and captured 531. The Apoists' present strategy is to raid Turkish villages.

In retaliation for the Tasleden attack, the Turks mounted a big operation to round up the terrorists, almost certainly members of PKK. A few days later 30 Turkish aircraft bombed the insurgents' mountain camps in the Sirat, Era and Alanis areas, on the Iraqi side of the border. Several hundred Kurds were killed.[2]

Retaliatory Turkish attacks are made with the approval of the Iraqi Government which permits Turkish armed forces to carry out 'hot pursuit' operations against the Kurds up to 10 km inside Iraqi territory. The air raids caused great anger in Iran, which had long claimed that Turkey was not as neutral in the Gulf war as it professed to be. Iranian leaders accused Turkey of 'aggression against the Muslim Kurdish people'. The pro-Iranian Kurdish rebels in Iraq also denounced the raid and threatened to avenge the 'bombing murders'. The Iranians believe that Turkey's ultimate purpose in its aggression against the Kurds is to reconquer some of the Iraqi land lost during World War 1—the Kirkuk and Mosul regions. The Turkish Government denies this and counter-charges that Iran has been trying for years to export its Islamic revolution to Turkey.

By March the conflict between the Turkish Army and the Kurdish insurgents in the remote eastern provinces had grown into something like a full-scale war. Thousands of troops, including commando units, were airlifted into the area and their commander was told to 'teach the Kurds a lesson they would never forget'.

The PKK's aim is to set up an independent 'socialist' republic, allied to the Soviet Union, with its capital in Diyarbakir.[3] To Western observers this might appear to be remote but Turkish Generals and the Government claim that they are cracking down not only on a troublesome minority but on Communist terrorists. The Prime Minister, Turgut Ozal, clings to the belief that the Kurdish problem can be solved by general economic development of the neglected eastern provinces. If the Kurds become prosperous, Ozal assumes, they will become apolitical. Meanwhile, Turkish generals are devising more sophisticated military techniques to cope with the insurgency. One move is to build up a special force of 1,000 policemen skilled in anti-terrorist methods. Among other things, they are learning Kurdish, the banned language.

Some influential Turks and military men advocate a large-scale military operation against the Kurds who attack Turkish targets from Iraq. They even suggest a 'pre-emptive takeover' of northern Iraq, including the Kirkuk area.

Syria Front

The Syrians cannot control their Kurds, who continue to make many minor raids into Turkey. For instance, on 7 March 1987 a guerrilla group threw hand-grenades into two buildings at Acikyol near the Syrian border and sprayed the occupants with machine-gun bullets as they tried to flee. The raid was only one of many made by Kurds using Syria as a base for hit-and-run raids. Immediately after the Acikyol massacre people in Ankara were calling for military action against the Syrians.

However, the Government gave Syria what its spokesmen called a 'soft warning', quite unlike the harder warnings to the Iranians. The Turkish government hopes that the regime of Hafez Al Assad will carry out promises made to stop Syrian Kurds from crossing the Turkish border. Many Turks, including Opposition members of parliament and influential newspapers, say that 'soft warnings' mean nothing and they demand stronger measures. For instance, they want the waters of the great Euphrates River, which originates in Anatolia, denied to the Syrians.[4]

Iran Front

Not all Kurds are fighting with Iran against Iraq. About 11,000 are fighting *against* Iran in Iranian Kurdistan. These guerrillas are the men of a breakaway group of the Kurdistan Democratic Party led by Abdorrahmen Qassemlou. Pro-Iraqi, he receives some aid from Iraq but denies that his group is dependent on Baghdad. This is true, because Abdorrahman, like all Kurdish leaders, knows how fatal it is for any Kurdish group to trust outsiders. The Iranian troops sent into Kurdistan heavily outnumber the Kurds and have pushed them out of the main towns in the region but the Kurds, as always, hold the rugged, mountainous ground.

References

1. Some copies of this 'secret' report reached diplomatic sources in Baghdad.

2. Turkish Minister of State, Hasan Celal Guzel.
3. PKK policy document.
4. Report in the leading newspaper, *Hurryet*. Some of the information in this description of the Kurds'
    wars comes from a British Foreign and Commonwealth Office Background Brief, 'The Kurdish
    Problem', July 1986. The Kurds were the victims of numerous atrocities in 1985-87, mostly at the
    hands of the Iraqis. Amnesty International has much evidence about this. Amnesty made a
    statement before the UN Commission for Human Rights on 10 March 1987.

Lebanon in Chaos

WAR AS A WAY OF LIFE

Background Summary

The conflict in Lebanon began in 1975 as a civil war, mainly between the 'Lebanese Forces'—the name used by the Maronite Christian militia—and the terrorists of the Palestine Liberation Organisation (PLO). The PLO had settled in southern Lebanon after expulsion from Jordan in 1970; it refused to obey Lebanese law and became a state within a state. The PLO region became known as Fatahland, after the name of the PLO faction commanded by Yasser Arafat, chairman of the PLO. When the Christians appeared to be losing to the PLO the Syrian Army went to their aid, but later the Syrians changed sides and backed the PLO.

The conflict became complex and other groups were involved. They are: Lebanese Shi'a Muslims of the south; Sunni Muslims of central-west Lebanon, and the Druse of the hills, notably from the Shouf Mountains. In the next 8 years at least 100,000 people were killed, many of them in massacres.

In 1978, in *Operation Litani*, an Israeli column attacked the PLO in southern Lebanon, in retaliation against PLO raids against Israel. The UN sent in a multi-national force, the United Nations Interim Force in Lebanon (UNIFIL). On 6 June 1982 Israel launched *Operation Peace for Galilee* and defeated both the PLO and the Syrian forces. The PLO split with the pro-Arafat faction evacuating Beirut in October 1982.

Christian militiamen massacred at least 800 Palestinians in two refugee camps. Meanwhile Iranian Shi'a Muslim agitators were active in the Bekaa Valley. US Marines, French paratroops, Italian and British soldiers were sent to Beirut where they were caught up in what had become a *jihad* or holy war. American and French casualties were heavy as a result of Shi'a suicide attacks. Israel made a phased disengagement and withdrawal but suffered casualties in attacks by suicide 'martyrs' driving car-bombs. With the help of the South Lebanese Army (SLA), the Israelis set up a buffer zone along the Israel-Lebanon border.

(For full details of the entire war see **WAR ANNUAL** 1.)

Summary of Operations in 1985

Artillery duels and street fighting, involving Maronites, Druse, Shi'a Muslims, Sunni Muslims and Syrians, continued in Beirut. Following collusion between the Syrians, Druse and the Shi'a militia *Amal*, the Sunni militia was virtually destroyed. In May and June *Amal* attacked PLO fighters returning to the refugee camps and massacred many civilians.

In the latter part of 1985 serious fighting took place around the northern

135

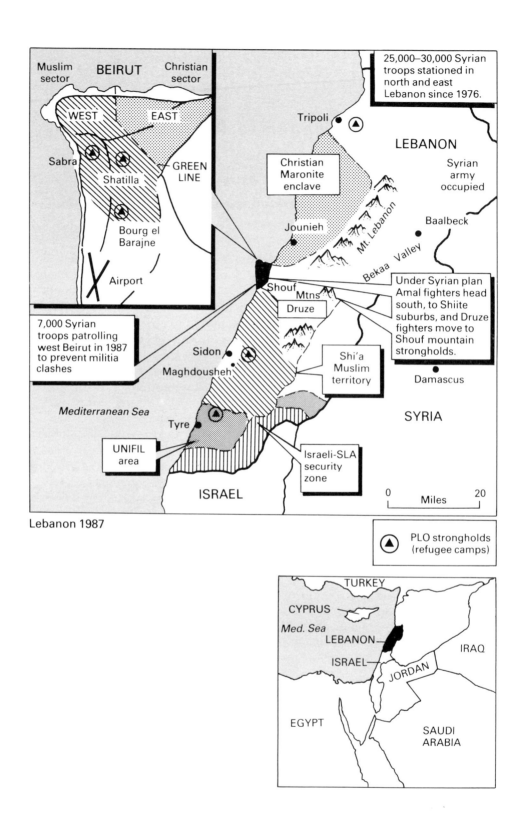

Muslim sector | **BEIRUT** | **Christian sector**

WEST | EAST

Sabra

Shatilla

GREEN LINE

Bourg el Barajne

Airport

7,000 Syrian troops patrolling west Beirut in 1987 to prevent militia clashes

Mediterranean Sea

UNIFIL area

Tyre

ISRAEL

Lebanon 1987

25,000–30,000 Syrian troops stationed in north and east Lebanon since 1976.

Tripoli

LEBANON

Syrian army occupied

Christian Maronite enclave

Jounieh

Mt. Lebanon

Baalbeck

Bekaa Valley

Shouf Mtns

Druze

Under Syrian plan Amal fighters head south, to Shiite suburbs, and Druze fighters move to Shouf mountain strongholds.

Sidon

Maghdousheh

Shi'a Muslim territory

Damascus

SYRIA

Israeli-SLA security zone

0   Miles   20

▲ PLO strongholds (refugee camps)

TURKEY

CYPRUS

Med. Sea

LEBANON

ISRAEL

JORDAN

IRAQ

EGYPT

SAUDI ARABIA

Lebanese city of Tripoli, when Sunni Muslim fundamentalists of the pro-Palestinian Islamic Unification Movement were attacked by the Syrians together with several Islamic militias. In the most bitter and intense fighting of the entire war 500 people were killed, 1,000 injured and 300,000 became refugees. By now the Syrians were strong enough to control and manipulate every group in Lebanon. They had also replaced all the arms and equipment lost in the 1982 war and had 30,000 troops in Lebanon.

The War in 1986-87

Tension became high because, in the early part of 1986, Syria seemed to be preparing for war against Israel on the Golan Heights. In two public addresses President Assad said: 'The Golan will be located in the heart of Syria and not on its border.' The Syrian military build-up was massive, with perhaps 350,000 troops stationed along and behind the Golan border with Israel. The Syrian Army numbered 470,000, with 2,000 tanks from Syria's total of 4,000 deployed between Damascus and the Golan. The intelligence services of several countries were convinced that Syria was planning a war against Israel at this time but it did not occur, largely because the Soviet Union, Syria's ally and supplier, advised against it. The Soviet assessment was that President Reagan, still smarting from American military inability to respond to terrorist acts against American targets, would welcome a chance to aid Israel against Syria, which, with Iran and Libya, the Americans considered responsible for terrorist acts.

With several conflicts, often unrelated, going on concurrently, it is better to look at each one in turn.

The Camps War

As pro-Arafat PLO fighters infiltrated back into Lebanon, the Shi'a Muslim factions, mainly *Amal*, feared that once again the PLO planned to take over southern Lebanon. The PLO is committed to armed attack against Israel while *Amal* is concerned with securing its power base in Lebanon's Shi'a community and a strong position for the Shi'a in the emerging political power equation.

The spectre of a PLO-controlled southern Lebanon deeply alarms *Amal*, which is led by Nabih Berri. By the time Israel invaded Lebanon in June 1982 virtually all the southerners, Muslim and Christian alike, had come to hate the arrogant way in which Palestinian terrorists held sway over the region, disrupting their lives and inviting the avenging wrath of Israel's armed forces. The Israeli raids were of less consequence than the PLO presence itself. The Palestinian state within a state was resented by all Lebanese and they are still willing to go to great lengths to ensure that it is not restored. This particularly applies to *Amal*, as it demonstrated in the Camps War, which began in 1985.

Amal was determined to destroy the PLO's bases, the big refugee camps of south Beirut—Sabra, Shatilla and Bourg el Barajne, and Rashidiyeh in south Lebanon. In this they were encouraged by the Syrian government—and more directly by Syrian officers from the Bekaa—which sponsors and equips its own faction of the PLO. This is the group led by Abu Musa which had split from Arafat's PLO in 1982. It is against the Syrians' interests for Arafat to become strong again in Lebanon.

These three Israeli soldiers are examining part of a large haul of weapons and ammunition found in a building in southern Lebanon. The Israelis thinly man a security zone to prevent terrorist infiltration into northern Israel. (Courtesy Israeli Defence Forces.)

The *Amal* militiamen sealed all entrances to the camps and daily bombarded them with mortar bombs and howitzer shells. Sabra, Shatilla and Bourg el Barajne, home of 50,000 Palestinian refugees, contain a network of underground passages and cellars where large quantities of supplies can be stored. These reserves sustained the Palestinians through long months of siege but by January 1987 they had been used up. The staple diet of many was a mixture of ground wheat mixed with grass picked from around the camp edges, even at the risk of being sniped by *Amal*. The besieged Palestinians were having to eat cats, dogs and rats.

Outside the Palestinian camps *Amal* waged an especially vicious war against the civilian presence of Palestinians. Hundred were captured; Palestinian homes outside the camps were looted and burnt. Palestinians living in the Shi'a neighbourhoods were murdered. In one suburb, Hay Sellum, where only a few Palestinian families remained, masked men broke into a wake and sprayed a room full of women with children with gunfire. According to a survivor, they shouted 'See how your children are going to die!'

PLO Versus Amal *in the South*

The Camps War was largely a siege war against armed civilians. In the south of Lebanon—but north of Israel's security zone—the combatants are PLO guerrilla fighters backed by the extremist Islamic *Hezbollah* (Party of God) movement, against *Amal* gunmen. The big PLO refugee camp at Rashidiyeh, near Tyre, was besieged by *Amal* for 68 days but *Fatah* fighters loyal to Arafat then broke out. In October 1986, in one of the biggest battles in Lebanon, they inflicted a humiliating defeat on the *Amal* militiamen, subsequently driving them from a string of villages. In November-December, Iran and Algiers sponsored an accord between the Palestinians and Shi'a Muslims. About 100 anti-Arafat Palestinian groups handed over some positions around Maghdousheh to pro-Iranian *Hezbollah* fighters, but pro-Arafat men were then allowed to reoccupy them.

Arafat has helped to fund and arm *Hezbollah*. *Hezbollah*'s motive for helping Arafat is that it wants to wrest the leadership of Lebanon's 1 million Shi'as from the more secular *Amal*. The *Hezbollah* leadership plans to create an Iranian-style Islamic republic in Lebanon. Most Palestinians, being Sunni Muslims, reject this objective but as Arafat needs southern Lebanon as a springboard for yet more terrorist attacks on Israel he collaborates with *Hezbollah*. In contrast, *Amal* does not want PLO terrorist raids on Israel because they will trigger further Israeli retaliatory strikes in southern Lebanon. The pro-Arafat PLO appears to have the upper hand. Arafat's men control a strategic swathe of territory where Syrian control does not reach—from the Maghdousheh Heights through the refugee camps, with their hardened PLO fighters, to the city of Sidon itself.

UNIFIL's War

UNIFIL's rules of engagement dictate that its soldiers may fire only in self-defence, and even then only when fired upon. Despite countless tense moments the UNIFIL troops managed for years to control their anger and exasperation. French soldiers of UNIFIL and the fighters of Shi'a *Amal* were friendly enough until 18

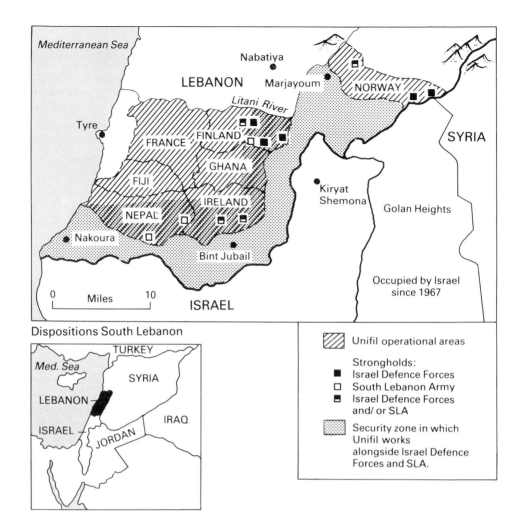

Dispositions South Lebanon

	Unifil operational areas
	Strongholds:
■	Israel Defence Forces
□	South Lebanon Army
⊟	Israel Defence Forces and/ or SLA
	Security zone in which Unifil works alongside Israel Defence Forces and SLA.

Map labels:

Mediterranean Sea
Nabatiya
LEBANON
Marjayoum
Litani River
NORWAY
Tyre
FINLAND
SYRIA
FRANCE
GHANA
FIJI
Kiryat Shemona
Golan Heights
IRELAND
NEPAL
Nakoura
Bint Jubail
Occupied by Israel since 1967
0   Miles   10
ISRAEL

Inset map labels:

TURKEY
Med. Sea
SYRIA
LEBANON
IRAQ
ISRAEL
JORDAN

August 1986, when French guards at a UN security checkpoint in the *Amal*-controlled village of Marrakeh attempted to disarm a local *Amal* commander. His bodyguard drew a revolver and the French soldiers responded with automatic fire that killed both the Shi'a gunmen. Within minutes more than 100 *Amal* fighters drove into Marrakeh in trucks and opened intense machine-gun fire on the UN positions. Nabih Berri negotiated a cease-fire 14 hours later; by then two other Shi'a fighters were dead and 18 French soldiers were wounded. Both sides issued statements calling the fighting a 'regrettable incident' but at the funeral of the dead *Amal* militiamen hundreds of young Shi'a chanted 'Death to the French!'

Until mid-1986 UN checkpoints consisted of little more than a sentry-box, some barbed wire and a couple of heavy iron tank traps to force vehicles to stop at the checkpoint. They are now strongly fortified. Many are protected by high concrete walls, as a defence against rocket and mortar attack from the surrounding hills. The UN troops are targets as a result of an Iranian policy decision to step up the conflict in south Lebanon, both for control of the local Shi'a community and against Israel. The offensive threatens not only the future of UNIFIL but also future relationships between Lebanon and Israel and between the Gulf War allies, Iran and Syria.

Christians Versus Christians

On 27 September, 1986 Elie Hobeika, who had been thrown out of his command of the Maronite Lebanese Forces, tried to fight his way into power. Openly allied with Syria, Hobeika launched his attack from the western or Muslim side of Beirut's 'Green Line'. The resulting fighting killed about 50 people but is more important for the new features it introduced into the complex pattern of war rivalries in Beirut.

The leaders of Lebanese Forces published detailed accounts of the arrangements which preceded the attack. While these were impossible to confirm it was widely accepted in Beirut that Hobeika's raiders could not possibly have made an attack from Muslim west Beirut without the knowledge and co-operation of the Syrians and of some militias in west Beirut.

For the first time in years the Lebanese Army showed itself capable of incisive command and decisive action. Under orders from President Gemayel, the army's 10th Brigade crushingly defeated the attackers. The reputation of Samir Geagea, commander of the Lebanese Forces, also improved as a result of the battle in the streets, but Hobeika's attack penetrated a mile beyond the Green Line before it was stopped.

Shi'a War Against SLA

Late in September 1986 Shi'a fighters inspired by religion but without allegiance to any particular group, made a night raid on the South Lebanese Army (SLA) at Sojod, on the edge of Israel's security belt. In a well-planned and daring operation, the Shi'as clambered up precipices overhanging Sojod and overran the SLA positions. In a 10-day period they killed 16 SLA fighters, demoralized the SLA and

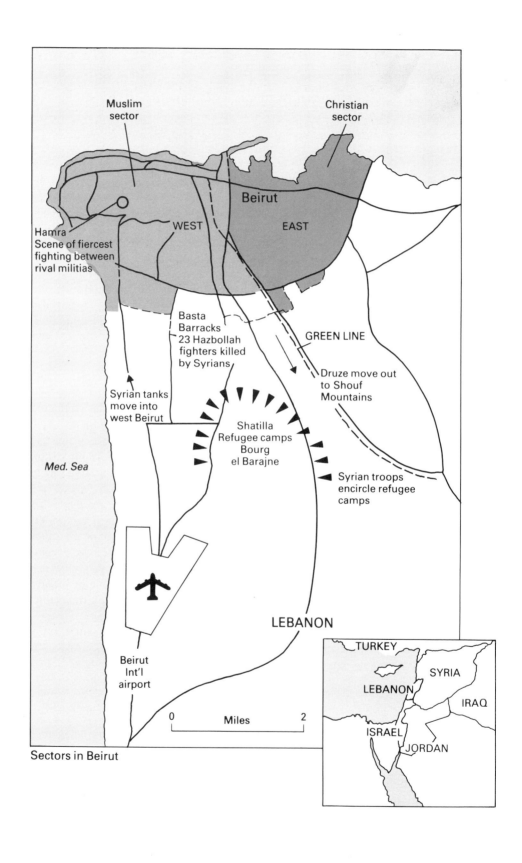

Muslim sector

Christian sector

Hamra
Scene of fiercest
fighting between
rival militias

Beirut

WEST

EAST

Basta
Barracks
23 Hazbollah
fighters killed
by Syrians

GREEN LINE

Druze move out
to Shouf
Mountains

Syrian tanks
move into
west Beirut

Shatilla
Refugee camps
Bourg
el Barajne

Syrian troops
encircle refugee
camps

Med. Sea

Beirut
Int'l
airport

LEBANON

0   Miles   2

Sectors in Beirut

TURKEY

SYRIA

LEBANON

IRAQ

ISRAEL

JORDAN

alarmed the Israelis. The attack was led by 15 young men originally from Sojod who know the country intimately.

The Israeli Army sent super-modern Markava tanks to Sojod to boost the morale of the SLA. The situation in southern Lebanon is difficult for Israel. The army has about 1,000 soldiers in the security zone but would like to withdraw them and cut loose from the Lebanese chaos. To do this the Israelis need the SLA to be strong; in 1987 it comprises about 1,800 men, two-thirds Christian to one-third Shi'a Muslim.

The commander of SLA, Major-General Antoine Lahad, is not as effective as its previous commander, the late Major Haddad. Unlike Haddad, Lahad is not a local man, but a Maronite from the north. He has aspirations to make the security zone a haven for all Christians in Lebanon but his co-religionists in the north have turned against him. On 2 January 1987 radical Shi'as attacked another SLA compound on a hill overlooking the village of Baraachit and killed six SLA men. The 30 Shi'a raiders, who attacked the SLA position from the rear, apparently suffered no casualties.

About 20 southern Lebanese villages are controlled by *Hezbollah* fanatics. As a result the pro-Iranian militia has moved from small-scale guerrilla operations to fully-fledged military assaults involving up to 50 men at a time.

Syrian Peace-keeping in Beirut

Towards the end of February 1987 the Syrian Army moved into parts of Beirut to impose order. Announcing a curfew, the Syrian commander, Brigadier Ghazi Kenaan, said that troops had orders to shoot on sight and after the first night 18 bodies were found dumped in the street while dozens of people had disappeared. When the Syrians took over a *Hezbollah* barracks they executed 23 *Hezbollah* extremists found there. Within a week 7,000 troops were in the city, much to the anger of the Druse militias and the Communists who had combined to fight the Syrian-backed *Amal*. The Syrians did not attack *Amal* fighters or their bases, but many *Amal* gunmen, taking no chances, fled from the city with their entire arsenal to evade the Syrian order that weapons must be surrendered.

The Syrians' return to Beirut in force was primarily a defeat for Nabih Berri whose militia forces have shown that, despite all the help they had received from Syria, they could not bludgeon the Palestinian camps into submission or impose a minimum of authority in Beirut's Muslim quarter.

Syria's 'War' in Tripoli

The Syrian Army has waged a long campaign against various Muslim groups considered to be enemies of the Assad regime, notably the Muslim Brotherhood. In the northern Lebanon town of Tripoli the army sanctioned and organized an onslaught against members of the Islamic Unification Movement, also known as the *Taweed*. This was a continuation of an operation which began in 1985.

On 18 December 1986 Syrian soldiers arrested a leader of the fundamentalist *Taweed* and in response *Taweed* ambushed and killed 15 Syrians. Syrian officers, some of them from the Intelligence section, organized retaliation. That night they used members of the pro-Syrian Arab Democratic, Lebanese Nationalist, Ba'ath and National Syrian Socialist parties to cordon off the suburb of Tabbaneh. Syrian Intelligence officers then named more than 200 people for summary execution. All were shot in the head. The massacre, the biggest since the Syrian Army slaughtered 20,000 people in the Syrian city of Hama in 1982, is taken to be a warning that Syria rules in Lebanon.

Morocco–Polisario War

Background Summary

The conflict concerns the ownership of Western Sahara, a former Spanish colony. Both Morocco and Mauritania claimed the territory but in 1975 an international court found that neither country had a legitimate claim. The overriding principle, the court decided, was self-determination by the West Saharans. Their exact number is not known but is estimated to be between 200,000 and 400,000.

Spain withdrew in February 1976 and Morocco and Spain partitioned the territory. The Popular Front for the Liberation of Saguia el-Hamra and Rio de Oro (Polisario) declared the whole area to be the Sahrawi Arab Democratic Republic (SADR). After military reverses Mauritania agreed to a ceasefire; Morocco then claimed the entire area.

The Polisario forces, a highly mobile guerrilla army, made it impossible for Morocco to occupy the region and Moroccan strategy became based on the 'Hassan Wall', a system of defences begun in 1980. The Western Saharan people were squeezed into the north-west or into refugee camps in neighbouring Algeria, which supports Polisario. Many countries and the Organisation of African Unity (OAU) recognise SADR but Morocco will not negotiate with Polisario.

Summary of the War in 1985

In 1985 the war went badly for Polisario, although the guerrillas continued their harassing tactics. SADR leaders believed that sooner or later Islamic fundamentalism would bring down the Moroccan monarchy and that the Moroccan people would reject the great cost of the war. The Moroccan Army made major gains during 1985 and in particular took over nearly all the northern territory, leaving only the stony plains of Rio de Oro in the south to the guerrillas.

Polisario had only one really powerful friend—the Soviet Union—whereas Morocco is supplied by the United States and France. Polisario could fight only a war of attrition but at least its bases were well protected. Tindouf, its main base, was defended by Algerian-supplied anti-aircraft guns and missiles.

The remarkable Hassan Wall dominated the territory. In 1985 it reached a length of 1,600 km. Built of sand 3 metres high, it is protected by barbed wire, radar and ground sensors. Behind the wall quick-response units were ready to deal with any Polisario breakthrough.

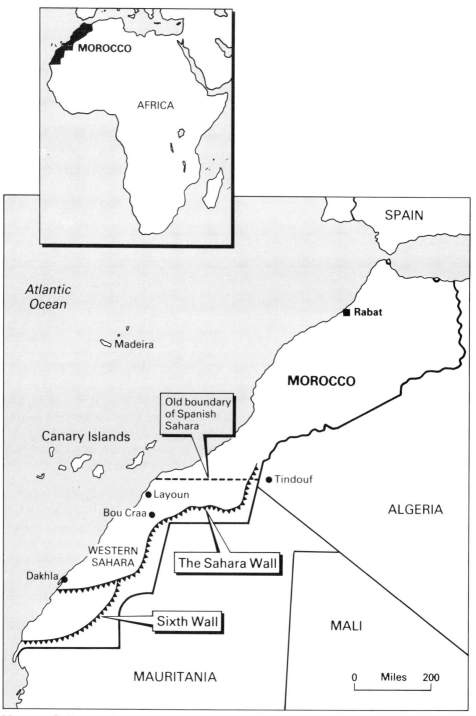

SPAIN

Atlantic
Ocean

● Madeira

Canary Islands

■ Rabat

MOROCCO

Old boundary
of Spanish
Sahara

● Tindouf

● Layoun

ALGERIA

Bou Craa ●

WESTERN
SAHARA

The Sahara Wall

Dakhla ●

Sixth Wall

MALI

MAURITANIA

0   Miles   200

Morocco-Polisario War

The War in 1986-87

On the 10th anniversary of the proclamation of SADR, 27 February 1986, more than 600 visitors—including delegations from Algeria, Cuba, Mauritania, Madagascar, the African National Congress (ANC) and South-West Africa People's Organization (SWAPO)—attended the celebrations in Tindouf. It was an indication of the wide support for SADR and Polisario. By that time 63 countries recognized SADR.

Whatever limitations the Hassan Wall might have imposed on Polisario's military capability it has not held back the growth of SADR institutions, which include a labour union, a women's union, a public health system and an educational programme.

During the anniversary parade Polisario displayed its captured military equipment. This included South African AML/Eland-90 armoured cars, British Cascavels and Austrian-French SK-105 tank destroyers, French WAB mobile administration units and US 106 mm recoilless rifles. To prove the effectiveness of their defensive fire, the Polisario fighters showed wrecked F5-E fighter bombers and French Mirage jets.

The military review was watched by Polisario General Secretary Muhammad Abdel-Aziz and a senior Algerian minister, Muhammad Abdel-Ghani. His presence indicated Algeria's readiness to continue as Polisario's main supporter. The cost of Algeria's role has risen since Libya withdrew its support for Polisario following the 1984 treaty between Morocco and Libya. This treaty was meaningless by 1986 but it is unlikely that Libya will again give aid to Polisario.

The Hassan Wall may be costing Morocco more than it is worth. Lack of water, inhospitable terrain and climate and constant harassment from Polisario mortar fire have weakened the morale of the 100,000 Moroccan troop stationed on the wall. Early in 1986 the Moroccans completed the last leg of the wall along the Algerian border facing Tindouf, thus bringing its total length to 1,760 km, a tremendous feat of military engineering. In fact, the Hassan Wall is more than one wall; in places it now consists of 5 or 6 separate walls, one behind the other.

By mid-1986 Polisario guerrillas were able to breach the wall and operate within a 10 km belt behind it. But even if it is periodically penetrated, the wall remains an obstacle to Polisario's military effectiveness.

The guerrillas move up and down the front with comparative ease. In the Smara and Mgala region Polisario operates within range of Moroccan artillery, travelling in Land-Rovers and being shielded from Moroccan surveillance systems by intervening hills. A typical Polisario harassing operation took place on 6 March 1986 when sustained shelling by concealed 120 mm mortars appeared to score at least 10 direct hits on a Moroccan base along the wall near Smara. The Moroccans returned their fire but the shells fell wide of Polisario positions. Within minutes the guerrillas had moved back from the hills on to level ground dotted with acacia and thorn trees, their retreat covered against air attacks by anti-aircraft batteries spread over a 3-km arc. Such operations are known to occur daily but they amount to little more than skirmishing.

The 11th anniversary—26 February 1987—of the founding of the SADR was one of the most remarkable days of the war. To celebrate the occasion Polisario made an attack with 110 armoured Land-Rovers and broke through the Hassan

Wall. The object was to show that it was not as impregnable as the Moroccan Army claimed.

The raid was a classic of its type. Under cover of darkness, Polisario specialists in mine detection cleared the way for the vehicles, which then fanned out to cover a front of about 12 miles. Several miles inside the wall, between Farsia and the oasis of Mahbess, they met the first line of Moroccan soldiers. With their defences breached, the Moroccan commanders were thrown into confusion, for if they fired on their own positions there could be heavy casualties among their own men. The Polisario raiders were on the Moroccan side of the wall for more than three hours. In that time they blew up a fuel-storage tank and an ammunition dump, killed or wounded an unknown number of enemy troops, captured 80 of them and seized much equipment.

They were gone, without losing any men, before the Moroccan Army could mount a counter-attack. Next morning Polisario showed off its booty: anti-tank missiles, mortars, bazookas, Belgian-made FAL automatic rifles, Soviet-made Kalashnikovs, Spanish Santana troop-carriers, a French AMX tank and much ammunition. To save face, the Moroccans claimed that Polisario had intended to establish a foothold across the barrier—which would have made no sense—and that the attempt was repulsed.

On the same day as the big Polisario raid, assassins presumed to be in the pay of the Moroccan government attacked the home of the SADR president, Muhammad Abdel-Aziz, in Tindouf refugee camp. The bombs they used would almost certainly have killed him had he been at home; he was away welcoming the Polisario raiders back from the desert.

It was learned during 1986 that Polisario has no more than 3,000 guerrillas but this small number, all well trained and most of them highly experienced, are more than enough to tie down the large 'Army of the Hassan Wall'.

The army is so bored for most of the time that many of the soldiers have taken to using hashish; they buy it from certain officers who reportedly sell it for three times the market price in the towns. Desertion to Polisario by Moroccan soldiers is not uncommon. Polisario has 2,100 prisoners but the exact number of deserters in this total is not known. Some are always paraded before the steady stream of visiting diplomats and journalists. Being a Polisario prisoner is also boring but prisoners tell visitors that it is preferable to being under the command of corrupt Moroccan officers. The 50 or so captured Moroccan officers are also paraded for journalists.

Interestingly, Morocco's military reputation is high among black African countries. Zaire, Senegal and Gabon have their officers trained in Morocco, which is providing technical military assistance to Chad, Togo and other African countries.

Polisario maintains an ever-growing 'war museum' of captured equipment but the amount is small compared with Morocco's huge reserves. Nearly half of Morocco's military equipment came from France in 1986-87 but each year the US contributes US$36 million worth of ammunition and spare parts. The Americans have three times refused to give King Hassan the F-16 aircraft he covets. They know very well that the planes are useless against elusive desert guerrillas operating in small numbers and they fear that Hassan might use them against Algeria; this could cause a major war. Saudi Arabian money pays the King's largest war bills—the specially high wages paid to Army of the Wall soldiers.

In mid-1987 the war reached the stand-off stage. The Polisario guerrillas could puncture the Hassan Wall but during daylight they could not exist inside it for more than a few hours. The few parties that have tried it have been wiped out.

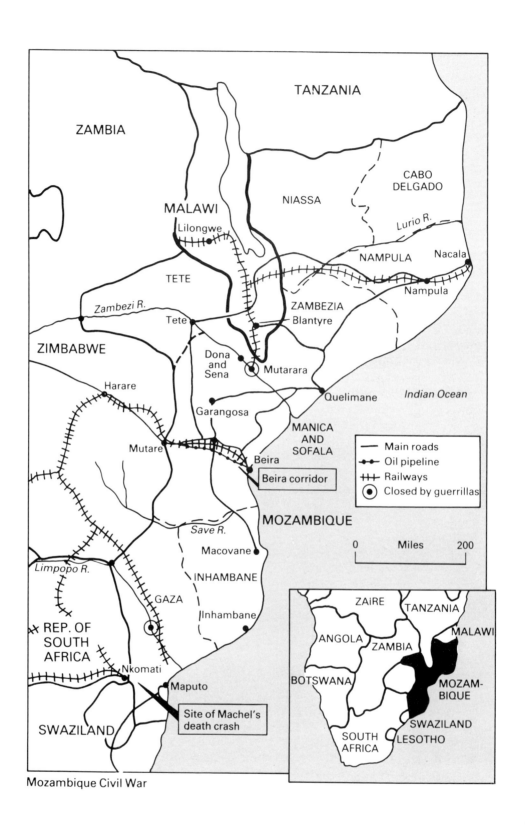

Mozambique Civil War

Mozambique Guerrilla War

THE CONFLICT INTENSIFIES

Background Summary

Mozambique, a former Portuguese colony, has been a battlefield since it became independent in 1975. The country's already poor economy was undermined by the mass flight of Portuguese skilled workers. The Mozambique Liberation Front (Frelimo), the Marxist faction which won control of the new nation, compounded already severe problems by investing scarce resources in inefficient nationalised farms and factories and keeping food prices so low that small farmers had little incentive.

In 1977 the Rhodesian Central Intelligence Organisation created the Mozambique National Resistance (MNR) which is better known as Renamo. At the time white-ruled Rhodesia was trying to reduce the amount of assistance which neighbouring black regimes might give to the Zimbabwean resistance, later to become the government.

Fighting between Frelimo forces and Renamo guerrillas, which was often savage and destructive, gradually destroyed Mozambique. In 1982 South Africa, which has a long border with Mozambique, embarked on a campaign to ensure that Mozambique would never become a threat to South African security. South African Defence Force (SADF) raided the capital, Maputo, blew up storage tanks at Beira, derailed trains and wrecked power lines. Also, South Africa financed, trained, armed and transported Renamo fighters.

In 1984 South Africa and Mozambique signed a peace pact, the Nkomati Accord. It brought South Africa more benefits than Mozambique but South African aid to Renamo was stopped. In return, Mozambique's President, Samora Machel, prevented the terrorists of the African National Congress (ANC) from using his territory. By now the United States was involved because the Reagan regime feared that Mozambique was following Angola into the Soviet-Cuban camp.

(*For a full description of the war see* **WAR ANNUAL** 1.)

Summary of the War in 1985

Mozambique covers an area of 303,769 sq. miles. In this large and difficult region half of Renamo's units were beyond command or control throughout the year. Yet supplies reached the organization and were reasonably well-distributed, much by air drop from the Comores Islands. Portugal, Morocco, Saudi Arabia, Zaire and Mozambican expatriates in Bavaria supplied the weapons and equipment, apart from South Africa. Total strength of the Renamo groups was estimated at 9,000, a large enough force to confront Mozambique's armed forces of only 15,500 trained soldiers. The army was augmented by 3,400 Zimbabwean soldiers doing guard duty on the railway and oil pipeline which served Zimbabwe from the Mozambique port of Beira.

After 8 years Renamo still had no coherent leadership, no political philosophy and nothing to offer in place of the leadership it wanted to destroy. Nevertheless President Machel was in a difficult position. While he had a defence treaty with the Soviet Union and relied on Russian and Chinese military aid, he accepted an American offer of army vehicles and uniforms and he was still being helped by South Africa.

Some major actions were fought, notably that at Manianje when the goverment troops captured a guerrilla base, and at Cas Banana, when guerrillas recaptured a major depot from the army.

The War in 1986-87

During the earlier part of 1986 the Machel government was virtually under siege because the guerrillas controlled at least two-thirds of the country and were active in several urban areas. In May, Renamo terrorists set off two car bombs in Maputo and injured 50 people. Because of terrorist activity—by both sides—and consequent disruption, more than 200,000 people became refugees in their own country; at least half of them live in more than 100 resettlement camps, most of them strung out along Mozambique's 1,500 mile coastline.

Giving aid and comfort to the refugees can be dangerous. In March 1986 a Mozambican official, David Campos, left the coastal city of Inhambane in a well-marked Red Cross Land Cruiser with medicine and food. Ambushed by three separate guerrilla groups, he ran the gauntlet of gunfire from the first two before being stopped by a bazooka blast from the third. The rebels dragged the seriously wounded Campos from his vehicle, shot him again and beheaded him.[1]

In each new area the rebels capture, they sweep away every vestige of government administration and replace it with one of their own. People are then left to live for themselves and, according to reports by several journalists who have travelled through such areas, the majority of peasants prefer this new 'freedom' to the government's coercive scheme. Under the Government's 10-year plan the whole rural population is to be resettled, in communal villages, state-run farms or co-operatives, by 1990. Renamo condemns all such settlements as concentration camps and burns them.

The Renamo rebels make a stark contrast to those of UNITA in Angola. While the UNITA men are well-armed and smartly dressed, the Renamo men wear a ragged mixture of civilian clothes and captured uniforms, many with jacket buttons embossed with hammer and sickle emblems. Webbing for their Russian Kalashnikovs is crudely sewn from brightly coloured plastic or cheap cotton cloth. According to Renamo leaders, all its guerrillas are volunteers. This is not wholly true; Renamo commanders sometimes order local chiefs to provide recruits. Their average age is young, probably no more than 17 years, but the fighters' status in bush society is high and they are envied their good-quality food.

The Renamo leader, Alfonso Dhlakama, now lives in what he calls the 'presidential camp', a collection of mud huts in the dense forest of the Gorongosa National Park. Until 1977 he was a Frelimo officer in charge of supplies in Beira. In

January that year, alarmed by Frelimo's ever more harsh Communism, he defected to Renamo.

In June 1986 Dhlakama claimed to have 18,000 men under arms, 2,000 of them in what he described as 'conventional battalions'.[2] They have no resemblance to Western army units but are roughly similar to UNITA's regular army units in Angola. The other fighters are formed into 'traditional guerrillas', in Dhlakama's terms. His figures are exaggerated but Renamo's numbers are certainly much higher than the 1985 figure of 9,000. Early in 1986 Renamo formed a women's battalion but its members have not been seen in armed action.

In an apparent attempt to win more friends abroad, Renamo made a key change to its leadership in July 1986. The Secretary-General, Evo Fernandes, who is of Indian descent, was demoted. Because of his background, Fernandes was seen by some Westerners as not 'African enough' to represent an indigenous anti-Communist rebel movement. Only days after his removal, the Heritage Foundation, a conservative Washington 'think tank' with close links to the Reagan administration, invited Renamo representatives to Washington for consultation.

Also, his removal prompted a Munich-based group of Mozambicans, known as the Committee for Mozambican Unity, to pledge loyalty to Dhlakama and the Renamo military command. Fernandes's demotion has also helped the rebels to gain support for Mozambique's small businessmen and commercial farmers. These groups viewed Fernandes as too pro-Portuguese and not in keeping with the nationalist image of Renamo. A pastoral letter issued by the Episcopal conference of Mozambique seems to indicate success for Renamo's propaganda campaign. In the Letter, the Catholic bishops for the first time referred to Renamo forces as 'guerrillas' rather than 'armed bandits', the government term for them.

Despite its attempts to create a better image, at times Renamo seems to be waging a war of starvation against the Mozambican people, though Dhlakama denies this. Only relief food destined for Government areas is stopped from getting through, he claims.

In groups of 300-500, the guerrillas often attack army posts. One target, in early June 1986, was Inhaminga, a hilltop town and a district capital in the central Sofala region. The action was typical. The Renamo fighters marched for several days through the bush so that the garrison would have no word of their approach. They moved in Inhaminga at dawn, swarming down the town's deserted main street and using the disused railway station as a base. The defending soldiers almost immediately fled from their posts and congregated in their barracks on the town's outskirts. From here they laid down mortar and rifle fire. After a few hours, the guerrillas pulled back with their wounded and besieged the barracks. Three times the government troops tried to break out and the commanding officer then called for an air strike. Two MiG 17s flew from Beira to strafe and bomb the rebel positions. The guerrillas fired back with three 14.5 mm anti-aircraft guns but the jets returned to the attack several times. Neither side gained any advantage and both suffered many casualties. That night the Renamo raiders destroyed much of Inhaminga and withdrew.

With or without official sanction, Renamo operated from Malawi for much of 1986. Then, at Machel's request, Zimbabwe and Tanzania landlocked Malawi's big neighbours, threatened Malawi's President, Hastings Banda, with a trade boycott unless he stopped protecting the Renamo rebels. He did so and Renamo was driven out of its Malawian bases.

Most of Renamo's overall strategy is decided by expatriates in Lisbon. The aim of the offensive which began in October 1986 was to capture the garrison town of Mocuba in northern Zambezia. Mocuba is the military headquarters of Zambezia, Mozambique's richest and most populous province. From there they could easily march to the Indian Ocean port of Quelimane and the town of Chinde on the Zambezi estuary and cut Mozambique in half. Renamo took control of much of the lower Zambezi River valley as part of its attempt to isolate northern Mozambique. One of Frelimo's greatest defeats was the loss of the bridge linking the towns of Dona and Sena across the Zambezi. Hundreds of Frelimo troops and 50,000 civilians were sent fleeing north into Malawi.

In early October more than 1,500 Mozambican troops fled from Malawi in the face of rebel onslaughts. Other soldiers deserted their posts throughout the country. About the same time South Africa applied a devastating sanction against Mozambique's collapsing economy by returning an estimated 60,000 Mozambicans working in South Africa. This action was supposedly in retaliation for a land-mine explosion that injured six South African soldiers on the Mozambican border. Lost income from the repatriation would cost the government US$75 million a year—more than a third of its foreign earnings.

On 19 October 1986 President Machel was killed in a plane crash. He was on his way from Zambia to Maputo when his Soviet-built and Soviet-piloted aircraft crashed, during bad weather, in South African territory. Also killed were Defence Minister Alberto Joaquim Chipande and Transport Minister Alcantara Santos.

The black African states accused South Africa of having caused the crash, either through a bomb or by having sent misleading radio signals. International investigators proved that the crash was the result of pilot error.

Machel was succeeded by Joaquim Chissano, an appointment welcome to the West and to his country. Chissano is a moderate and as Foreign Minister for more than ten years his had become the recognized voice of Mozambique abroad. He is thought to have been the main influence in persuading Machel to move away from doctrinaire Communism towards a more pragmatic relationship with the West. In mid-March 1987 Chissano reached an agreement about mutual defence with Malawi's President, Hastings Banda. Within hours Alfonso Dhlakama warned Banda not to send troops to protect the Nacla corridor, which connects Malawi with the Indian ocean. 'We advise President Banda not to play with fire,' he said.

Zimbabwean operations in Mozambique in support of the Government, have steadily increased. The Zimbabwe air force showed surprising range in February 1987 when it led a two-day attack on Mutarara and four other lower Zambezi River towns held for months by Renamo. The air and ground assault capped a successful two-month drive by Frelimo and the Zimbabweans to roll back Renamo's 1986 gains in Tete, Sofala and Zambezia provinces.

The Government has 1,500 Cuban, 350 Soviet and 80 North Korean military 'advisers'. Many are known to be instructors while the others are technicians. In addition, there are about 200 East German security advisers, some of whom personally protect government leaders.[3] A Tanzanian Army contingent of 3,000 troops guards important installations but it is the Zimbabwean contingent that is most vital. It grew to 10,000 in 1987 and even this large number is increased for special operations and in emergencies.

Mozambique's armed forces in 1987 appeared more impressive on paper than their performance in the field; this is largely because they are notoriously ill-led. Also, they have spent the available money on the wrong equipment for the type of warfare in which they are involved. The army has a total strength of 30,000, out of a population of nearly 13 million. About 75% of its manpower are conscripts, who serve two years.

The Army's Establishment

The army's establishment comprises:

1 tank brigade, which also forms the Presidential Guard, 7 infantry brigades, each comprising 1 tank battalion, 3 infantry, 2 motorised, 1 artillery and 1 air defence battalion, 2 independent mechanized battalions, and 7 anti-aircraft artillery battalions.

Equipment: 250 tanks, a mixture of T-34, T-54 and T-55, 46 armoured fighting vehicles; 200 armoured personnel carriers; 200 pieces of artillery; 300 mortars and some howitzers.

Backing the army is an air force with 69 combat aircraft and 22 helicopter gunships.

Tanks, artillery and armoured fighting vehicles are virtually useless for combat against Renamo because of the unfavourable terrain and vegetation. Few of the combat aircraft are airworthy but in any case are little use against guerrillas in jungle. Helicopter gunships are the best weapon against the Renamo guerrillas but Mozambique has too few of them, and even fewer skilled pilots. The armed forces' best asset would be well-trained and well-led commando-type infantry. The Soviet and Cuban instructors appear to be unable to bring Frelimo's infantry to the necessary degree of professionalism.

Renamo's guerrillas were active in 13 of the 14 provinces in mid-1987. This was proof that Frelimo was not in control of the insurgency and evidence that the suffering of the peasant population was far from over.[4] Renamo's preconditions for cease-fire talks remain unchanged: free elections and the withdrawal of all foreign troops from Mozambique.

References

1. The story was told by Campos' assistant who, though wounded, survived the ordeal.
2. A report froma Portuguese journalist, Almerigo Grilz, who spent five weeks with Renamo.
3. Diplomatic sources in Maputo.
4. Oxfam described the situation in Zambezia, in March 1987, as 'terrible'. All relief organisations echo this assessment. UN officials estimate that between 1975 and March 1987 more than 250,000 people died as a direct result of the war. The US State Department's 1986 Human Rights Report describes the rebels as 'brutally violent'.

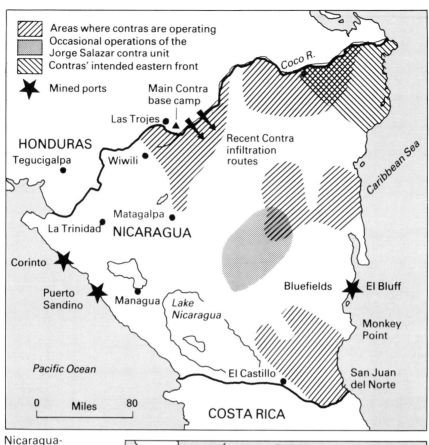

Legend:
- ⧄ Areas where contras are operating
- ▦ Occasional operations of the Jorge Salazar contra unit
- ⧄ Contras' intended eastern front
- ★ Mined ports
- △ Main Contra base camp
- Recent Contra infiltration routes

Coco R.

Las Trojes

HONDURAS
Tegucigalpa   Wiwili

Matagalpa
La Trinidad   NICARAGUA

Corinto

Puerto Sandino   Managua   Lake Nicaragua

Pacific Ocean   El Castillo

Bluefields   ★ El Bluff

Monkey Point

San Juan del Norte

Caribbean Sea

0   Miles   80

COSTA RICA

Nicaragua-
Sandanistas
versus Contras

JAMAICA   CUBA HAITI DOMINICAN REP.
BELIZE   HONDURAS
GUATEMALA   Caribbean Sea
EL SALVADOR
NICARAGUA   VENEZUELA   GUYANA
COSTA RICA   SURINAM
PANAMA COLOMBIA   FR. GUIANA
ECUADOR

US view
of Sandinista
intervention
in Latin America   PERU   BRAZIL

BOLIVIA

Shaded countries are those
cited by President Reagan
as places where radicals
have received aid, ranging
from safe haven and false
documentation to arms and
military training, from the
Sandinista government.

PARAGUAY
CHILE
URUGUAY
ARGENTINA

Source: State Department and White House.

Nicaragua—The Contra War

Background Summary

The Sandinistas, the ruling party in Nicaragua, take their name from Augusto Sandino, an army general who rebelled against the corrupt Somoza family which ruled Nicaragua for decades. Sandino was assassinated in 1933. Anastasio Somoza fled the country in 1979, after a war in which 45,000 died, and was later murdered.

The *junta* which gained control of the country was led by radical Left-wingers such as Daniel Ortega, his brother Humberto and Tomas Borge. Their Sandinista National Liberation Front (FSLN) is Marxist-Leninist and élitist: It has a nine-man Directorate, an 80-member Committee and party membership is pegged at 5,000. In November 1981 President Carter assured Congress that the Sandinistas were not assisting Left-wing insurgents in other countries but President Reagan, only three days after assuming office in November 1981, stated that Nicaraguan weapons were reaching El Salvador. He cut off American aid to Nicaragua.

At the same time he approved funds for covert war against the Sandinistas. The war was to be waged by Contra (opposing) right-wing rebels. Between 1981 and 1983 the CIA directed the Contra operation.

Strengthened by Soviet-bloc weapons reaching them through Cuba, the Sandinistas forced 12,000 Miskito Indians out of the country's north-east. Their homeland was needed for military purposes and as Cuba's bridgehead on mainland America. Most of Cuba's military 'advisers' based themselves in this region.

During 1984 the CIA mined Nicaraguan harbours and the US Administration spoke of sending American troops to Nicaragua if other anti-Sandinista efforts failed. The Contras were frequently given money and weapons. The term Contras covered several guerrilla groups. The largest, the Nicaraguan Democratic Force (NDF) was 9,000-strong before 1985 and led in the field by Colonel Enrique Bermudez, a former Somoza officer. It operated in the north and from over the Honduras border. In the south was the Democratic Revolutionary Alliance (ARDE) with 3,000 fighters led by 'Commander Zero'—Eden Pastora Gomez. In all the Contras numbered 15,000.

(*For a full description of the war see* **WAR ANNUAL** 1.)

Summary of the War in 1985

With Humberto Ortega as nominal commander-in-chief, the Nicaraguan Army had 60,000 regulars and 120,000 reservists, of whom 30,000 were on duty at any one time. Against such a large, well-armed and generally well-trained army the Contras fought a guerrilla war in the mountains, river valleys and coastal swamps. In 1985 the Americans responded with a war of nerves against Nicaragua, with warships on inshore surveillance, spy planes (SR-71 type) regularly overflying the country and the army 'manoeuvring' in Honduras and Panama.

Soviet-bloc activity also increased markedly. The number of Cuban advisers increased to 7,000. On Russian advice the Sandinistas set up a 'directorate of state security' staffed by 400 Cubans, 70 Russians, 50 East Germans and 25 Bulgarians. Ortega carried out Soviet advice to move 50,000 peasants from five northern provinces to deprive the Contras of a popular base and make it difficult for them to find shelter. Trained by the Cubans and East Germans, an 'Irregular Warfare Battalion' was formed to fight the Contras using the Contras' own guerrilla tactics.

The large-scale Contra attack on the town of La Trinidad on 1 August 1985 shocked the Nicaraguan Army and impressed foreign observers. But the battle turned out to be the peak for the Contras and a costly one at that. The army, after chasing the guerrillas back into the hills, estimated that only half the rebels escaped unhurt. The Contras have never since staged such an ambitious raid.

After the battle of La Trinidad the Contras changed their tactics and attacked soft targets—villages without protection, state-owned farms, government health centres, agricultural co-operatives. The aim was to cause administrative collapse. The government met this threat with a public relations campaign designed to induce Contras to return to civilian life, but it had only limited success.

Simultaneously the army experimented with 'hot pursuit' tactics—chasing the Contras into their refuges in Honduras. The Contras, beset by many problems, nevertheless prevented the Sandinistas from running Nicaragua efficiently. Pastora Gomez's ARDE lost its main camps near the Costa Rican border. President Reagan, unceasing in his efforts to get aid to the Contras, warned Americans that Nicaraguan terrorists and subversives and their allies were 'only two days driving time from Harlingen, Texas'.

The War in 1986-87

The first 11 months of 1986, when the rebels' official US aid was limited to US$27 million in humanitarian assistance, saw no serious Contra attempt to take the initiative. Rather, the Contras' largest military force of 10,000 to 12,000 men, was bottled up in its Honduran base camps, hemmed in by Nicaraguan ground troops and artillery. Small groups raided Government-owned enterprises but the Sandinista Army was never seriously engaged.

Having made Miami, Florida, their political and financial capital, the Contra leaders planned strategy and the absorption of aid in the quiet suburb of Kendall. The headquarters of the United Nicaraguan Opposition (UNO), the umbrella organization for most Contra groups, is situated there. About 70,000 Nicaraguans live in Miami, including Adolfo Calero and Arturo Cruz, two members of the triumvirate which until recently ostensibly directed the insurgency. The third, Alfonso Robelo, lives in Costa Rica. Six of the seven leaders of UNO's advisory committee live either in Kendall or Key Biscayne. Wounded Contra guerrillas are sent to Miami to recuperate in a farmhouse turned into a hospice.

Money, with or without US Congress approval, has never been a problem for the Contras. Washington has asked many countries for help in financing them, including the Gulf states, Saudi Arabia and Portugal. The Sultan of Brunei, the wealthiest man in the world, contributed US$10 million for humanitarian aid for

Central America at the request of US Secretary of State George Shultz. The money went to the Contras through a numbered bank account in Switzerland.

The Contra leaders might not have worries about cash flow but they are deeply concerned about their image as bandits who burn, loot, rape, torture and murder. This image is more applicable to the Sandinista security forces, the Contra leaders allege. They see themselves as crusaders rescuing Nicaragua from Communism and Cuban-type dictatorship.

Late in 1986 they hired a young Nicaraguan lawyer, Marta Patricia Baltodano, to be the Contras' human rights director. Marta Baltodano set up offices in Tegucigalpa, Honduras, and in San Jose, Costa Rica, and trained 45 senior Contra members in the significance of the Geneva Convention on warfare. In particular she stresses the Convention's regulations on treatment of civilians, prisoners and the wounded. With a brief to bring about a 'change in mentality', to curb human rights abuses by Contra fighters and to implement new enforcement procedures, Baltodano sent her 45 officials into the field to train FDN troops. The next step is for the troops of each unit to elect a Human Rights Officer.

Baltodano wants guerrillas to report any comrades who are guilty of human rights abuses. Paid directly by the US State Department, Baltodano says that she is careful not to work too closely with the FDN. She is in no way responsible for Contra strategy and tactics in the field. Her problem is that in most of Nicaragua, particularly in the north, co-operative farms and other enterprises are defended by civilians who have had no more than basic military training. As they are the first line of Sandinista defence some are bound to be killed in an encounter against Contras. Thus massive human rights abuses are almost inevitable. If unarmed civilians are killed in such attacks rebel commanders are unlikely to hand over their men for investigation.

In any case it is difficult for Human Rights Officers to convince all 20,000 men who make up the groups of the United Nicaraguan Opposition that human rights must be respected. Most of the rank and file are former peasant farmers who feel they themselves have not been accorded a fair share of human rights.[1]

The 70 officers absent in the US when the Sandinista Army invaded Honduras (see p. 146 below) were given a 6-week course run by the US Army Special Force Groups ('Green Berets'). This included lessons on guerrilla tactics, infiltration, planning, rapid reaction, psychological operations and Intelligence-gathering. During 1987 about 600 Contra unit commanders were to undergo similar courses.

In January 1987 the Contras became very active in efforts to help President Reagan convince the US Congress and others that theirs was not a lost cause. More than 1,000 guerrillas were infiltrated from Honduras to the central province of Chontales and Boaco. Crossing the northern border far to the east of normal entry points, they avoided the heavy Sandinista military presence deployed in the northern mountains to protect the coffee crops. Once across the border the Contras faced a 45-day trek across the steep mountain ranges to the great cattle lands.

By increasing their activities in Nicaragua's centre, the Contras hoped to force the Sandinista High Command to withdraw some of the troops operating on the northern border. The units posted there included 11 of the army's 18 Irregular Light Battalions, known as BLIs. These units, first sent into the field early in 1986, are said to be a great military success.

The Contras hoped to tie up government forces in the centre, thus leaving gaps in the border defences; the main Contra force of 8,000 would then pass through the gaps. Even more important, the Contra leadership and its advisers calculated that they would counter criticism that the FDN was unwilling or unable to fight deep inside Nicaragua.[2]

The ranching country of central Nicaragua offers a number of advantages to the insurgents. The owners of the many private farming estates are anti-Sandinista. The area around Acoyapa was a traditional recruiting ground for the brutal National Guard that kept in power the dictatorship of Anastasio Somoza. In this region the infiltrators linked up with an FDN unit based inside Nicaragua—the Jorge Salazar regional command. The Jorge Salazar unit has the only real base inside Nicaragua on which the FDN can build.

In the last week of March 1987 the Contras ambushed state forestry workers in the ravine of El Infierno and killed eight of them. This made a total of 23 foresters killed by Contras in 30 months. In the village of Aguas Calientes ten co-operative farmers were killed in an attempt to dissuade others from participation in the Sandinistas' rural programme. All forestry workers and many farmers are armed with Kalashnikov rifles. The FDN, in a communiqué broadcast over Radio Liberacion, the rebel radio station, repeated an earlier FDN warning that anyone bearing arms or wearing uniform would be considered a legitimate military target.[3]

The Hasenfus Affair

On 5 October 1986 an American pilot, Eugene Hasenfus, took off from Ilopango airport, El Salvador, in a C-123K transport plane. Hasenfus regularly flew between Ilopango, the Contra bases at Aguacate, Mocoron and Catacama in Honduras and a secret airfield in northern Costa Rica.

Over Nicaragua the C-123 was hit by a rocket from a shoulder-held launcher fired by a soldier of the Gaspar Carcia Laviana Light Hunter Battalion. Hasenfus, who happened to be wearing a reliable parachute given to him by his brother, baled out and survived. Two other US nationals and a South American, all without parachutes, died in the crash. The soldiers found in the plane 50,000 rounds of ammunition and many rifles and grenades as well as other supplies. Also found were documents giving details of the Contra supply operation. Official US aid for the Contras was banned at the time. The biggest catch was Hasenfus himself, the first US national to be taken alive in Nicaragua.

Under interrogation, Hasenfus stated that he was working for the CIA as part of an extensive undercover operation to supply the Contras. His story was denied by the CIA and the Reagan administration. However, the 'Portland Air Services', for which Hasenfus claimed to work, was found not to exist. The capture of Hasenfus, who had worked for the CIA in South-east Asia in 1966-73, was a propaganda coup for the Sandinistas. He was sentenced to 30 years imprisonment but, at the request of President Ortega, the Nicaraguan Assembly voted on 18 December to pardon him. Hasenfus was, in fact, part of Colonel Oliver North's team.

The CIA has since moved the base for supply runs from Ilopango and Aguacate to Great Swan Island, a Honduran island 150 miles off the country's north-eastern coast. Under the new plan US military aircraft fly supplies from America to the island. From there private planes similar to the C-123K transport make the drops in Nicaragua. The move relives US pressure on El Salvador and Honduras to accommodate Contra operations. Under the US aid arrangements of 1987 a Congressional ban prohibits US advisers from approaching nearer than 20 miles to the Nicaraguan border.

Sandinista Expedition into Honduras

For some years Contra guerrillas have occupied a wedge of Honduran territory called Las Vegas Salient. In 1986 the number grew to several thousands. In March that year 1,000 Sandinista troops moved into the same area, which they called 'New Nicaragua', a label the Hondurans regarded as provocative. Occupying an easily defendable stretch of high ground, the Sandinistas intended to show both the Contras and the long-suffering Hondurans that they too could use Honduran territory.

The Sandinistas were sniped at but no effort was made to drive them out and they remained quiet, hoping to accustom the Contras to the non-aggressive presence of enemy troops. Then, on 1 December 1986 they launched a surprise attack. The 1,000 troops already across the border were joined by 4,000 more, supported by artillery and Soviet-made helicopter gunships. The objective was to strike the Contras a crippling blow and drive them deeper into Honduras before 70 middle-ranking officers returned from a training session in the US.

The Honduran Army usually turns a blind eye to Nicaraguan incursions. Most Honduran officers are politically sympathetic to the Contras but resent their presence in Honduras and fear that, if they were defeated they could turn to armed banditry in Honduras or even seek to overthrow its government. It now became clear that they resented even more the presence of a large force of Sandinistas on their soil.

The Honduran President, Jose Azcona Hoyo, had ignored 60 Sandinista Army incursions during 1986. Now he ordered the army to hit back. It did so, first with howitzer fire and then with Super Mystere fighter-bombers which, on 7 December, attacked the Nicaraguan town of Wiwili. The Honduran High Command chose Wiwili for attack because it is a Sandinista 'project town'. Three years ago Wiwili received financing from a private German group to bring running water from a spring six miles away. The project was delayed because the army felt that it could not protect the workers or the finished product from Contra attacks. This changed when the Sandinistas began to mass troops on the border to push the Contras deep into Honduras. The project was finished just before the Honduran aircraft bombed it.

The same day 14 American Chinook helicopters from the Palmerola air base ferried hundreds of Honduran troops to an airstrip at Jamastran, 17 miles from the Nicaraguan border. Their position here was tactically threatening and the Sandinista invaders pulled back.

Honduras has been likened to 'an aircraft carrier at Nicaragua's doorstep'. From this 'aircraft carrier' the Pentagon could, if the order were given, destroy Nicaragua in 30 minutes. There are military bases, training-camps, strategic routes and landing strips that can accommodate big Hercules-type transport planes. Colonel Bermudez, the former Somozan National Guard officer who is now the Contra chief of military staff, was incautious enough to speak to an Argentine

A student who had been engaged on the coffee harvest in Nicaragua does military duty in defensive positions outside Managua. Military service against the Contras is compulsory. (Courtesy Laurie Lewis.)

Nicaragua is so much a nation under arms that even when picking coffee women are armed to defend themselves against possible Contra attack. This woman, mother of two children, has been trained to use the AK47 she is carrying. (Courtesy Steve Lewis.)

The uniforms worn by Nicaraguan soldiers are of good quality; many are made in Cuba. This student-turned-soldier is expected to do three months' service before returning to university.

Three of the Nicaraguan Army's 20,000 conscripts, who are required to do 2 years' service. The youngest of the group is 17. (Courtesy Steve Lewis.)

newspaper of the 'American Plan' to invade Nicaragua. Army staffs all over the world prepare plans for all kinds of contingencies. The one drawn up by the Pentagon for a future 'Operation Nicaragua' has been well known for two years. The American Army runs almost continuous exercises in Honduras. More than 10,000 troops took part in the major exercise of 1987, called *Operation Big Pine*.[4]

Contragate, Irangate, Northgate

By whatever name the highly unpopular US-Iran arms-for-hostages deal is known, it badly affected the Contras. They were the recipients of the money which the Iranians paid for American arms. When the scandal first broke, many American diplomats and officials were convinced that the Contra programme was irremediably damaged.

Since this book is primarily concerned with military actions it is worth looking at the way in which Nicaragua so profoundly attracted several of the men involved in Contragate.

Many former CIA agents who had operated in South-east Asia influenced members of the Reagan administration with their ideas about low-intensity conflict (guerrilla war), with its psychological operations and civic-action projects. They were convinced that this was the way to deal with uprisings in the Third World. Central America could be the place to use the style of war practised by the CIA in Vietnam.

In Nicaragua, in particular, the insurgency was to be modelled closely along the lines of the CIA's secret war in Laos. Indigenous bands of guerrilla Contra fighters would live inside Nicaragua and be supplied by small aircraft capable of taking off and landing on rough airstrips. When Lieutenant Colonel Oliver North of the US Marines was put in charge, in 1984, of the operation to keep the Contras supplied, despite the Congress's denial of money, he turned to a network of people with experience in clandestine operations. His first contact was Richard Secord, a former Air Force General who had directed air operations in Laos 20 years before.

North already knew, from Laos, General John Singlaub, a prominent American advocate of the Contra cause. He had been head of the Studies and Observations Group which had conducted secret missions in Laos, Cambodia and North Vietnam. Others brought into the operation include Theodore Shackley, a former deputy director of clandestine operations at the CIA, and Thomas Clines, a former CIA man widely credited with helping to create the Contra supply network.

The Contra connection with Laos became even more complicated. General Heine Aderholt, now chief of the Air Commando Association which has flown 'non-lethal' supplies into Central America, was an air force pilot assigned to the CIA in its secret war in Laos.

According to reports in summer 1986, the Contra network was seeking recruits among the Meo tribesmen of Laos, now living in California, who once formed part of the private 30,000-man CIA Army in Laos. Vang Pao, the General of that army who now lives in the United States, heads a Laotian group that supports the Contra war.

Colonel North built up a militarily impressive system which not only supplied the Contras with money and arms but with expertise about how to operate effectively against the Sandinista armed forces.[5]

The Balance of Power

The balance of military power seems firmly in the Government's favour. The rebels' southern front is in disarray and their fighters there number no more than a few hundred. Most of the Miskito Indian guerrillas on the Atlantic Coast are observing a cease-fire or negotiating with the Sandinistas.

In any case, bitter divisions among Miskito leaders prevent any serious armed opposition to the Sandinista regime. Three men are specially prominent. One is Steadman Fagoth, a former Miskito Contra leader who returned to Honduras in January 1987 after a year of exile in the United States. Fighting to retain his influence in the face of Mr. Fagoth's comeback is Wycliffe Diego, leader of the Kisan movement, which is associated with UNO. Watching from his base in Costa Rica is Brooklyn Rivera, an old rival of Fagoth's for Miskito loyalties. Rivers controls the Misurasata organization, which is not linked to UNO.

On top of these problems, the Contras' UNO leadership collapsed in February-March 1987. First Adolfo Calero resigned from the triumvirate directorate which controls the UNO, though as leader of the most powerful Contra fighting group, the FDN, he is still the single most influential Contra. In March Arturo Cruz, whom the Americans favoured most among Nicaraguans, resigned. He was, he said, 'fed up with the whole mentality' of the Contra movement. Cruz and his ally on the triumvirate, Alfonso Robelo, wanted all fighting groups to be co-ordinated by UNO. Calero did not want FDN's activities 'co-ordinated'. Cruz thought he had a chance of success when Calero stepped down from the directorate but Calero's nominee as replacement backed the FDN chief in arguing for a free rein for the various Contra fighting groups.

The Nicaraguan Army is the largest and best organised in the history of Central America, and has probably absorbed as much heavy equipment as it can handle. The emphasis now is on greater mobility, hence the delivery of large numbers of lorries and troop-carrying helicopters from the Soviet Union via Cuba.

Some rebel leaders, acknowledging this situation, put their faith in a popular insurrection against the government; they point to the Sandinistas' own victory in 1979 over the superior forces of President Somoza. The FDN leader Adolfo Calero is confident that if his men can wage 'generalized guerrilla warfare that it is impossible to hide', Nicaraguans discontented with their government will become aware of the vulnerability of the Sandinsta regime. A popular rising will be the result, Calero says. Few diplomats in Managua share this belief.

The poor prospects for an insurrection have led some Contra advisers, notably Arturo Cruz Jr., son of the UNO leader Arturo Cruz, to consider what they call a 'long march' approach. Cruz expressed his thinking in a magazine article[6] in which he discounted the chances of either an insurrection or a US invasion. He argued that the Contra force should be prepared to wage a long-term struggle 'to buy the time it needs to strengthen its political base in Nicaragua and beyond'.

The significant question is whether the FDN's military chiefs are capable of carrying out a short, intensive war or a prolonged war of attrition. One of the Contras' main weaknesses is their lack of tactical skill in organizing small-unit operations. The Contras acting either as an invasion force or a guerrilla group cannot overthrow the Sandinistas or force them to negotiate seriously.

Nicaraguans are often disappointed with members of the Sandinista leadership but the idealism of the country's youth is linked with 'Sandinismo' and its image of romantic rebellion. Just over 35% of the 3.2 million Nicaraguans are under 24 years of age. The Contras mean nothing to young Nicaraguans—partly as a result of state control of the media—and they have little appeal to anyone old enough to remember the bloody Somoza days.

The Baldizon Testimony

In July 1985 a Nicaraguan government official, Alvaro José Baldizon, defected to Honduras and travelled on to the United States. Baldizon had headed a Nicaraguan Government commission for the investigation of political crimes and human rights violations and in this job was a close colleague of Nicaragua Interior Minister, Tomas Borge.

Baldizon alleged that between 1979 and 1985 more than 2,000 people, mostly peasants and Miskito Indians, were murdered by Sandinistas. His commission investigated 700 cases, of which he personally checked 200. Most charges turned out to be justified. Interior Minister Borge used the information to 'invent the most credible possible lies', Baldizon claimed.

The guidelines under which he operated as head of the commission stipulated, among other things, that the terms 'execution', 'physical elimination' and 'firing squad' were not to be used; the phrase 'special measures' replaced them. Requests for 'special measures' to be taken had to be submitted by district heads of the state security service. Baldizon gave details of mass executions. In June 1984 his commission investigated the massacre of 300 peasants on the orders of a Lieutenant Javier Lopez. Torture is practised in all prisons operated by the state security service, Baldizon stated: 'Torture is regarded as an essential means of protecting the Sandinista revolution.' Prominent members of the opposition were not subjected to such treatment. It is used mostly on peasants and minor opposition leaders but by no means only on individuals who have resisted the Sandinistas by force or co-operated with the Contras.

References

1. Information on the Contras' human rights programme from Marta Baltodano and diplomatic sources in Tegucigalpa.
2. FDN sources in Miami.
3. Radio Liberacion broadcast, 25 March 1987.
4. Diplomatic sources in Tegucigalpa.
5. The facts of the Contragate affair—in relation to Nicaragua—came to light during Congressional committee inquiries.
6. *Commentary*, January 1987.

Baldizon appeared at Press conferences in Washington but his disclosures were not widely reported. The respected Swiss *Neue Zurcher Zeitung* checked Baldizon's credibility with two independent sources before publishing an article by a Dutch journalist who interviewed the defector. It was later picked up by the *Swiss Review of World Affairs*, which also checked Baldizon's information as well as his credibility.

Northern Ireland Terrorist War

MORE VICIOUS THAN EVER

Background Summary

In modern times violence in Northern Ireland dates from the late 1960s. The basis of the bitter confrontation is the demand by the nationalist organization Sinn Fein for the union of Northern Ireland with Eire (the Irish Republic) and the insistence by the Protestant or Loyalist community that Northern Ireland remains part of the United Kingdom.

Since the split in the organization in 1969, Sinn Fein's military arm has been the Provisional Irish Republic Army (often known as 'Provos'). In practice Sinn Fein and the IRA have the same command. The IRA wages a terrorist war against the Protestants' 'Defence' groups, some of which are also terrorist. The British Army's overall objective is to protect Protestant and Catholic communities while at the same time fighting the terrorists.

Since 1977 the British Army has not been responsible for law and order. In that year this became the responsibility of the Royal Ulster Constabulary (RUC). Any operations which the army undertakes are carried out in co-operation with the RUC and at its request.

Summary of the War in 1985

Fewer than 9,000 British regular soldiers were stationed in Northern Ireland in 1985, compared with 22,000 in the early 1970s. The Ulster Defence Regiment comprised the larger portion of the army presence, with 6,500 men and women. In over 85% of the province the UDR was alone responsible to the RUC for support in defeating the terrorists and maintaining law and order.

Terrorists found it more difficult to operate in 1985, partly because of their fear of soldiers of the Special Air Services (SAS). Of the 13 IRA 'active service unit' men killed on operations between December 1984 and mid-1985, nine died in SAS stake outs. More than 200 terrorists were convicted by the courts in 1985. Nevertheless, the IRA caused numerous casualties, including nine officers killed when a mortar bomb landed on the police post at Newry; four others were killed by a massive remotely detonated car bomb south of Newry.

The Hillsborough Agreement signed by Britain and the Irish Republic late in 1985 was designed to reduce terrorism by improving co-operation between the two countries. The objective was achieved but the Protestant majority in Northern Ireland—62% of the population—rejected the agreement and resorted to violence. The illegal Ulster Defence Association, the Protestant equivalent of the IRA, threatened 'armed conflict to protect the Loyalist community from Irish domination'. The IRA also opposed the Hillsborough Agreement because it

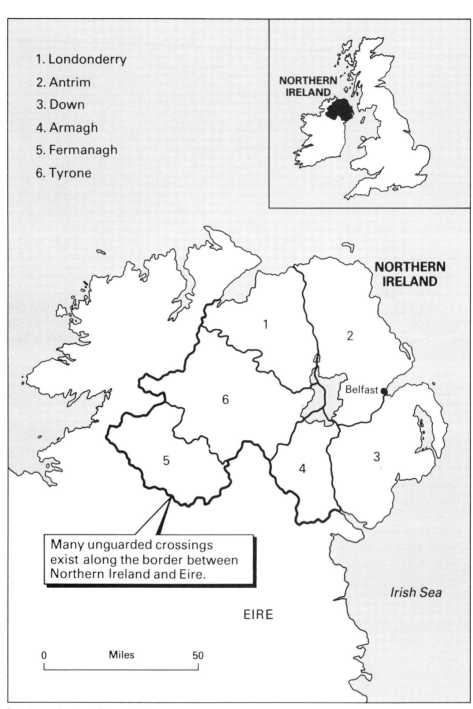

1. Londonderry
2. Antrim
3. Down
4. Armagh
5. Fermanagh
6. Tyrone

NORTHERN
IRELAND

NORTHERN
IRELAND

Belfast

Many unguarded crossings
exist along the border between
Northern Ireland and Eire.

EIRE

Irish Sea

0   Miles   50

Northern Ireland Terrorist War

threatened their terrorists' freedom of action. Protestant attacks on the homes and families of the RUC were the most disturbing aspect of the war in Northern Ireland. Unable to harm the British government for its 'treason and perfidy' in co-operating with the Irish government the Protestants made war on the RUC men as 'servants' of that co-operation.

The War in 1986-87

The war against the terrorists started well in 1986—in Amsterdam. On 18 January a Dutch anti-terrorist squad raided an Amsterdam flat, threw in stun grenades and arrested three IRA terrorists, two of them escapers from the Maze Prison. From a container in a storage depot near Amsterdam's Olympic stadium police recovered 14 semi-automatic rifles, 2 hand grenades, 100,000 rounds of assorted ammunition, 30 plastic containers and 4 oil drums filled with nitro-benzine, a constituent in making explosives. The raid was the result of patient undercover work by British Intelligence. One of the captured men was Brendan McFarlane, a convicted bomber who was in charge of the IRA's attack on Ulster's security services.

Irish police uncovered an IRA arms cache in a series of raids in County Sligo and Roscommon in January 1986. Consisting of sophisticated assault weapons and ammunition, and worth £1.2 million, the hoard had come from Libya. A long surveillance by both Irish and British security forces led to the discovery of the weapons in isolated farm houses.

The trend of nationalist para-military activity since 1983 has been a shift out of Belfast and Londonderry. A total of 71% of all fatal casualties caused by the IRA occur outside these two centres in most years.[1] Attacks against the constabulary and defence regiment are selective but often opportunist. The victims are selected at police stations, on patrol on lonely farm roads, coming out of church services and in private homes. The IRA terrorists frequently attack Catholics in an effort to discredit the security forces. The IRA tactic is meant to intimidate Catholics from joining the security forces, thus making the propaganda point that the RUC, the UDR and the British Army are entirely sectarian organizations which discriminate against Catholics.

Easter traditionally marks the beginning of a period of rising tension in Ulster, often resulting in rioting and death as Catholics commemorate the 1916 Easter Monday Rebellion against British rule. In 1986 there was a difference. While the Catholic observances were notably peaceful—except in Londonderry where a British soldier was wounded by a sniper—Protestants erupted in a fury of violence in Portadown, Belfast and other parts of the province. UDA members and others attacked not only Catholic homes but members of the RUC, in protest against the Hillsborough Agreement.

The sudden turn against the RUC, the one force which Protestants have long relied on to protect them, began a new phase of the long conflict. The main battleground was a grey stone bridge over the River Bann where RUC men in riot gear attempted to block marchers from crossing into the downtown area. Whole towns became 'no-go' areas as hard-line Loyalists in paramilitary uniforms set up roadblocks, 650 of them in one day.

Leader of the UDA since 1973 is Andrew Tyrie, who calls his command 'the largest nationalist organization in Britain and the most misunderstood people in Europe'. Tyrie told a journalist: 'The Northern Ireland problem is not a religious problem. It's not a social problem. It's a problem of territory. I'd rather have an independent state than go Irish.'

A fugitive IRA killer, Seamus McElwaine, died in a dawn shoot-out with the SAS, on 26 April 1986, as he planted a roadside bomb just inside the Northern Ireland border at Rosslea, County Fermanagh. He is believed to have murdered between 10 and 15 people. McElwaine had operated in a border gang of four, frequently in Fermanagh, where 13 soldiers, 12 UDR men and 10 policemen have been murdered by terrorists since 1969.

In one week in July 1986 two people were murdered and more than 200 injured; there were 100 reports of intimidation and dozens of families were forced to move out of their homes. In the autumn of 1986 Sinn Fein and the IRA made preparations for what they predicted would be civil war against the Loyalists. A Sinn Fein leaflet asked people with medical experience to come forward. Lists of the elderly, sick and handicapped were drawn up to ensure that in a siege they would be supplied with necessary medicines. Vigilante squads were organized to combat Protestant murder squads. Owners of small vans and lorries were mobilized so that people under threat could be quickly taken to safe areas.

The Ulster Clubs, a new Protestant organization, appeared in 1986. The Clubs are modelled on the organization established in 1912 by Sir Edward Carson to oppose Irish Home Rule. They provide a link between the political parties and the gunmen and their activities are designed to harass the police and civil authorities.

Several court convictions in 1986 put terrorist gangs out of action. In June four members of the extremist Marxist group Irish National Liberation Army—two sisters and two men—were gaoled for the murders of 11 off-duty soldiers, five civilian women and a teenage boy in a bomb attack on the 'Droppin' Well' disco bar in December 1982. The same month a court convicted the three leaders of the gang which blew up the Grand Hotel, Brighton, in 1984, killing five sleeping guests attending the annual Conservative Party conference. The same gang had also planned a series of 16 bombings in hotels at English seaside resorts that year.

One of the most bizarre events of the terrorist war took place in mid-August 1986 when about 150 masked men armed with cudgels 'invaded' the Irish republic and took over the Irish border village of Clontibret. Leader of the invasion was Peter Robinson, deputy leader of the Democratic Unionist Party and a Westminster MP. He was arrested and some months later heavily fined by a court in Dublin.

With the first anniversary of the signing of the Hillsborough Agreement yet another group was formed to oppose it. This is the Ulster Resistance Organization, which, launched with waving banners and pipe bands, was headed by the Reverend Ian Paisley MP, leader of the Democratic Unionist Party.

During 1986 the IRA stepped up its tactic of making threatening telephone calls to construction companies to prevent them from repairing or rebuilding damaged police stations and army posts. The IRA's drive to stop all civilian work in security bases had, by November 1986, left parts of rural Northern Ireland without police stations and had cost 2,000 building workers their jobs. Threats from Protestant extremists against Catholic workers and families in mainly Protestant areas and workplaces forced 350 families out into IRA-controlled ghettoes.

A total of 14 police stations, including the RUC's training centre, were partially or completely out of action because the IRA first bombed them, then threatened to kill anybody who worked on rebuilding them.

In August the terrorists widened their hit-list of 'legitimate targets' to include anyone supplying bread or milk to the army or police, telephone engineers, cleaning contractors, even people responsible for restocking vending machines. To underline the threat the terrorists murdered four contractors—two Protestant, two Catholic—and a young electrician who occasionally did work in police stations.

In September 1986 blood transfusion staff refused to accept British servicemen as donors for fear of IRA retaliation. About 3,000 of the 10,000 soldiers were registered blood donors but pressure from doctors and staff in the wake of IRA threats led to regular donor sessions at army bases being scrapped.

During 1986 the British Army's ordnance branch developed its technology to meet the increased threat posed by the terrorists' 2,000lb bombs, which are powerful enough to wreck a building. These bombs are now often made safe by remote-controlled Mark 8 'wheelbarrow' robots. The wheelbarrow is an improved version of the small caterpillar-tracked vehicle first developed in the 1970s, and used to break up a bomb so that its components separate, preventing it from detonating. In many cases it is able to defuse bombs, which previously had to be tackled by hand, by bomb disposal experts. Cylinders fixed to robot arms are aimed and fired at the device by remote control, breaking up the interior of the bomb with a jet of water expelled by an explosive charge. The Mark 8 wheelbarrow can operate at a distance of up to 200 metres from its control van.

Other remote control devices now being used by bomb disposal teams are a 'maxicandle' for blowing open the doors and boots of cars to provide access to terrorist bombs planted inside, and steel 'flat swords' used with explosives to open metal containers such as milk churns and gas cylinders containing bombs.

Bomb experts in Northern Ireland say that the IRA has the modern micro-chip technology and knowledge of electronic circuitry to plant bombs 18 months before they are due to explode.

The army has improved its surveillance of the border at strategic points in South Armagh by erecting observation towers of concrete and corrugated iron, supported by scaffolding and protected by sandbags and barbed wire. Nearby each post a television camera on a pole monitors the movements of passers-by.

The IRA extended its field of operations into West Germany in March 1987 when it made a car bomb attack on the joint British Army and RAF headquarters at Rheindahlen. The terrorists used 300lb of superior RDX type explosive which injured 31 people, mostly Germans visiting the British base.

In the early part of 1987 some members of the terrorist organization Irish National Liberation Army broke away to form the Irish People's Liberation Organization. This resulted in a murderous struggle for power and several notorious terrorists, were killed. One of the victims was Mary McGlinchey, wife of Dominic 'Mad Dog' McGlinchey, ex-leader of the INLA who is now in prison. Each group has labelled the other 'agents of British imperialism'. Mary McGlinchey is believed to have been involved in more than 20 killings herself and is said to have murdered at least six people personally.[3]

Despite the many attacks on personnel and the constant tension to which they are subjected, the RUC maintained its morale in 1986-87 and has no shortages of recruits. In 1987 the Constabulary was at full strength with 8,250 policemen and

A variety of firearms seized by the security forces in Northern Ireland. They include 20 different types of revolvers and pistols and 30 different rifles as well as sub machine guns and a light machine gun. Many are of American origin.

The British Army in Northern Ireland works closely with the Royal Ulster Constabulary. A police officer on road identification duty is covered by a soldier. A tour of duty in Northern Ireland is as tense as any service in British military history.

IRA terrorists packed this car with explosive and used it as a bomb in an ambush against an Ulster Defence Regiment Patrol. The car bomb remains the single greatest cause of casualties among the security forces in Northern Ireland.

policewomen. There are also 2,000 full-time reservists on a three-year contract and 1,500 part-time reservists.

The British Army in Northern Ireland in mid-1987 consisted of 10,200 men in these units: 2nd Infantry Brigade HQ; 10 infantry battalions; 1 SAS unit; 1 engineer squadron; and 2 squadrons of the Army Aviation Regiment.

American Help for Irish Terrorists

One of the IRA's major sources of support is in the Bronx, New York. It is called the Irish Northern Aid Committee (Noraid) and its fund-raising letters explain its activities:

> Our support goes exclusively to the Provisional IRA and those who are working with them. . . . Our funds are channelled through Joe Cahill of Belfast to be used for the advancement of the campaign in Northern Ireland . . . . We are fighting a guerrilla war and will continue to do so. We regard ourselves as members of the Provisional Irish Republican Army and will fight and die until victory is ours. Remember, the Irish Northern Aid Committee is the only organization in North America which supports the Provisional IRA.[4]

Michael Flannery, the co-founder of Noraid, was arrested on charges of conspiring to ship arms to the IRA—a 20 mm cannon, 47 machine-guns, a flame-thrower and numerous rifles. He was acquitted when a jury accepted his claim that the CIA had led him to believe that he was co-operating with an undercover operation. Flannery's right-hand man, Martin Galvin, Noraid's publicity director, on a visit to Northern Ireland gave a speech praising the IRA for soaking a young private in the British Army in petrol, burning him alive, and then riddling his charred body with bullets.

An American writer says of American aid to the IRA:

> When other terrorists around the world cause the same kind of carnage, American politicians and media are quick to assail those who back them with money and propaganda. Not so with the IRA. This is strange. . . . While we bitterly condemn Middle Eastern states that fund Palestinian terrorists and urge the Europeans to abandon lucrative links with Libya and Syria, the world mocks our hypocrisy and inconsistency over the question of support for the IRA.[5]

References

1. Statistics from the London-based Irish Information Partnership.
2. *The Observer*, London, 20 April 1986.
3. British Special Branch sources.
4. These letters are distributed to Irish-Americans in scores of thousands.
5. T.K. Jones, *Washington Post*, 14 February 1987.

Peru's 'Shining Path' War

GUERRILLAS IN THE ANDES

The South American Andean country of Peru has suffered from a guerrilla war since 1980 when the Left-wing Maoist movement *Sendero Luminosa* or Shining Path took to violence.

Shining Path is one of the world's strangest guerrilla/terrorist organizations. It was founded in 1970 by a university professor of philosophy, Abimael Guzman, who brought together a group which lived and preached in the barren Andean town of Ayacucho. The top leadership is drawn from the provincial intelligentsia which espouses a barely intelligible philosophy.

The leaders dismiss all forms of democratic politics as 'parlimentary cretinism' designed to hoodwink the people and perpetuate the rule of banks and landowners. Peru is to be the crucible of a worldwide revolution some time in the next few centuries. Nobody knows if Abimael Guzman is alive or not but his followers hail him as the 'fourth sword of the revolution' because of his promises to complete the world revolution begun by Marx, Lenin and Mao. The group has no proven links with any foreign government and China itself has long since discarded Shining Path's brand of Maoist fundamentalism.

The movement attracted half-educated peasants from poor backgrounds and with few career prospects, migrants from the countryside who found themselves living in city squalor and unable to get out of it, and some peasants who remain in the mountains and back Shining Path because it has made them an offer they cannot refuse—support us or be killed. Collectively they have become South America's most fanatical and mysterious subversive movement.

Between May 1980 and January 1987 an estimated 9,000 people died as a result of Shining Path's operations. They include 370 police and military officers and possibly 2,500 guerrillas; the rest were peasants killed by one side or the other. The peasants had long been at risk from heavy-handed military action. They had no sympathy for the guerrillas but equally no affection for the army, which ruled the country from 1968 to 1980.

In July 1985 a social democrat, Alan Garcia, became president of Peru at the age of 37. He has achieved immense popularity with the poor and an opinion poll in early 1986 gave him a 97% approval rate. His supporters call him Caballo Loco—Crazy Horse—but there is nothing crazy about Garcia. He has striven to be just and he has shown much political courage.

When soldiers massacred 69 peasants in the Andean village of Accomarca in September 1985 Garcia dismissed two senior generals. One was Wilfredo Mori, a Sandhurst-trained commando officer, who was the political and military commander of the Ayocucho emergency zone, the other was Sinesio Jarama, the army's fifth-ranking officer, who was commander of the important Lima military region.

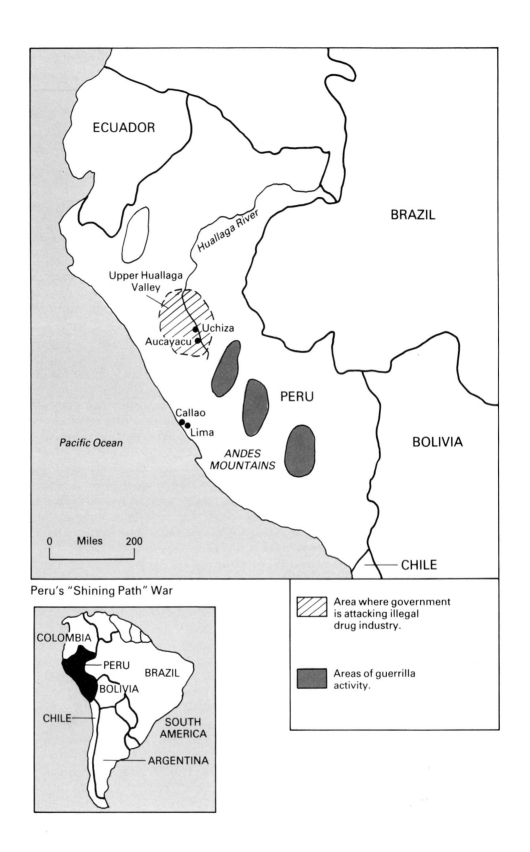

ECUADOR

Huallaga River

Upper Huallaga
Valley

Uchiza
Aucayacu

BRAZIL

PERU

Callao
Lima

Pacific Ocean

ANDES
MOUNTAINS

BOLIVIA

0   Miles   200

CHILE

Peru's "Shining Path" War

COLOMBIA

PERU

BRAZIL

BOLIVIA

CHILE

SOUTH
AMERICA

ARGENTINA

Area where government
is attacking illegal
drug industry.

Areas of guerrilla
activity.

Directly confronting the powerful military, he reduced an US$800 million order for French Mirage jet fighters from 26 to 12.

Coping with the Shining Path guerrillas, who will neither talk nor negotiate, is more difficult. In May 1986 Garcia admitted that the guerrilla problem had no early solution. 'Subversion will continue to be the major preoccupying issue,' he said. 'For it is a historical problem, not just a matter of tactics . . . . We are not facing a small armed and uniformed group which can be easily identified and localized. We are grappling with a structure of violence spread out in many regions in the country. Terrorist commando units are not always linked. They do not necessarily belong to Shining Path . . . .'

They could belong to the *Tupac Amaru* Revolutionary Movement, which concentrates on urban terrorism and is not, in military terms, a guerrilla force. Shining Path and *Tupac Amaru* have no connection at top level but there is known to be operational liaison between them in Lima and the other cities.

Drugs complicate the war against terrorism. The cocaine barons' exports from Peru are reckoned by the Peruvian police to have a US$12 billion street value in foreign countries. President Garcia's biggest moral problem is that cocaine profits are helping to keep afloat an economic boom that is Garcia's best hope for outflanking the Shining Path guerrillas. With less poverty fewer people are likely to be attracted to Shining Path.

Even so, a state of emergency was proclaimed in February 1986 and twice renewed because of guerrilla activity. Law and order in Lima and the nearby port of Callao are enforced by the military. In addition, several Peruvian provinces have been under virtual military control since 1983 when the then President, Fernando Belaunde Terry, gave the army broad military powers. Sudden death has become an occupational hazard for anyone in uniform. In a country where 40% of the 20 million population are under 15 and youth unemployment is high, the guerrillas have been able to recruit many of their assassination squads among schoolchildren of both sexes. Several senior commanders are teenage girls. A youthful hit team killed Admiral Carlos Ponce, a member of the naval General Staff, in June 1986.

On 18 June 1986 Shining Path prisoners in three government prisons rebelled and President Garcia put the jails under temporary military control. The prisons had developed into remarkable institutions, particularly the one on the island of El Fronton which Shining Path had converted into its own private camp. The guerrillas could not escape but their flag was raised at the prison every morning and lowered with equal ceremony at night. Classes in Maoist theory were held regularly, Press conferences held and discipline strictly enforced. According to Army Intelligence much of the terrorism in Lima was planned in this prison. One of the inmates' demands was to be given the status of prisoners of war.

Without the President's authority or knowledge, the troops stormed the three prisons and killed at least 300 prisoners; some reports say 1,000. According to a reliable source in Lima, Garcia first heard about the incident from a general who came to him to report on the operation. 'One hundred per cent success,' the General said. 'No survivors.' The soldiers had slaughtered all the Shining Path prisoners.

Garcia found that at Lurigancho prison about 100 prisoners were executed by the paramilitary Republican Guard after they had surrendered. The appalled President dismissed the head of the Republican Guard and had 100 guardsmen arrested; the Minister of Justice resigned. Few senior officers appear to understand Garcia's insistence that there must be a humane alternative to slaughter as a response to terrorism and guerrilla warfare.

On 15 January 1987 Shining Path terrorists launched one of their most violent assaults, simultaneously hitting the electricity networks of more than six Peruvian provinces, two of the country's largest textile factories, banks, television stations and commercial establishments. One of Shining Path's terrorists boasted to his captors: 'Our objective is to turn Lima into a second Beirut, demolish the national productive apparatus and paralyse national industry.' Textiles is the industrial sector which has the highest growth rate, hence the terrorists' attacks which completely destroyed the plants.

A week later Shining Path repeated its attacks on power stations, blacking out the country. On 30 January death squads assassinated Dr. Cesar Lopez Silva, national secretary of the ruling party, the American Popular Revolutionary Alliance (APRA).

In February 1987 President Garcia announced the reorganization of the country's Intelligence system and called on each citizen to become 'an integral part of a new strategy to root out subversion'. Appealing to each Peruvian to become a security agent, Garcia said that the government was setting up a telephone hot line to enable citizens to report suspicious activities or individuals in their neighbourhoods, whether in town or country.

On the morning of 13 February police and soldiers carried out surprise raids on three universities. The universities are known to have student populations which identify with Peru's Leftist parties. Walls at San Marcos University are covered in guerrilla slogans. Nearly 800 students were rounded up while police searched for guns, explosives and 'subversive' materials. They found little but the government defended the decision to raid the universities, calling them breeding grounds for the Shining Path and *Tupac Amaru* guerrillas.

Because senior army officers do not want to risk being accused of killing innocent civilians, they have ceded large areas of the Andes to the guerrillas. However, in other areas towns and villages which had been abandoned by their people when they became guerrilla strongholds are now being resettled. A military guard is essential. The resettled town of Huambalpa in the central Andes was not at first given protection and one morning four Shining Path gunmen arrived. They accused a village teacher of being a government spy, tortured and then murdered him. They left a warning: 'This is how infiltrators will die, and this is how anyone who buries this infiltrator will die.'

While the President tries to make his army more humane he still has to strengthen the police. At the beginning of 1987 only 60% of the police force of 70,000 were armed. Now all are armed. A self-defence force or people's militia—the *Rondas Campesinas*—is being formed.

The young and still popular President faces daily challenges in his handling of the war. If he does not allow the military to be firm enough he risks a military coup. General Julio Julian, head of the armed forces, is the man most likely to lead a coup though so far he has supported Garcia. Some generals would like to give the army's seven independent 'jungle' infantry battalions and its four other independent battalions free rein to scour Peru for Shining Path guerrillas. Garcia knows that the problem is much too militarily and socially complex for such crude tactics.

He fears that foreign agents may offer support to Shining Path and other subversive groups in order further to destabilise Latin America. If this should happen his guerrilla war could turn into a civil war.

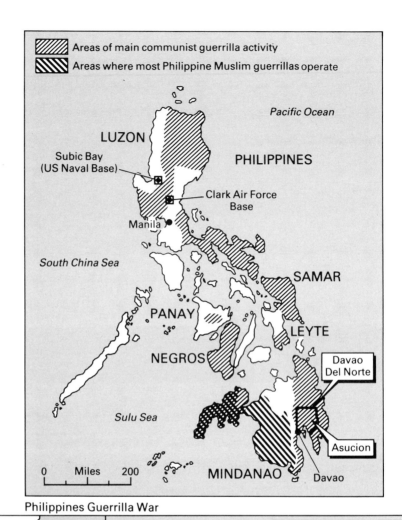

Areas of main communist guerrilla activity

Areas where most Philippine Muslim guerrillas operate

Pacific Ocean

LUZON

PHILIPPINES

Subic Bay
(US Naval Base)

Clark Air Force
Base

Manila

South China Sea

SAMAR

PANAY

LEYTE

NEGROS

Davao
Del Norte

Sulu Sea

Asucion

0   Miles   200

MINDANAO

Davao

Philippines Guerrilla War

Philippines

Mariana
Is.

SUBIC

CLARK

Manila

US front
line in the
Philippines

Cebu

Davao

Zamboango

Cotabato

Clark air base

13th Air Force

Area: 55,000 hectares
Military personnel: 8,000
Civilians: 800
Dependants: 12,000
Value to local economy: $115 m.
Capacity: 800 aircraft

Subic naval base

Radar and supply depot of
US 7th fleet

Area: 26,000 hectares
(11,000 water)
Military personnel: 7,000
Civilians: 500
Dependants: 6,200
Value to local economy: $200 m
Ships in port daily: 12

Philippines 'Communist War'

GUERRILLAS MAKE THE RUNNING

Background Summary

During the period 1969-72 the Communist Party of the Philippines (CPP) and its military wing, the New People's Army (NPA) came into being. NPA was soon engaged in a 'people's war' against the regime of President Marcos. When in 1976 Marcos's troops captured Victor Corpus, NPA's chief of training, the NPA was assumed to be finished. But it quickly revived and in 1977 joined the Muslim rebels of Mindanao. Marcos relocated the Mindanao population into supervised settlements to deny popular support to the insurgents, but the scheme failed. The NPA and the Muslims split later.

The NPA, which had operated in groups of three to nine guerrillas, changed to companies of 200 fighters in 1983 and a year later was active in 60 of the 73 Philippines provinces. The NPA was so threatening that the army launched a general offensive against it, though without significant effect.

(*For a full description of the entire war see* **WAR ANNUAL** 1.)

Summary of the War in 1985

The government appointed General Fidel Ramos as Commander-in-Chief of the armed forces and he announced that the 'barbarians of the NPA' would be wiped out. In response, an NPA squad killed a retired general who was hated for his corrupt practices and a sniper seriously wounded another general near his headquarters in Mindanao. The NPA caused trouble out of all proportion to its numbers—20,000. This was mainly because of the guerrillas' popularity with the peasants, many of whom had suffered under army brutality.

General Ramos evolved a three-pronged political military strategy: (1) greater military effectiveness following an American offer to supply new arms and equipment; (2) punishment for army violence against civilians and training of soldiers in dealing with the public; (3) greater priority for social and economic development.

The NPA continued its successes against the army and the Government, in desperation, formed a counter-insurgency force, the Civil Home Defence Force. Planters living in guerrilla areas were required to raise security squads from among their workforce. The NPA treated them as traitors and murdered several. The army continued to be so brutal that scores of Catholic priests took to the hills with the guerrillas.

In Mindanao the NPA tried to force out foreign owners of sugar plantations by bomb attacks; they also exacted blackmail money by threatening to burn the plantations. With no outside source of funds, virtually all NPA's weapons are captured from soldiers. The CPP's only financial backer in 1985 was the National Democratic Front, which was ideologically opposed to CPP but in pragmatic alliance with it in opposition to the Marcos regime.

The guerrilla war alarmed the US government and its armed forces because the Philippines play a pivotal role in US strategy. American bases at Subic Bay (naval) and Clark Field (air force) are the most important in Asia and the largest in the world. (Clark covers 140,000 acres.) When Mrs. Corazon Aquino was elected as President and Marcos fled the country some observers believed that the NPA would no longer be a threat. This was unrealistic. President Aquino was in no position to reform the economic and social system quickly or thoroughly enough to meet the NPA's demands and she could do little about the demands by the Filipino Muslims for autonomy.

The War in 1986-87

Numerically and in arms and equipment the Filipino armed forces are overwhelmingly superior to the guerrilla groups which oppose them. These groups are the Philippine Communist Party's New People's Army (NPA), the *Bagsa Moro* Army, which is the armed wing of the Moro National Liberation Front (MNLF), the Moro Islamic Liberation Front (MILF), the Cordillera People's Liberation Army (CPLA) and some private armies.

The Filipino Army, Navy and Air Force have a total strength of 113,000, backed by 42,000 men in paramilitary units and reserves of 48,000. In addition, the Civil Home Defence Force has grown to 65,000. The army alone has a strength of 70,000. In a country of many islands the navy is important and comprises 26,000 men, plus 9,000 marines and 2,000 coastguards. It has 7 frigates, 10 corvettes, 86 patrol craft and 102 amphibious craft. For counter-insurgency work the air force has 32 North American T-28D aircraft, 62 Bell UH-1H helicopters and 17 Sikorsky helicopters. The air force transport command, also important in the scattered islands, is well equipped with Fokker, Douglas and Hercules aircraft.

The guerrilla forces actively involved as fighting men and women total 33,000, of whom 22,000 are in the NPA. They have no aircraft, no vessels, no artillery, no tanks and no artillery beyond some mortars. Yet the security forces rarely have a military success against them and the Government's chances of eventually winning what it calls the 'Communist War' appear to be remote. The NPA, in particular, is increasingly impressive, though its power varies from province to province and island to island. Its leaders are intelligent, educated, and dedicated, and they impose strict discipline.

The NPA considers Samar Island, 200 miles south-east of Manila, as the 'centre of gravity' of the insurgency—a realistic assessment in military terms—and part of its strategy is to force the Government to concentrate its forces there so that rebel groups elsewhere have a chance to expand.

Samar has been notorious for human rights violations by Government soldiers and by private armies controlled by local warlord plantation-owners. During the ceasefire of January-February 1987 the army made no effort to improve its image with the civilians. In contrast, the NPA fighters used the ceasefire to parade through the towns and visit their families; the guerrillas made a favourable impression on the townspeople.

In Samar's mountainous and marshy Catubig province NPA controls about three-quarters of the 560 villages and is rapidly expanding its influence in the six large towns of the region. It has a training base far up the Catubig river which is a model of organization. Easily collapsible bamboo huts have been placed on small hills, each higher than the next, so that an attack on one group of huts can be readily repulsed by fighters on the next hill. An approach by land requires a five-hour trek through rice fields, knee-deep in mud, or a difficult canoe journey along the Catubig river.

The security forces have 2,000 men in the province—soldiers, police and militia—but only two helicopters. NPA commanders say that army officers know the location of the rebel camp but are unwilling to risk their helicopters in an attack.

An important explanation of the NPA's durability lies in the close bonds of fellowship among the rebels. It seems to satisfy a deep need common among Filipinos to belong to some kind of extended family. They like to have their behaviour and values shaped and approved by the group. The NPA takes its social structure as seriously as it takes its rules. For instance, rebels' marriages have to be blessed by the Communist Party and no rebel may marry a non-rebel.

Before marrying, a guerrilla couple must have courted for at least a year, except for women over 30. Any woman asked for a date by a man cannot simply refuse. She must give a reason. Divorce requires permission at high Party level and requires a waiting period of one year. To have a child also requires Party permission.

Breaches of the rules are often punished by execution; according to the Filipino Army more than 600 Communists were executed by their comrades in the period January–March 1987 because they dared suggest the possibility of accepting an amnesty. Army spokesmen are not reliable sources but their claims about these deaths are supported by Catholic priests.

The NPA tries to avoid actions which affect civilians. The guerrillas do not sabotage electricity pylons, blow up bridges or mine rural roads. In this they are different from the guerrillas of many other countries.

By a process of slow military advance, political organizing among the peasantry and pressures on landowners to change—and to pay 'revolutionary taxes'—the NPA claims to have achieved a series of reforms in the areas in which it operates. On Negros Island they have redistributed thousands of hectares of land to peasants, reduced peasants' rents and forced landowners to cut interest rates. In addition they have set up co-operatives.[1]

The Government is campaigning to divide the rebel Communists. It wants to split them regionally and to separate the rank-and-file from the leadership. It continually stresses that the NPA is largely composed of non-ideological non-Communist elements and admits that they have a genuine grievance. These elements must be won over. One Government tactic is to try to induce the rebels to accept regional ceasefires but the NPA commanders are too astute to be tricked into this. The Government can easily whisk its troops from island to island, but the rebels cannot. If a ceasefire were arranged in Mindanao, for instance, the government would be able to take troops from there to northern Luzon.

The 60-day general ceasefire between the guerrillas and the Government, which ended on 11 February 1987, took the parties no nearer a peace settlement. The realistic guerrillas had never anticipated that it would because they knew that President Aquino could not give them the sweeping social, economic and land reforms they want. Captured Communist Party documents[2] reveal that the decision to start peace talks in 1986 was merely a tactic to hold the movement together and win popular support.

Hardliners were secretly assured that they would not really have to lay down their arms. During the ceasefire the Communist leaders performed well in television interviews and the rebels got the chance to regroup in the field and to rally their supporters.

For a few weeks 50 of the hitherto faceless men and women who had built up the NPA and slowly undermined the Marcos dictatorship appeared in public. Armed with Government safe-conduct passes for the duration of the peace talks, they put across a revolutionary political message which had been censored for years. In Manila one of the most popular and sought after guerrillas was Victoria Justiniani or 'Comrade Vicvic'. The daughter of a plantation-owner, she shocked her family in 1973 by abandoning her studies at the age of 17 and leaving for the hills, at the time that Marcos declared martial law and began a wave of repression. Comrade Vicvic is the main spokeswoman of *Makibaka*, the 'Nationalist Movement of the New Filipino Woman'.

When the guerrilla spokesmen and spokeswomen had milked the peace talks of all propaganda value they broke them off, claiming that their lives were in danger from Rightists in the army who were preparing yet another coup against Mrs. Aquino.

Trouble in the armed forces has been commonplace. One of the most serious disturbances took place on 27 January when about 400 soldiers, led by Colonel Oscar Canlas, attacked the Villamore air base in Manila, the Sangley Point naval base south of Manila and radio and television stations in the capital. Loyalist troops fired a few tear-gas shells into the television station. The rebel commander telephoned General Ramos to say that the tear-gas was 'embarrassing' him and the Government attack was at once called off. The mutineers surrendered next day.

A massacre took place outside the presidential palace in Manila on 22 January when marines fired into a crowd of demonstrators, killing 12 and wounding 100. Unknown to senior generals, the 300-member marine guard detachment was under the command of a corporal.

The army sometimes has very bad days. On 17 March 1987 19 soldiers were killed in a guerrilla ambush. By then the rebellion was claiming an average of eight lives a day. President Aquino had made little progress with her alternating policies of talking to the guerrillas and shooting at them. Fewer than 500 guerrillas have defected from the NPA, whose numbers increased overall from 22,000 in 1986 to 24,000 in 1987.

During or shortly after almost every clash between the army and the NPA the peasants suffer most of all. The massacre of Numulandayan, 90 miles north of Manila, was only one of the more tragic examples. On 12 January 1987 NPA guerrillas ambushed an army patrol at Numulandayan, (population 170) killing a lieutenant. The rebels, who had been hiding in huts, made a quick getaway. The soldiers, furious that the rebels had escaped almost unharmed, continued shooting. They killed 17 villagers; four were children between 4 and 13 years and two were in their 80s, one of them a blind woman. The mayor told investigators from Manila that many of the victims were shot in the head.[3]

Mistrust between the army and the Government has persisted despite the crushing of several attempted military coups. A general and two colonels who went underground after a failed coup in January 1987 organized private armies and set out to kill Communists. A shady group of American mercenaries was also operating, though it was uncertain who was paying them. They are said to be linked to a retired American general, John Singlaub, an avowed anti-Communist, who was associated with Colonel Oliver North in the Nicaraguan 'Contragate' affair. With other American veterans, General Singlaub set up an office in Manila in November 1986.

The official story is that Singlaub has obtained permission from the Philippines Government to search for a horde of treasure hidden in the jungle by a Japanese general during the 1939-45 war. Many Filipinos speculate that the Americans may really be preparing a 'Filipino Contra' army to fight the NPA on its own terms—as guerrillas.[4]

Simultaneously with the Communist guerrilla war, the Government and army face a Muslim insurrection, notably on Mindanao Island. But for the deep ethnic divisions within the Muslim community of 5 million the danger to the Government would be even greater than it is. President Aquino herself widened the divisions into a feud between Muslims. On 5 September 1986, in a dramatic gesture of reconciliation with the Muslims, she met the MNLF leader, Nur Misuari, on Jolo, an island controlled largely by his rebels.

Her gesture, in effect, appointed Misuari as the sole Muslim representative. The meeting, which was arranged by the President's brother-in-law, Agapito Aquino, excluded a breakaway faction of MNLF, the Moro Islamic Liberation Front (MILF) led by Hashim Salamat. Salamat's group is bigger and stronger than MNLF and he and Misuari are often in conflict. The Aquino-Misuari meeting made him implacably angry. The real battle between the two Muslim groups may be over who will eventually assume leadership of a new autonomous government in Mindanao.

Some Muslim leaders have their own private army and none is stronger than that of Sultan Muhammad Ali Dimaporo, known as the 'Mad Dog of Mindanao'. His army of *barracudas* is 5,000 strong and, as a multi-millionaire, Dimaporo has no trouble in paying them. Dimaporo is a Marcos supporter and a warrant has been out for his arrest for more than a year, but the Muslim millionaire, who has a mansion in Los Angeles, has friends in high places. The army group in Mindanao which is supposed to disband his guerrillas instead provides him with an escort against Communist attack.

Oplan Eagle Operation

Oplan Eagle is a pilot counter-insurgency operation mounted in Davao, the Philippines' second largest city, by Commander-Colonel Franco Calida, with the help of the anti-Communist radio commentator, Jun Pala. It is regarded in the Philippines as one of the greatest successes against the NPA and other governments facing insurgencies may copy it.

Davao is a key region which the government believes it must control. It does so through the work of Pala and Calida. Pala, for five hours, morning and night, denounces the evils of Communism, names suspected Communist sypathizers and orders residents of the city's outlying Communist strongholds to leave 'or prepare to die'. While Pala's fiery words keep emotions running high, Calida has organized civilians into an armed anti-Communist group known as *Alsa Masa* (People's Uprising), which has set up an Intelligence network and roadblocks to assist military operations.

In the first week of March 1987 General Fidel Ramos endorsed *Alsa Masa* as a 'suitable' national counter-insurgency strategy. Local Government Secretary Jaime Ferrer advocated the organization of similar groups by local government officials. Just two weeks after Colonel Calida delivered a 'surrender or die' ultimatum over Pala's radio programme Davao was transformed. Districts where the 'Red Fighters' and Communist ideologues ate and slept were festooned with anti-Communist banners and patrolled by armed civilians and military Intelligence officers.

General Ramos now describes *Alsa Masa* as 'a major blow to the NPA'. In Davao city, Colonel Calida, known as 'the father of *Alsa Masa*' has coaxed hundreds of armed Communists to surrender and then persuaded them to join the fight against former comrades. 'The only way to fight insurgency is to let the people fight it,' he said. 'To cook the terrorists in their own oil. The *Alsa Masa* uses the NPA's own methods—shoot them in the head and bury them two feet under the ground'.

Inside the sealed-off battle zones on the edge of Davao city, rows of houses lie empty while crowds of evacuees huddle in schools and churches and observe the nightly curfew. The evacuees, once NPA sympathizers, are told by the military to join *Alsa Masa*. Hungry, and confused by the radio barrage and the military commands, they are prepared to join any group which will bring them food and peace.

Observers in Davao doubt the long-term effectiveness of the *Alsa Masa* approach. The CPP rallies of the NPA have not conceded defeat, only that the guerrillas have been handicapped in their movements. NPA liquidation squads are still operating and their hit-list is growing. At the top of it are Jun Pala and Colonel Calida.

The Four-Day War

On 12 January 1987 the *Bagsa Moro*, in the name of the Moro Islamic Liberation Front, (MILF), declared war against the Aquino Government and its army. *Bagsa Moro* was in conflict for years with the Marcos regime and lately with the Aquino regime but sometimes it intensifies the conflict and a war is declared. This declaration of war was made by Al Hadj Murad, the deputy leader of MILF and also chief-of staff of *Bagsa Moro*.

Most of the early casualties were among civilians as Muslim guerrillas threw grenades into homes, set fire to hotels and killed rice-planting peasants with sporadic howitzer fire. The biggest operation took place at Lake Buluan, where *Bagsa Moro* fighters attacked a Civil Home Defence Force (CHDF) post. The CHDF is a notorious organization whose 100 members at Buluan call themselves the 'Crocodiles of the Lake'. After a rebellion in February 1987 the Crocodiles lost their official status but retained their weapons and their territory.

The Muslims attacked the Crocodiles in Buluan and the battle lasted all day. Just as the Crocodiles were on the point of surrender the army arrived to reinforce them. Probably ten Crocodiles were killed and six Muslims, including the field commander of Zone Six, Janid Salimbato, known as Commander Cobra.

Hadj Murad arranged a truce with the Aquino Government but military operations continued in the area. The CHDF, who had been mauled by the Muslims, wanted revenge and the army helped them to get it by 'clearing' the area. This meant more casualties among peasants who had nothing to do with the brief war.

References

1. Assessment of NPA from diplomatic sources, Catholic Church reports, foreign Intelligence estimates.
2. Seen by foreign diplomats in Manila.
3. Report by Philippine Government's official investigator.
4. US State Department sources.

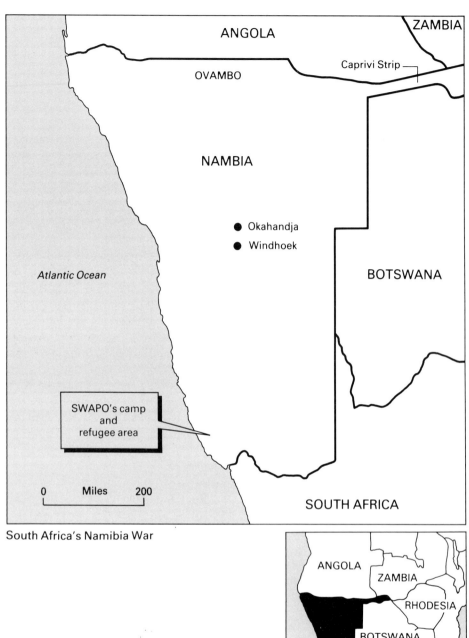

South Africa's Namibia War

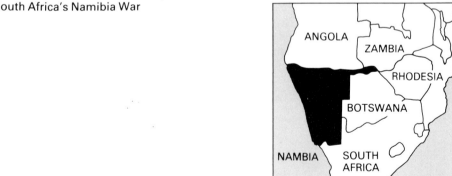

South Africa's War in Namibia

*(In **WAR ANNUAL** 1 the conflict in Namibia was linked with that in Angola. While the two are politically and militarily connected, they are separate wars.)*

South Africa took over the territory known as German South-West Africa during World War 1 and has held it ever since, despite political opposition from many countries and armed opposition, since 1966, by the South-West Africa People's Organization (SWAPO). The territory is now known as Namibia.

On 4 March 1986 the South African President, P. W. Botha, announced that a UN plan for Namibian independence, drawn up in 1978, would be set in motion on 1 August. This surprise announcement was welcomed by several Western governments. Diplomats pointed out, however, that Botha made clear that the plan would be implemented only if 'a firm and satisfactory agreement can be reached before that date' on the withdrawal of Cuban troops from neighbouring Angola.

The Government in Luanda has never accepted any linkage between the Cuban troops in Angola and Namibian independence. Luanda supports SWAPO as the 'sole legitimate representative of the Namibian people', and permits SWAPO to have bases in southern Angola.

Namibia has its own government, the Multi-Party Conference (MPC) but SWAPO regards the MPC politicians as traitors and collaborators. SWAPO is committed to a guerrilla war until UN-supervised elections are held and South African troops are withdrawn.

The first shot in the conflict between SWAPO and the South African security forces was fired in August 1966. It is thus the longest bush war in Africa's last colony. The rainy season, December-April, is the combat period. The commanders of the People's Liberation Army of Namibia (PLAN)—SWAPO's military wing—call it 'the killing time'. During the wet season the tactical advantage lies with the guerrillas, who make use of the dense growth and the downpour. Muddy roads and poor visibility hamper the operations of the South African Defence Force (SADF) and South-West Africa Territory Force (SWATF).

They are determined to show that armed struggle does not always win, despite much theorizing and teaching to the contrary. After the 1986 rainy season the commander of the SADF troops in Namibia, Major General Meiring, said that PLAN's offensive had been less 'dangerous' than in previous years. While 16,000 guerrillas were active in 1978 the number had dropped in 1986, he claimed, to 9,100. Of this total about 3,500 were fighting in Angola against Savimbi's UNITA Army. Sooner or later, Meiring said, PLAN and SWAPO would be nothing more than a nuisance.

The South African strategy is to ensure that PLAN does not recapture the initiative. During the whole of 1985, according to SADF figures, 599 guerrillas were killed. The figure for 1986 was less, probably because fewer guerrillas were operating. SWAPO and its army have self-inflicted problems. They are weakened by factional squabbling as well as rivalry among the leaders. Its internal enemies betray SWAPO's plans and South African agents have penetrated the organization. By mid-1986 SWAPO was more demoralized than at any time in 20 years.

Nevertheless, it is certainly more than a 'nuisance' to South Africa. The military cost of countering SWAPO is said to be US$550 million annually. Something like 2,500 South African servicemen died in the period 1976-86, though this figure includes casualties from disease as well as enemy action.

SWAPO resorts to outright terrorism whenever it embarks on intimidation campaigns to prevent Namibian groups from co-operating with the South Africans. For instance, in November 1986 guerrillas kidnapped Amupolo Gabariel, pastor of the Evangelical Lutheran church of Ovambo and shot him dead. The apparent intention was to cow the people of the Ovambo tribe; with the Damara tribe, the Ovambo make up half of Namibia's population.

The South-West Africa Territory Force (SWATF) is regarded as the basis of the defence force which will protect a future independent Namibia. In 1987 SWATF provided 60% of all troops in combat operations against PLAN and about 40% of the total military strength. SWATF's mobilization strength is 22,000 and, while selective national service is in force, it is often not needed. SWATF's 101 Battalion proposed to raise a new company of 205 men; more than 3,000 applications were received.

SWATF's organisation is based on three separate commands—the Standing Force, the Reaction Force and the Area Force. In detail these are:

Standing Force: Six regional light infantry battalions; the SWA Specialist Unit and a reconnaissance regiment. Most of the men are regulars.

Reaction Force: 91 Motorised Brigade; SWA Parachute Battalion and a light aircraft squadron. The force is a mixture of regulars and ready-call territorials.

Area Force: A better title might be Areas Force because this command has 4 main sectors and 26 units, each responsible for a specific region.

The emphasis is on counter-insurgency operations and SWATF has its own military school at Okahandja. Logistically the entire force is self-supporting, with its own engineering, signal, commissariat and transport units. Equipment is largely South African, suitable for the terrain and vegetation. Casspir Armoured personnel carriers, with protection against mines, are used to get trackers into the bush. Working in pairs, the Casspirs are extremely effective in chasing PLAN raiders after a raid—and often enough before a raid. Helicopter-borne support troops can be called up in minutes should the tracking units find PLAN guerrillas in strength.

One of the most interesting units is the SWA Specialist Unit which trains mounted and motorcycle infantry, trackers and dog-handlers. Mounted infantry, a military arm which has virtually disappeared from the world's battlefields, operates at platoon strength in support of infantry companies. A great advantage of horses over motorcycles is that they can move quietly.

In one way the Area Force units are the most important of the entire command. Concentrating on one area, a unit's members have an intimate knowledge of the region which they guard. Officers and NCOs are expected to know the names of every farmer in their region and to be able to recognize their black farm workers.

As the SWATF became more efficient in 1987 the SADF main forces were reduced. SADF's strike force consists of four infantry battalion groups, a mechanized battalion group and a light infantry battalion; this key unit specializes in reconnaissance in the form of long-range bush and jungle scouting. It also makes frequent raids against SWAPO and PLAN bases in Angola.

The South African High Command knows that SWATF could comfortably hold Namibia against SWAPO without army help but the presence of more than 30,000 veteran Cuban troops in Angola is an ever-present threat. The South Africans are convinced that, should they relax their vigilance and reduce their strength, the Cubans and Angolans would quickly march into Namibia. The Angolan Government has made 'plataforma proposals' under which 5,000 Cuban troops would be withdrawn from southern Angola once South African troops in Namibia had been reduced to 1,500. Cuban troops would conduct no manoeuvres south of the 16th parallel and the remaining troops in the south would be withdrawn over three years.

Between 17-20 September 1986 the United Nations in New York held a special session on Namibia and adopted a Resolution by 126 votes to nine against, with 24 abstentions. The Resolution's main points were these:

- Namibia had a right to independence.
- South Africa's occupation of Namibia was condemned.
- The support of the international community was sought to uphold the legitimacy of Namibia's struggle by all means 'including armed struggle'.
- SWAPO was commended as the Namibians 'sole and authentic representative'.

The European Economic Community abstained. Its spokesman rejected the call to give increased military assistance to SWAPO 'because the general and primary duty of the UN is to promote peaceful solutions . . . .' The EEC was also against any group being designated in advance the sole and authentic representative of the Namibian people.

With the African National Congress (ANC) steadily increasing the strength of its military wing, *Umkhonto we Sizwe*, the South Africans are even less likely to make concessions about Namibia. The president of the ANC, Oliver Tambo, has declared a 'people's war' against South Africa and the ANC already has 10,000 trained fighters. Up to 3,000 are based in Angola. Terrorist groups from ANC carried out several terrorist attacks in South African cities in 1986-87.

SRI LANKA: Tamil areas

Sri Lanka Tamils descend from South Indian settlers and leftovers of invasions 1000–2500 years ago.

Indian Tamils descend from workers imported for British teafields 70–120 years ago.

Country's population:15m	
SINHALA	74.0%
SRI LANKA TAMIL	12.6%
INDIAN TAMIL	5.6%
MOOR	7.1%
OTHER	0.7%

1981 Census

Over 50% Sri Lankan Tamil

20–35% Sri Lankan Tamil

Up to 47% Indian Tamil

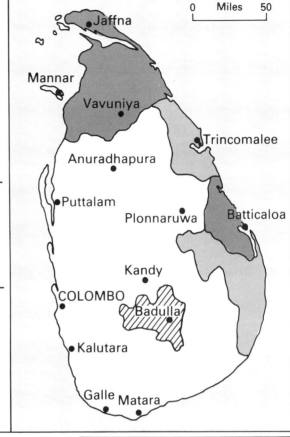

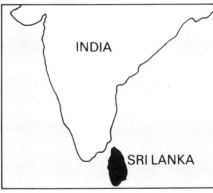

Sri Lanka: Tamil areas

Sri Lanka Civil War

A CONFLICT OF REPRISAL AND RETALIATION

Background Summary

Sri Lanka, formerly Ceylon, became independent from Britain in 1948 and from that year the ethnic animosity between the Buddhist Sinhalese and the Hindu Tamils increased steadily. The Sinhalese are dominant in numbers: there are 11 million compared with 3 million Tamils and 1.5 million Muslims. Sri Lanka covers 25,332 sq. miles and the Tamils are heavily concentrated in about 1,000 square miles, mainly in the north but with smaller areas in the centre and on the east coast.

In 1948 the Sinhalese gained several advantages. For instance, Sinhala was proclaimed the official language and the Sinhalese gained control over the police, the army and the universities. The Tamils demanded a separate state, which they would call Eelam. In 1977 Tamil was recognised as a second official language but this did not placate the Tamils, especially when Buddhism became the official state religion.

Open violence between the communities began in July 1983. The army deployed troops in the north. Young Tamils from Jaffna called them an army of occupation. Calling themselves freedom fighters, the Tamils organized many guerrilla groups. The best known were: Liberation Tigers of Tamil Eelam (LTTE), the People's Liberation Organization of Tamil Eelam (PLOTE); the Tamil Eelam Liberation Organization (TELO), the Eelam People's Revolutionary Liberation Front (EPRLF) and the Eelam Revolutionary Organization and Supporters (EROS) founded in London in 1975. There was also the political body, Tamil United Liberation Front (TULF), which included members of parliament.

In their first major assault the Tigers ambushed an army patrol on Jaffna peninsula, killing 13 soldiers. The repercussions were far-reaching. The next evening when the bodies arrived in the capital there was an outbreak of anti-Tamil hatred that quickly turned to slaughter. Within a week an estimated 1,000 people, nearly all of them Tamils, were killed by Sinhalese mobs. Many victims were burned alive. Tamils refer to these riots as 'the Holocaust'. Tens of thousands of middle-class Tamils fled to Madras. All TULF MPs were forced out of parliament when they refused to take an anti-separatist oath. Over the next year several attempts to reach an accord between the two ethnic groups ended in failure. As money poured in from Tamil expatriates in Australia, Britain and other countries, militants began buying weapons and setting up training camps.

The majority of Tamils wanted a completely separate state; others wanted at least Tamil control of the police and of land use in Tamil areas. This group also demanded that the Tamil districts be administered as one province with its capital in Trincomalee. The Government of President J.R. Jayawardene opposes a Tamil state in Sri Lanka, contending that the Indian state of Tamil Nadu, just across Palk

Strait, is adequate for the Tamils. The headquarters of several Tamil groups are in Madras, Tamil Nadu and the province has a Tamil population of 50 million. In Sri Lanka tension and conflict increased throughout 1983 and 1984.

(For a full description of the entire war see **WAR ANNUAL** 1.*)*

Summary of the War in 1985

Neither side was militarily prepared for a civil war. The Government turned to the United States for financial aid to buy arms and equipment, but in 1985 the army was still so ill-equipped that the Government launched a 'help the forces' campaign and asked citizens for equipment ranging from rain-capes to wheelbarrows. The Tamils looked to their own Tamil community in Tamil Nadu and to India generally. PLOTE sent some of its men to Damascus to be trained by Palestinian terrorists.

Generally, the Tamil groups attacked Government forces, stole and burnt state property and attacked Sinhalese civilians whose property encroached on traditional Tamil territory. Each group tends to specialize. The Liberation Tigers are fighters; TELO specialized in spectacular coups, such as blowing up troop trains; EROS concentrated on economic sabotage; PLOTE's tactics were to harass the Government and individual leaders by threat, blackmail and political pressure.

Attacks, reprisals and counter-reprisals proliferated. In a Tamil reprisal attack in Anuradhapura (May 1985) 146 civilians were killed. A Sri Lankan naval party boarded a ferry off Sri Lanka's north coast and hacked 39 Tamils to death. Tamil tactics included raids on foreign development projects, a move designed to bring foreign pressure to bear on the Sri Lankan Government. During 1985 the morale of the Tamils was higher than that of the ill-disciplined and often young Government troops.

As guerrillas, the Tamils were opportunist in their tactics; the national army was deliberate. The army devastated the island of Mannar, where some Tamil groups had training camps, and turned it into a 'no-go' area. Elsewhere soldiers destroyed Tamil villages. In a single series of raids Commodore Jayasuria, commanding in the Trincomalee region, attacked 23 villages and burnt more than 1,000 homes.

During 1985 the Indian authorities confiscated weapon supplies consigned to the Tamil fighters. This was taken as an indication that the Gandhi regime's support for the Tamils was being scaled down.

Sri Lanka's Muslims were drawn into the conflict by Sinhalese *agents provocateurs* who told them that the Tamils, if they gained political power, would outlaw the Islamic religion and seize Muslim land. As a result Muslim mobs attacked Tamil shops and homes.

At the end of 1985 the Tamil freedom fighters, of ten known simply as 'the boys', had become true guerrillas; that is, they were operating without fixed bases in Sri Lanka. Unable to find them in the hills or jungles the army attacked their sympathizers. Subjected to atrocities, the Tamil populace quickly came to tolerate the guerrillas' violent tactics.

The War in 1986-87

President Jayawardene, frustrated in his attempts to find a political solution and spending one-fifth of the national budget on the war, set out to achieve 'a military solution', as he put it. To do this he used his air force's six Cessna 337S and six Siai Marchettis to drop bombs almost daily on the Jaffna district. Since more than 97% of the district's population is Tamil any casualties were acceptable. Elsewhere the army embarked on sustained terror campaigns. A Catholic priest in Batticaloa told reporters that if 'slow genocide' was to be avoided all Tamil boys aged 14–17 had to be got out of Eastern Province. It is at this age that Tamils first become fighters.

On 26 March 1986 the railway from Colombo to Jaffna was sabotaged just inside the Tamil area, which meant that the only remaining land route was along a heavily mined road, vulnerable to ambushes. Government convoys had to be protected by armoured vehicles with helicopters overhead.

Some serious Tamil in-fighting occurred during 1986. The Government had already claimed that it had proof that the Tigers intended to eliminate their rivals and in April 1986 the Tigers did indeed turn on TELO, the second largest group. Its leader and at least 100 members were killed. There are two 'official' versions by the groups themselves of the conflict.[1]

The TELO version: LTTE (the Tigers) kidnapped four members of TELO as 'a first step in its planned conspiracy to cover up robberies and murders it had committed a month ago'. Two were subsequently released after severe torture. To secure the release of the remaining two, TELO abducted two LTTE men. When the LTTE men arrived to negotiate they opened fire on the TELO camp. At the same time several TELO camps and safe houses were attacked. The clashes were most fierce at Kalliankadu where Sri Sabaratnam, the leader, was staying. Sabaratnam escaped to Kondavil where he was tracked down and murdered.

The LTTE version: On 25 April the Sri Lankan Navy sank a LTTE boat in Palk Strait, and one of those killed was the area commander, Major Aruna. In his memory LTTE organized a *hartal* or Hindu festival. TELO called for a *hartal* in memory of ten TELO lives lost in a similar attack on 25 April. There was a poor response to this call and TELO members tore down posters that had been put up in memory of Aruna at Kalliankadu, a TELO stronghold and Aruna's birthplace. In addition, TELO had abducted and beaten up Basir Kaka, an LTTE central committee member. TELO then shot another LTTE leader, Lingan, sent as a mediator. According to LTTE, 'this abduction and murder sparked a wider clash'. According to A.S. Balasingham, spokesman for LTTE, his organization was justified in its action against TELO on the grounds that it had become 'a base for international forces of imperialism'.

Foreign observers believe that one reason for the action LTTE took against TELO was the decision of LTTE to retreat to the Jaffna peninsula after a series of defeats inflicted upon it by the Sri Lankan security forces. TELO, too, seems to have decided to make the Jaffna peninsula its base and had massed its people from the eastern and southern ends of the peninsula. LTTE saw this as a threat in Jaffna, which it considered its preserve. Whatever the background to the conflict, TELO was finished as a guerrilla force.

Until May 1986 Colombo appeared to be escaping major repercussions of the fighting in the north and east. Then came a series of terrorist attacks. On 3 May a bomb exploded on an Air Lanka jetliner on the tarmac at Sri Lanka's international airport; 16 people, most of them foreign tourists, were killed and 20 were injured. On 7 May a bomb went off in the Colombo's Central Telegraph Office, killing 14

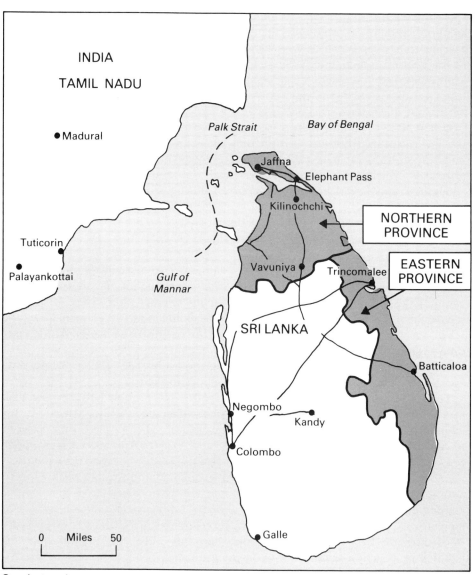

Combat regions

people and wounding 100; the EROS group claimed responsibility. On 2 June a bomb in a railway station killed eight and wounded 54 people. On the same day a bomb hidden inside a delivery truck exploded at a soft-drink bottling plant, killing ten people.

On 17 May the army launched a major operation to relieve the beseiged garrisons at Jaffna, Palaly and at smaller posts, and to regain control over the vital Elephant Pass and the Thondamaru bridge. The offensive was repulsed at all points and 1,200 troops who had sallied out from the 11 besieged bases were driven back in.

After this reverse parties of soldiers tried to break out but were quickly stopped, often in ambush, with RPG 7s and small-arms fire. The troops were safe enough in their bases because they had cleared the ground around them and supplies arrived by helicopter or by sea.

Tamil strategy is to increase still further the pressure on besieged military bases in Tamil-inhabited territory in the hope that the troops' morale will break. They have realized, as the British knew a century ago, that the Sinhalese are not 'natural' soldiers and their Buddhist background of humility and non-violence inhibits them.

The peninsula's normal population of 800,000 was swollen, in the summer of 1986, by more than 100,000 Tamils from other areas. For the first time the Tigers set up a form of civil administrative control in their Jaffna area of operations. Schools were encouraged to re-open and hospitals were helped to improve their services; taxes were collected in an orderly way.

The Tigers opened an arms factory which produces 25 mortars and 100 grenades a month. All Government employees, normally paid by the state, continue to receive salaries. Not self-sufficient in food, the Tigers smuggle food in from Tamil Nadu across Palk Strait despite the danger from Sri Lankan naval patrol boats. The Tigers also started small factories which make jam, soap, fruit juice and arrack.

The Tigers claim to have five military camps near Jaffna; their recruit training centre produces 80 trained men every three months. If true, this would be a considerable regular reinforcement.

One of the senior Tigers, known as Kittu, is the commander in Jaffna and the most wanted man on the Sri Lankan security forces' terrorist list. He has carried out many attacks on military and civil targets and has a price of US$20,000 dollars on his head. One of Kittu's victims in August 1986 was the headmaster of a Jaffna school who was murdered for the crime of playing football with the army. Two moderate Tamil politicians were kidnapped and murdered, probably to deter any others who favour a political solution. Kittu says[2] that the Tigers are revolutionary socialists whose ultimate aim is the creation of a 'one-party socialist state'.

The nature of the war can be illustrated by two events which occurred in the first week of June 1986. Both were described by Marguerite Johnson of *Time* Magazine.[3]

> **1:** 'The rice-growing settlement of Siripura [in Sri Lanka's Eastern Province] was in shock. Red and white paper lanterns, strung up to celebrate Vesak, one of the holiest Buddhist festivals, lay in tatters on the ground as smoke rose from the ruins of 25 thatched mud huts. At the entrance to one village women wept at the sight of the charred remains of a young couple who had been shot and left to die in their burning home. Down the road, beside the irrigation ditch, the bodies of ten other villagers, including several children, lay in a row

where they had been gunned down. The day before, 12 people had been killed in nearby villages in the district of Trincomalee. The victims in both attacks were Sinhalese . . . who had been settled in the area by the government as part of a controversial land-development program. Their assailants were Tamil guerrillas . . . .

Outraged Tamils charge that the Government's intent is to increase the number of Sinhalese in areas that are predominantly Tamil.'

2: 'To the north-east of Siripura, on the Jaffna peninsula, Tamils were also mourning their dead and wounded. Less than a week before, Government forces using helicopter gunships and fixed-wing aircraft rocketed and strafed the commercial centre of the city of Jaffna. The central bus terminal, several shops and six wards of Jaffna General Hospital were hit. "Miraculously", reported a doctor, "only one patient and two visitors were injured because we got all the patients under the beds or down to the ground floor . . . ." At the end of the 4-day military offensive at least 34 civilians and guerrillas were dead. Tamil sources said that 60 people were killed and at least 100 others injured. . . . The military routinely rounds up Tamil males and holds them in camps like the notorious Boosa prison. . . . Amnesty International says that last February security forces in the Amparai district surrounded a rice paddy where Tamils were threshing rice . . . and shot at least 47 workers . . . .".'

Taken together the two events show the implacable reciprocal hostility between Tamils and Sinhalese and give some idea of the ruthlessness of the war. The intention of the fighting men of both sides dictates the strategy and tactics used.

Officials in Colombo claimed in November 1986 that they had proof that Libya and the Palestine Liberation Organization were supplying weapons to the Tamils.[4] The supplies were first going to Tamil Nadu and then by boat across Palk Strait. Libya and the PLO are both diplomatically represented in Colombo but Sri Lanka has not formally protested about the weapons 'because of fear of Middle East extremist factions'.

Serious efforts to reach a peace settlement were made late in 1986. President Jayawardene told the Tamils that they could at last have a genuine degree of autonomy. The Government proposed to set up nine provincial councils, to be given money by the central government but also to be allowed to raise some revenue themselves. The provincial councils would run the police, though top ranking officers would be appointed by Colombo.

While TULF is attracted to the idea, many on both sides of the conflict oppose it and there is a long way to go before a solution is found. Jayawardene's proposals do not go far enough for the Tamils but too far for the Sinhalese. For them it would mean giving 12.7% of the population, the Tamils, more than 25% of the land.

On 6 February 1987 the Sri Lankan security forces began their biggest offensive in the northern peninsula, Jaffna and the eastern areas since 1983. In what amounted to a full-scale invasion at Jaffna, the troops captured a 500-metre area beyond Jaffna Fort and advanced 3,000 metres along Vasvilan road. More than 80 Tamils were killed in a few days. As 5,000 troops combed the jungles, gunboats patrolled the coast to prevent guerrillas from crossing Palk Strait to India. According to Tamil sources about 200 guerrillas swallowed their issue cyanide capsules rather than be captured by the security forces.

According to the Tamil Information Centre, London, British pilots have been flying helicopters and aircraft in attacks on Tamil areas and other British mercenaries are leading ground attacks. The Information Centre quotes Simon Winchester, a senior and experienced British journalist, who discovered during the first week of May that two Britons and a South African had been manning helicopter gunships attacking targets in Tamil areas.[5]

The security forces resorted to aerial bombing because they do not have troops willing to go into battle.

A security firm partly staffed by former members of the British SAS, Keeni Meeni Services, has been retained by the Sri Lankan government to advise the armed forces on counter-insurgency.

Most Tamils support 'the boys' not necessarily because they believe in a separate Tamil state—which few want or even believe will ever happen—but because they represent the best defence against the brutal behaviour of the Sinhalese Army. But then, the Sinhalese point out, the army behaves the way it does because it has been provoked by Tamil terrorism. More than 150,000 Tamils have fled from Sri Lanka, inspired by fear and desperation. Some have been smuggled into Canada, Britain and West Germany.

One military analyst paints what he calls a 'black scenario'.[6] Should the Tamils gain their Tamil Eelam, the Tigers might take the war on to another phase—to extend by military means the area they originally claimed. This would lead to an all-out ethnic war which could only be contained by a United Nations peace-keeping force rushed to the island to man the partition line.

In the meantime, Sri Lanka is virtually a partitioned country consisting of separate Tamil and Sinhalese communities, though many people within the country and abroad find this difficult to concede. Each side fears and distrusts the other.

In late April 1987 the Sri Lankan war became more violent and bloodier than at any time since 1983. On 19 April an estimated 50 Tamil terrorists stopped three buses and two lorries in an ambush on a lonely road near Trincomalee. The passengers were mostly Sinhalese but included Tamils. Many were returning home after the New Year holiday. They were forced out of the buses and machine-gunned; 126 people were killed in the massacre and another 60 wounded. The victims included 66 servicemen returning to camp after leave.

Next day 15 Sinhalese villagers were slaughtered. On 21 April on enormous bomb exploded in Colombo's main bus station during the rush hour, killing 155 and wounding more than 200. The Government claimed that the outrages had been carried out by the Tigers in association with EROS and the following day strafed Tamil bases on the Jaffna peninsula. About 80 people were killed.

From a base in Madras, the Tigers denied any complicity in the terrorist attacks at Trincomalee and Colombo but they were the most likely suspects and their denials were not believed. The atrocities ended any hope of an early settlement between Sinhalese and Tamils.

The Sri Lankan Armed Forces

The Sri Lankan Commander-in-Chief is Lieutenant General C. Ranatunga. Even with the available auxiliaries, his forces are too small to crush the insurgency. The military quality of the Tamil fighters is high and the army requires more manpower

Tamil 'Tigers' in an ambush position on a road leading into Tamil territory in Sri Lanka. Heavily funded by Tamils living in India, the Tigers have plenty of modern weapons and equipment.

A soldier of the Liberation Tigers of Tamil Eelam Army in the jungle of the Jaffna peninsula, Sri Lanka. The Tigers have the strongest military force among the several groups demanding independence.

Tamils under fire from units of the Sri Lankan Army on the north-eastern part of Sri Lanka. Such outposts, built into gardens, sandbagged and barricaded, are common in the Tamil defence system.

and much more modern equipment to defeat them. The Government understands this and is obtaining more armoured vehicles, helicopters, aircraft, coastal craft and modern weapons adequate for a long campaign. The 1987 strength of the armed forces, all volunteers, is as follows:

Army: 30,000 men. 5 'Task Forces', actually infantry brigades of 11 battalions in all: 2 reconnaissance regiments; a field artillery regiment: a field engineer battalion; a signal battalion; a Special Forces Task Force—a type of commando unit—of 4,000 men.

Arms and equipment: 18 Saladin, 15 Ferret and 12 Daimler armoured fighting vehicles; 160 armoured personnel carriers; a variety of guns and mortars but in inadequate numbers.

Navy: 4,000 men in bases at Trincomalee, Karainager, Colombo, Tangalla and Kalpitiya. Five large (40-metres) *Jayesagara*, 56 light patrol boats and 8 amphibious landing craft.

Air Force: 3,750 men, with ten Bell helicopters from Singapore, only two of which are attack helicopters; 2 Dauphin helicopters. The transport wing has Douglas, Heron, Cessna and Siai Marchetti aircraft. During 1987 another 6 counter-insurgency helicopters were delivered and the Government has another 6 on order.

Strategic Importance of Sri Lanka

Trincomalee on Sri Lanka's east coast is one of the few good harbours in the vast expanse of the Indian Ocean and is the only one capable of basing a large surface fleet; the ports of Colombo and Galle complement Trincomalee. One analyst[7] claims that in the hands of the Soviet Union Trincomalee could be turned into the Cam Ranh Bay (Vietnam) of the Indian Ocean. In addition, the principal airport of Katunyake is a key stopover for many airlines operating routes to the Eastern Pacific. In international crises the airport has great strategic importance.

In 1954 Sri Lanka permitted US Globemasters carrying French troops to Indochina to use its airfields; Sri Lankan bases were used by Pakistan in 1971 during its war with India. The Soviet Union has been taking an interest in the Indian Ocean and access to Trincomalee would give the Russians a commanding if not dominant position in the Indian Ocean.

Violence in Tamil Nadu

Following a street brawl in Madras on 30 October 1986, members of EPRLF fired more than 60 rounds from automatic weapons at a crowd, causing a number of casualties. The security forces, until this time tolerant of Tamils with weapons, arrested 10 EPRLF members and seized six automatic rifles, six machine guns, pistols, ammunition and grenades. Following further provocation on 8 November, the Indian security forces made a pre-dawn sweep—*Operation Tiger*—in Madras city and ten other districts and seized a large quantity of weapons, including Ak-47 (Kalashnikov) rifles, surface-to-air missiles, rocket-launchers and mortars.

Soon after the seizure of weapons Tamil Nadu's chief Minister, M. G.

Ramachandran, informed the senior rebel leaders that if they wanted to continue their fight they would have to move their bases to Sri Lanka; they have 39 camps in Tamil Nadu. Until this time Ramachandran was widely believed to have helped to finance the activities of the Sri Lankan Tamils.

Several guerrilla leaders were placed under house-arrest. Among them were two prominent chiefs of the Liberation Tigers—Velupillal Prabhakaran, the leading guerrilla tactician, and the group's spokesman and theoretician, Anton Balasingham, a Marxist teacher from London. Prabhakaran has an office in a white villa in a Madras suburb which looks like a shrine, with photographs of massacred Tamils lining the walls. Dominating all is a large poster of Prabhakaran himself in a Tiger camouflage uniform, a sub-machine gun cradled in his arms.

References

1. These explanations were made public by LTTE and TELO.
2. In an interview with John Swain of the *Sunday Times*, London, 10 August 1986.
3. *Time* Magazine, 9 June 1986.
4. Confirmed for War Annual by diplomatic sources in Sri Lanka.
5. *Sunday Times*, London, 11 May 1986.
6. Edgar O'Ballance, *Armed Forces Magazine*, London, December 1986.
7. Penelope Tremayne, *Terrorism in Sri Lanka*, published by Institute for the Study of Terrorism, London, 1986. Tremayne says: 'What is going on in Sri Lanka today has been called a separatist movement and an insurgency. But properly speaking it is neither of these things. Its real objective is not the establishment of a viable separate state and the Tamil population have not risen against the government, nor are they trying to do so. A small number of ambitious Left-wing activists is attempting to seize control of the state, using a rather larger number (but still very much a minority of a minority) of young men with no jobs, or no judgement or neither.'

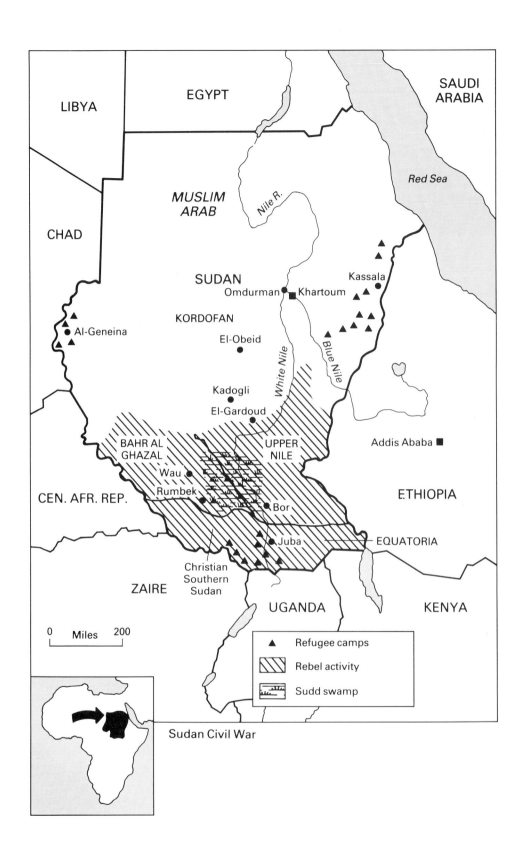

Sudan Civil War

Sudan Civil War

Background Summary

Following Sudanese independence from British rule a civil war was fought (1955-72) between the Muslim Arabs of the north and the Christian negroes and animist tribes of the south. Because of Islamic pressure against the Christians and equally because of army oppression, the southerners formed the *Anyanya* ('venom of the viper') guerrilla army. This grew into a more conventional military force, the Sudan People's Liberation Army, (SPLA) and in 1982 Colonel John Garang became its leader.

Under Abdullah Chol, *Anyanya II* came into being as a rival of SPLA. *Anyanya II* was willing to cooperate with the Khartoum Government of President Gaafer Nimeiri; SPLA wanted the south to secede from Sudan.

(For a description of the entire war see **WAR ANNUAL** 1.)

Summary of the War in 1985

Showing great skill as a guerrilla leader—and utter ruthlessness—Garang used sabotage, kidnapping and threats to close down work on the oilfields and irrigation projects. His proclaimed aim was to take over power in the whole of Sudan but as a Christian he had no chance of doing this; Muslims outnumber Christians by at least 2 to 1.

With 10,000 fighting men, in 1985 he controlled two of Sudan's three southern provinces. Propaganda from his powerful SPLA Radio station reached Khartoum. He sank two Nile steamers, killing 150 passengers and capturing 300.

On 5 April 1985 President Nimeiri was overthrown in a military coup led by General Swar al-Dhahab. Garang refused an offer of negotiation and extended SPLA's operations into northern Sudan, where his men captured much livestock, sank two more river steamers and shelled Government garrisons. Thousands of miles from their base, SPLA fighters raided air force bases near Khartoum and destroyed several aircraft.

Anyanya II's William Chol sought a separate peace with Khartoum and, to show his good faith, he and his men fought with the army against SPLA. Chol was killed in a fight at Fangak, Upper Nile. Many of his followers then joined Garang and *Anyanya II* collapsed.

The War in 1986-87

The Sudan conflict is not a struggle for 'hearts and minds',—the label given to a war in which one side or the other, or both, try to persuade the civilian populace that they are humane and care for the welfare of the ordinary people.

During 1986-87 the civilians of the war area—the south—suffered cruelly as a consequence of the strategy of both the Government and the SPLA. The SPLA's object was clearly to suppress, strangle and annihilate; in particular it proposed to starve Government-held southern towns into submission.

The Government set out to tribalize the conflict by organizing 'friendly forces' hostile to the Dinka tribe, to which John Garang belongs, by giving them licence to raid, steal cattle and burn crops. This campaign has been successful and limits the SPLA's ability to expand from the Dinka areas or to call itself a national force. But the Government is not strong enough to break permanently the SPLA siege of the three major regional capitals of Wau, Malakal and Juba.

Changing completely from guerrilla warfare to conventional methods of attack, the SPLA shelled and then stormed army garrisons, On 5 March they captured Rumbek in this way. Garang's tactics were to demoralize the soldiers by making them fear sheer annihilation so that, at times, he used 3,000 men to overwhelm an enemy company of 200. A propaganda war has become part of the military strategy of both sides. Khartoum's line is that the SPLA is dominated by the Dinka tribe to dissuade southern tribes, which do not like the Dinka, from joining Garang's army. The SPLA projects itself as a national movement and church leaders in the south speak well of it.

In April 1986 elections brought to power the nation's foremost political figure, Sadiq al-Mahdi. Garang had hoped to negotiate with al-Mahdi but the new Prime Minister backed the army and Government and accused Garang of being the tool of Marxist Ethiopia.

Food has become a principal weapon of war. The Government and the SPLA are convinced that any food given to the other side will strengthen its capacity to fight. The Government refuses to allow donor food into rebel areas and the rebels threaten to shoot down relief aircraft. The UN *Operation Rainbow* flew in only 300 tons of medical supplies and food to the starving people of southern Sudan before SPLA anti-aircraft fire became too dangerous for the flights to continue.

When a rebel Sam-7 missile shot down a Sudanese civilian airliner on 16 August 1986, killing 60 people, the relief effort was stopped. The rebels had already tried unsuccessfully to shoot down a UNICEF plane in March and they warned that they would shoot at any aircraft flying over southern Sudan without SPLA permission.

The relief agencies want to distribute food only to civilians, on the basis of strict need. The Government argues that Westerners, new to the country, are unable to distinguish between genuine civilians and rebels. The SPLA wants to distribute the food in rebel-controlled areas but the Red Cross is concerned that the grain might not reach the needy. It is noticeable that the SPLA's 20,000 men do not usually go hungry. Pressure to supply food to one side while denying it to the other is one of the biggest problems facing the relief agencies. Distributing food in areas being fought over is practically impossible.

The effect of the war on the country and its people is best seen by focusing on a single town, Malakal. About 600 miles south of Khartoum, on the Nile, Malakal is an army garrison town, deep in the war area. Because of drought and the consequent famine, and poor administration, the 80,000 people of the town are suffering acutely and United Nations agencies have struggled to bring in emergency supplies. Yet army planes continue to fly ammunition, cigarettes and soap for sale on the black market—never food or medicines.

The SPLA cut road, river and civilian air links so Malakal had no links with the outside world between October 1986 and March 1987. In November an army-escorted barge convoy arrived six months late. It was only the third to arrive throughout 1986; Garang's forces captured the others. Most of the garrison's soldiers, Arabs from the north and west, hate the Malakal district. The wet season keeps them penned in the town and in the dry season they risk their lives on constant patrols. The army suspects that local people help the rebels and there is constant friction. The locals resent the money being made by the soldiers in black market selling. Some officers have become rich.

The Government's militia troops cause much trouble. They are supposed to fight the rebels in the rural areas, leaving the regular soldiers to concentrate on protecting the garrison towns. However, the unpaid militiamen, without discipline, education or proper training, spend much of their time stealing cattle and killing anyone who tries to stop them. On average about 50 people a month are believed to die at the hands of the militia.

The Catholic Archbishop of Wau, Joseph Nyekindi, is one of the most credible witnesses of the war. In a report to the Vatican late in October 1986 he said:

> Actual fights between the army and the SPLA are in single figures. The army is not prepared to take the risks and the SPLA avoids direct attacks on military targets. The civilians are the real targets and thousands have died. For over three years the Government has done nothing to protect and maintain the railway line to Wau, knowing this is the main lifeline to Bahr al Ghazal. Neither has it made alternative arrangements to supply at least the armed forces. Meanwhile the SPLA moves around in large groups looting all foodstuffs and clothes, moving to the next village, leaving the poor people naked, without anything. In fact, villagers call the SPLA 'human locusts'. Guerrillas rape women and girls. Anyone who shows resistance to the SPLA is tied to a tree by the hands and legs. A rope is passed through the mouth and the person is left for hours or until relatives pay a ransom. Government troops shoot most suspects on sight and torture those they take prisoner. John Garang knows that the destruction is among his own people and Sadiq al Mahdi should support a constitutional conference, including the SPLA, to achieve a lasting peace.

Garang insists that the SPLA is neither a Christian nor an African movement but a Sudanese nationalist movement. There is probably some truth in this and Western diplomats in Khartoum and Addis Ababa believe that Garang is not entirely a puppet of the Ethiopian regime. However, they say, the Marxist Ethiopians use him as a weapon with which to punish Khartoum for allowing Eritreans and other dissidents to operate from Sudan.

SPLA fighters receive most of their weapons, which are always in good condition, from Ethiopia. Much of their equipment is Soviet-made but some is American, including their 60 mm mortars.

To say that Garang's guerrillas move confidently in battalions of up to 1,000 men is a contradiction in military terms. In units of this size, marching in single file through the vast tree-studded plains and malarial swamps, they are a regular army.

They move with surface-to-air missiles, many encumbrances such as bedsteads and frequently they balance pieces of dismembered cows—their rations—on their heads. The SPLA has hardly ever been attacked from the air; the Sudan Air Force seems unable to locate them. It has never attacked Garang's headquarters on Buma plateau.

Sudan has never had much unity. The largest country in Africa, it covers 1 million square miles and has 160 different ethnic tribes among its 22 million people; two-thirds of them are Muslim. At the end of 1987 unity was obviously not going to come out of the barrel of a gun. For both sides the delayed action tactics of hunger, crop destruction and siege seem to hold the key to the war.

Surinam Guerrilla War

BUSH NEGROES VERSUS CREOLE DICTATOR

In 1975 Surinam, formerly Dutch Guiana, gained its independence but within a few years its ethnic jumble of European settlers, descendants of African slaves, native Amerindians and contract labourers from India and Java were thrown into conflict.

Desi Bouterse, an Afro-European or Creole aged 40, became dictator after a military coup in 1980. He promoted himself from sergeant to lieutenant colonel and did away with ethnic bickering by suspending parliament. In an effort to give legitimacy to his government he revived, in 1986, the old East Indian, Creole and Javanese parties. The Bush Negroes—English for the Dutch *boschnegers*—reacted violently because they feared exploitation by the other groups. The Bush Negroes are descendants of escaped slaves whose armed attacks 200 years ago forced the Dutch colonists to grant them autonomy in the forest region.

Since then Bush Negroes have isolated themselves from national life, building a unique society with its own language, religious rituals and political structure. They make up 20% of Surinam's population of 500,000. Their guerrilla leader is Roddy Brunswijk, aged 26, a former bodyguard of Bouterse who broke with him in 1986. Brunswijk promoted himself from sergeant to captain. His headquarters are at Stoelman's Island, deep along the great Marowijne River.

Under Colonel Bouterse, Surinam's Press has been muzzled, foreign currency reserves depleted and genuine political parties banned. The necessities of life are scarce and *per capita* income is extremely low. He lost US$100 million in Dutch aid in 1982 when he had 15 of his political opponents killed, and the country's income from bauxite exports has dropped.

Despite his country's economic problems, Bouterse has been able to get all the cash and arms he needs from Colonel Gadaffi of Libya. Surinam and Libya signed a US$66 million trade-and-aid deal in December 1986. Gaddafi's interest in Surinam is twofold. In the first place he is eager for any kind of alliance, and secondly Surinam is next door to a *departement* of France, Guyana. Gaddafi sees France as an enemy of Libya second only to the United States.

Gaddafi offered Bouterse manpower which Bouterse originally declined. In January 1987 he changed his mind and accepted and a 100-strong Libyan contingent of instructors and troops was quickly sent. Bouterse, who now prefers to be called Commander Bouterse, has defeated six attempted coups and appointed six cabinets. His international reputation sank when his second-in-command was convicted in Miami, in September, 1986, of conspiring to import cocaine into the United States. He implicated Bouterse.

Roddy Brunswijk's guerrillas were first known as the Jungle Commandos but now have the title of Surinam National Army of Liberation. Trained by three

VENEZUELA

Atlantic
Ocean

GUYANA

Paramaribo   Moengo

Kourou

Stoelman's
Island

SURINAM   FR. GUIANA

Marowijne River

BRAZIL

0   Miles   200

Surinam Guerrilla War

SURINAM

SOUTH
AMERICA

British mercenaries and a few American and French mercenaries, they control an area much bigger than the original colonising nation, The Netherlands.

Eddie Jozezoon, one of Brunswijk's three senior advisers and one of the few rebels with an education, is the armaments procurer. He has sought aid from the Dutch, French, Brazilian, Venezuelan and US governments. Largely unsuccessful—except in the case of Brazil—he has obtained a war chest through appeals to the 200,000 Surinamese who live in The Netherlands.

Brunswijk's guerrillas have yet to capture and hold a town against Bouterse; in turn Bouterse has yet to recapture any great area of the forest. The guerrillas' strategy is to cause disruption and this they do by blowing up electricity pylons and raiding government installations. In one raid they hijacked a Surinam Airways Twin Otter aircraft and a privately owned light plane. With rifle fire they brought down an army helicopter.

The insurgents have their main camps along Surinam's border with French Guyana and control perhaps six forest airstrips. They do not have the strength to defeat the army and in December 1986 the army went on the offensive in the eastern part of the country and recaptured the vital bauxite-mining town of Moengo.

In December an exiled political leader, former President Henk Chin-A-Sen, a medical doctor, returned to join the rebels. His participation in Bouterse's government had lent it legitimacy but his opposition to Bouterse's excesses and threats to his own life caused him to flee.

One of Brunswijk's principal lieutenants in the jungles is Irwin MacDonald, a Bush Negro despite his name. His guerrillas might be poorly armed but they are inspired by belief in 'obeah' or magic. Every fighter wears a cloth amulet around his neck and another of wire on his upper left arm. The amulets are prepared by tribal medicine men.

The people of the capital, Paramaribo, have not risen against Bouterse, partly because of distrust and fear of the Bush Negroes. Nobody has a clear idea where Brunswijk and his followers stand politically. Eddie Jozezoon says they have a 'commitment to democracy' but foreign diplomats in Paramaribo say that the rebels have only a vague idea of democracy in practice.

The war is more serious for the West than it might appear to be. Just over the Marowijne River is the base for France's and Europe's space programme. The French fear that Gaddafi might take revenge in Guyana for his reverses in Chad. A bomb set off at an Ariane satellite launching could cripple the commercial prospects of the European rocket.

In February 1987 the French armed forces carried out *Operation Red Flag*; Mirage jets flew along the border of Surinam and Guyana in plain warning to Bouterse and his Libyan friends to keep to their side of the river. Four battalions of soldiers are based at Kourou, Guyana.

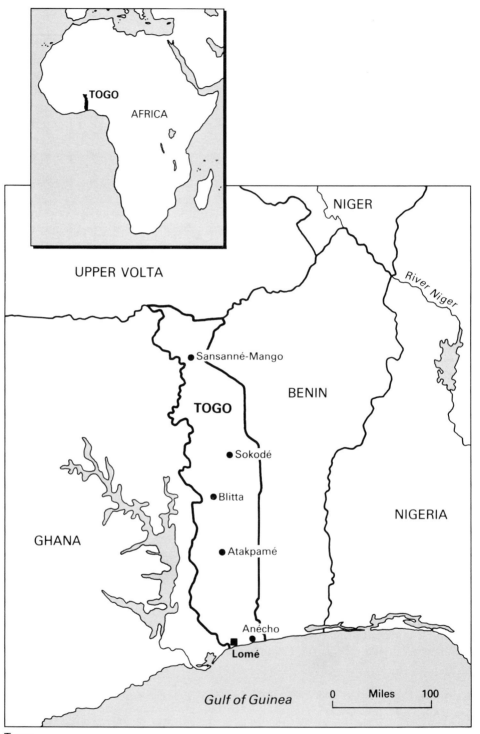

Togo

Togo

Before dawn on 24 September 1986 Ghanaian soldiers invaded Lomé, the capital of neighbouring Togo, in an attempt to mount an uprising against President Gnassingbe Eyedema, President since 1967.

It was not a particularly serious invasion and involved only 50 raiders but the 'small war'—as the French protectors of Togo called it—indicates the brittle nature of African politics. Shooting went on for seven hours and the invaders had seven killed and 19 captured. Five Togolese and a West German were also killed.

Foreign ambassadors were shown the seized equipment—explosives, rockets and grenades and the usual Kalashnikov rifles.

The 'small war' threat came directly from Ghana's 'progressive' Lieutenant Jerry Rawlings, President of Ghana, who is said to have 'imperial' ambitions.

At the request of the Togolese Government the French rushed 150 paratroopers and three Jaguar fighter aircraft to Togo. Zaire sent 50 paratroopers. The French-Togolese defence agreement of 1963 pledges France to help its ex-colony against an 'external threat'.

President Eyedema staged Africa's first *coup d'état* in January 1963, overthrowing President Sylvanus Olympio. At the time Eyedema boasted of having personally killed Olympio. He handed over power to a civilian government but four years later, in a second coup, he threw out President Grunitsky. A former sergeant in the French Army, Eyedema rose to the rank of Lieutenant Colonel and promoted himself to General when he became President.

Ghana has sheltered the family of President Olympio since 1963. Though descended from Brazilian re-emigrants to Africa, the Olympios are affiliated to the Ewe people who live both in Ghana and southern Togo. The Togolese Ewes resent rule by General Eyedema, who comes from the northern Kabra tribe.

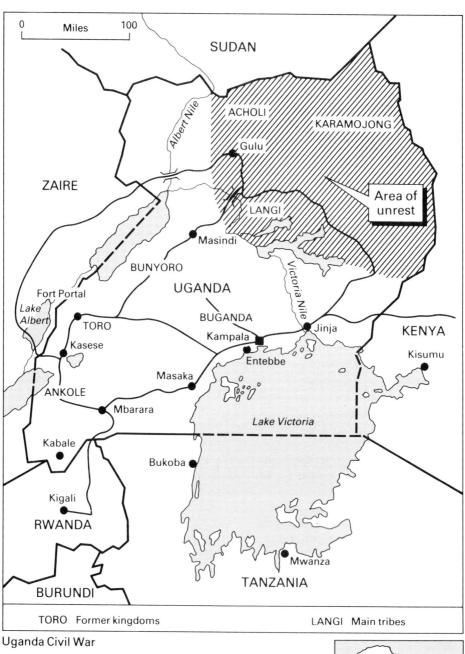

0 |——— Miles ———| 100

SUDAN

ACHOLI

KARAMOJONG

Gulu

Albert Nile

ZAIRE

Area of
unrest

LANGI

Masindi

BUNYORO

Victoria Nile

UGANDA

Fort Portal

Lake
Albert

TORO

BUGANDA

Kampala

Jinja

KENYA

Kisumu

Kasese

Entebbe

Masaka

ANKOLE

Mbarara

Lake Victoria

Kabale

Bukoba

Kigali

RWANDA

BURUNDI

Mwanza

TANZANIA

TORO Former kingdoms

LANGI Main tribes

Uganda Civil War

UGANDA

Uganda Guerrilla War

ANOTHER ROUND OF CONFLICT

Background Summary

After the cruel and incompetent Idi Amin was overthrown, Milton Obote became President in 1980. The Defence Minister, Yoweri Museveni, claiming that the election had been rigged, took to the bush to wage a guerrilla war against Obote. Styling his force the National Resistance Army (NRA), Museveni gathered 6,000 fighters who were largely armed by Libya. In its pursuit of the NRA, the Ugandan Army was guilty of countless atrocities against civilians, at least 300,000 of the 16 million population were killed.

(*For a full description of the war see* **WAR ANNUAL** 1.)

Summary of the War in 1985

Most fighting took place in the Lowero Triangle, which was virtually depopulated. The army shot any peasant suspected of helping the NRA guerrillas. Tribal rivalries affected much of the fighting. For instance, in June the army chief-of-staff, General Acak, sent Acholi soldiers to counter the NRA threat at Fort Portal. They were posted to Magamaga barracks where soldiers of the Langi tribe were already stationed. The two parties had a bloody shoot-out for no better reason than that they were traditional enemies.

On 27 July Brigadier Okello overthrew Obote and asked General Tito Okello (no relation) to become President. At this point the national army, which was now no more than a rabble, went on the rampage in Kampala and other towns and many people were killed. Museveni and his NRA, now numbering 8,000, moved out of the Triangle and extended their operations to a third of Uganda's area. He declared that he would restore democracy and security to Uganda.

Meanwhile, pro-Amin bush fighters from the West Nile region moved back into Kampala, keeping alive the public fear that Amin might return. Without Museveni's support the Okello government could not last, especially as Okello made the mistake of assessing the NRA as just another armed faction. In fact, it was a disciplined and trained army and foreign observers predicted that it would defeat the ill-disciplined and brutal Ugandan Army.

The War in 1986-87

On 26 January the NRA easily captured Kampala. Museveni threw out Okello and was himself sworn in as President a few days later. His priority was to create a new national army with his own NRA as the core, together with those men of the national army whom he considered could be redeemed.

217

Museveni is the first southerner to hold presidential power. Most of his officers come from tribes in Uganda's west but the bulk of the rank-and-file are Bugandans. As he built up the new army, Museveni planned to send back to school the many young boys who had been trained to fight. Known by the colloqial Swahili word *bakadogo* (little ones), most of them did not get their official demobilisation papers until the end of 1986 or early 1987. They were ordered to put aside their guns, take off their army uniforms and report to one of one of two special colleges to resume normal schooling. Any found roaming around armed or in uniform without a pass from school were liable to arrest and disciplinary action by the security forces.

The order ended a lengthy debate about the future of the child-soldiers and widespread criticism of Museveni's government for allowing them to carry out law and order duties for so long after the NRA came to power. Museveni tried to answer his critics by saying that his NRA force had not set out to recruit the *bakadogo*. Many children were left homeless orphans when the murderous soldiers of Obote and later Okello killed their parents. The NRA took them along to protect and feed them and gradually the children learnt how to use weapons to protect themselves.

After Museveni came to power the consensus in Uganda was that the young guerrillas should return to school but opinion was divided on whether they should mix with other children or go to special institutions of their own. Many teachers and parents opposed mixing on the grounds that they would be unruly and pass on militaristic ideas to their classmates.

Meanwhile, in the north General Basilio Okello, based at Gulu, established a resistance force to fight Musevini. It was built around the 800,000-strong Acholi warrior tribe and many of its members were boys, some as young as 8 years old. The war flared up again in July 1986, especially in the north. Tribal enmity was the main cause but men who had held great power and lost it to Museveni were determined to regain it.

In October and November 1986 the Kampala Government began to try to organize Uganda in the image of Libya and many members of the National Resistance Movement were trained in civil administration. Libyan-style 'people's committees' were given more power, especially in matters of political indoctrination and policing. They are also entrusted with the distribution of imported essentials. In November increasing numbers of Soviet and other Communist bloc 'advisers' and experts were active in Kampala, as well as Libyans. Ugandans were sent to Tripoli to learn how popular revolutionary committees work.

Despite all his foreign help Museveni had a hard time fitting deeds to words. Arbitrary arrests—often on denunciations—were increasing and jails were overflowing during 1986. The discipline and self-control of the NRA was even then deteriorating. Misusing the power they had, they treated ordinary people just as their predecessors had done. Near Masaka a passenger in a taxi was shot at a roadblock because he was not quick enough to open his bags. A member of the French Embassy security staff, a British teacher in Kampala and an Australian Franciscan priest in the eastern part of the country were killed. Many Ugandans expected better behaviour from the NRA, though it is true that many criminal acts have been committed not by genuine NRA soldiers but by men who served previous regimes and are now in the national army.

A bizarre battle occurred at Corner Kilak, 200 miles north of Kampala on 18

January 1987, between the rebels 'Holy Battalion' of the Uganda National Liberation Army (UNLA) and Museveni's NRA. At first the battle went well for the NRA. About 300 rebels attacked at 6.40 am and in a 90-minute fight more than 200 of them were killed. Only two government soldiers died.

More UNLA rebels then attacked and many of the NRA force ran in panic. Some of the men rallied, dug in and fought back. The NRA deputy army commander, Fred Rwigyema, brought in reinforcements and prepared for another battle.

The rebels were mostly former soldiers from the defeated armies of deposed heads of state, Obote and Okello. A woman named Alice Lukwena had convinced them that her fetishes and voodoo ceremonies would save their lives in battle. Lukwena means Messiah in the Acholi dialect used by many of the rebels. The priestess told the rebels that she had risen from the Indian Ocean. She brewed potions from local nut oils together with sticks and water and made voodoo models of tanks, anti-aircraft guns and helicopters from pieces of wire. These were scattered in a 'magic circle' in the centre of the area she advised as the battlefield.[1]

The magic failed; more than 350 rebels were killed in a seven-hour battle. Even so, the NRA suffered 38 dead and 116 wounded, the highest Government casualties from fighting in the north during the rebel offensive. The rebel leader, Lieutenant Colonel Eric Odwar, was killed. A prisoner of war—found by NRA soldiers hiding near the battlefield—told journalists that the men had been told that once the magic potion had been administered it prevented them from 'fighting lying down'. They became charging, valiant warriors. This accounted for their heavy casualties.

In mid-January Museveni's army received a trainload of field guns through the Kenyan port of Mombasa. Such weapons did not win the hearts and minds of the northern Ugandan people—and they did not help the President to control his own men. A year of peace has eroded the discipline of the NRA still further. Museveni dismissed the commander of the northern brigade, which was set up to combat insurgency, for heavy drinking. During an engagement at Kitgum the 35th Regiment of the NRA deliberatly threw down its weapons for the rebels to take up. The regiment was disbanded.

Sometimes NRA troops perform well. In the last days of January 1987 they crushed an armed rebellion by forces loyal to Obote in Uganda's eastern district of Soroti. The rebels hoisted the flag of Obote's Uganda People's Congress Party and occupied the town for three days. The uprising followed the arrest of six former members of the Congress party. Near Kaberamaido trading centre, 235 miles from Kampala, NRA soldiers fought their way out of a rebel ambush and killed 15 rebels. Nevertheless, the army is underpaid and unstable and with so many enemies inside and outside the country Museveni may not be able to prevent his once-proud NRA from being infected by the general unrest and indiscipline.

In mid-April the Uganda Freedom Movement (UFM) withdrew from the government and returned to the bush to pursue armed struggle. Francis Bwengye, a leader of the UFM, accused Museveni of creating a totalitarian Marxist state and of following 'a policy of arbitrary arrests and massacres'. The decision was largely caused by the murder in March of the UFM's leader Andrew Kayiira, a former Cabinet Minister in Museveni's government. Francis Bwengye accused Peter Magara, the intelligence officer of the 19th battalion of the NRA, of the murder on the orders of Fred Rwigyema, the NRA's deputy commander.

In going back to the bush the UFM became a serious military threat to Museveni. This group claims to have support in the Buganda region, where Museveni successfully waged his guerrilla war against Obote. The UFM has probably 1,000 trained fighters and is training hundreds more.

Militarily stretched already, Museveni is using soldiers from North Korea, East Germany, Cuba and Libya. About 400 Libyan military staff arrived at Nakasongala, 60 miles north of Kampala, in March, and another 750 were expected towards the end of 1987.

Uganda and the NRA face a potentially greater threat than those posed by internal rebellion and the presence of foreign troops in Uganda. The army is specially vulnerable to the AIDS virus which has reached epidemic proportions in Uganda. In February 1987 a team of Cuban doctors completed a two-month survey of AIDS infection in the army and found that one soldier in three is infected. The effect on the army in terms of morale and efficiency is incalculable.

More than 16,000 ordinary people, out of 500,000, are infected in Kampala alone. At least 5,000 babies born each year in Kampala catch the virus in the womb. At this rate, and without any changes in sexual habits, almost every adult in the capital will have the virus within 10 years. The capital is not Uganda's worst-hit area. Its infection rates follow, with a delay of about two years, those in the south-west of the country, the part of Uganda closest to the world's worst-affected areas—Burundi, Rwanda, eastern Zaire and the West Lake district of Tanzania. Most of the soldiers come from the heavily-infected southern regions.

Uganda has all the elements for another revolution, including 200% inflation. The Museveni administration is spending four times faster than Obote's government. Until adverse publicity stopped it, the Procurement Department proposed to buy 100 Mercedes cars for a Cabinet of 50 members. Museveni wears a bullet-proof vest and drives around in an armour-plated Mercedes which is followed by a Land-Rover on which is mounted a machine-gun.

The Ugandan Armed Forces, in terms of arms and equipment, is one of the weakest in Africa. It has only 13 tanks, 10 of them of Soviet manufacture and all of them unreliable, and 150 armoured personnel carriers, all of them poorly serviced. There are 60 76 mm guns and 20 120 mm. The air force has only six planes and a few command helicopters.

Reference

1. Details about Alice Lukwena come from Reverend P. J. Naseby, a Canadian Methodist missionary. Alice Lukwena was interviewed by western journalists, including *The Guardian* and *The Times* correspondents, present at the battle of Corner Kilak.

The United States' Raid on Libya

Contingency and even actuality planning by the Americans for military attacks against Libya began in the summer of 1985. The State Department summoned home the US ambassador to Egypt, Nicholas Veliotes, to help plan a joint US-Egypt military attack on Libya. Both countries were angry with Colonel Gaddafi because of his support for terrorism and his attempts to organize a coup against President Mubarak of Egypt.

Head of Intelligence Analysis for the CIA, Robert Gates, wrote a paper in which he estimated that an American-Egyptian operation against Libya would present an opportunity 'to redraw the map of North Africa'. The CIA director, William Casey, ordered a study of military targets in Libya that would be subject to US attack.

Under a plan known as *Operation Rose* prepared by the National Security Council (NSC), Egypt would attack Libya and capture half its territory, with the help of American air support. This would bring about Gaddafi's downfall. The US Joint Chiefs of Staff estimated that the operation would require six US combat divisions which would have to come from NATO and would thus weaken the Alliance.

Veliotes, did not like the scheme and neither, apparently, did the Joint Chiefs-of-Staff. The invasion was reduced to contingency planning in case of some clash with Libya.

On President Reagan's behalf, Admiral John Poindexter, Deputy National Security Adviser to the President, flew to Cairo to brief President Mubarak. Mubarak was doubtful about the attack and made it clear that if an invasion took place it would be based on an Egyptian plan. American contingency planning continued.

Following the terrorist bombings at Rome and Vienna airports on 27 December 1985 the US considered a military strike at Libya. No involvement in these atrocities could be traced to Libya but a major US naval and air exercise—*Operation Prairie Fire*—took place in the Gulf of Sidra, off Libya. Gaddafi has always insisted that the Gulf is entirely Libyan territorial waters. Under the rules of engagement, President Reagan would order attacks on certain Libyan targets should a Libyan attack cause American casualties.

The exercise angered Gaddafi but the Libyans took no hostile action. However, on 24 March 1986 Libyan forces fired missiles at US warplanes. The Americans retaliated quickly with a strike against a missile site and two Libyan patrol boats, both of which were sunk. Following this Gaddafi proclaimed: 'It is time for confrontation—for war.'[1]

On that day it was reported that US Intelligence agencies had intercepted messages from Tripoli to Libyan missions in eight countries ordering them to attack American targets. On 5 April a West German discotheque, *La Belle*, crowded

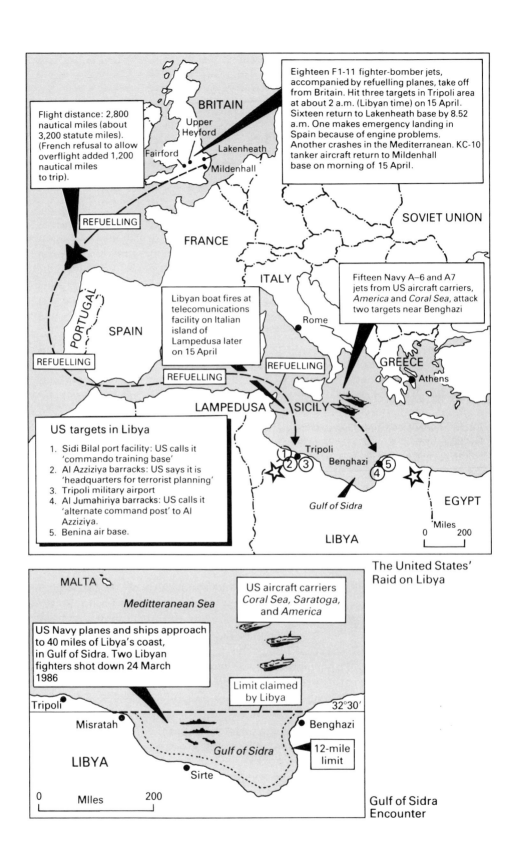

Eighteen F1-11 fighter-bomber jets, accompanied by refuelling planes, take off from Britain. Hit three targets in Tripoli area at about 2 a.m. (Libyan time) on 15 April. Sixteen return to Lakenheath base by 8.52 a.m. One makes emergency landing in Spain because of engine problems. Another crashes in the Mediterranean. KC-10 tanker aircraft return to Mildenhall base on morning of 15 April.

Flight distance: 2,800 nautical miles (about 3,200 statute miles). (French refusal to allow overflight added 1,200 nautical miles to trip).

BRITAIN
Upper Heyford
Fairford
Lakenheath
Mildenhall

REFUELLING

FRANCE

SOVIET UNION

PORTUGAL

SPAIN

ITALY
Rome

Libyan boat fires at telecomunications facility on Italian island of Lampedusa later on 15 April

REFUELLING

REFUELLING

REFUELLING

Fifteen Navy A–6 and A7 jets from US aircraft carriers, *America* and *Coral Sea*, attack two targets near Benghazi

GREECE
Athens

LAMPEDUSA   SICILY

US targets in Libya

1. Sidi Bilal port facility: US calls it 'commando training base'
2. Al Azziziya barracks: US says it is 'headquarters for terrorist planning'
3. Tripoli military airport
4. Al Jumahiriya barracks: US calls it 'alternate command post' to Al Azziziya.
5. Benina air base.

Tripoli
Benghazi
① ②③   ④⑤

Gulf of Sidra

EGYPT

Miles
0   200

LIBYA

The United States' Raid on Libya

MALTA
Mediterranean Sea

US aircraft carriers *Coral Sea, Saratoga,* and *America*

US Navy planes and ships approach to 40 miles of Libya's coast, in Gulf of Sidra. Two Libyan fighters shot down 24 March 1986

Limit claimed by Libya

Tripoli   32°30'

Misrath   Benghazi

12-mile limit

LIBYA   *Gulf of Sidra*

Sirte

0   MIles   200

Gulf of Sidra Encounter

with American service personnel was bombed. An American soldier and a Turkish woman were killed and 230 others were injured.

Libya was said to be responsible for the *La Belle* outrage and its complicity confirmed in an intercepted message. In direct response President Reagan ordered F1-11 bombers to attack selected targets in Libya on 15 April 1986. The attack, code-named *Operation El Dorado Canyon*, required much logistical co-ordination, largely because the American planners wanted the cooperation of their allies. A joint operation with even slight NATO involvement would carry much more political weight than if the United States acted alone. The British Prime Minister, Mrs. Thatcher, permitted some of the aircraft to leave from American Air Force bases in Britain. No other leader would co-operate and France and Spain refused to permit the warplanes to overfly their territory.

The first aircraft took off from the US bases in Britain at 6.36 pm British time on 14 April. By 8 pm an air armada had assembled in British skies: 24 F1-11s from the 48th Tactical Fighter Wing at Lakenheath; 5 EF-111 electronic counter-measure aircraft from Upper Heyford; 28 KC10s and KC135s—all petrol tankers—from Fairford and Mildenhall. Later they were joined by a high-flying SR 71 Blackbird reconnaissance jet from Mildenhall.[2]

Repeatedly refuelled in mid-air, the aircraft skirted France and Portugal before turning into the Mediterranean for the final approach to their target. The strike was scheduled for 1 am. Meanwhile the aircraft carriers *Coral Sea* and *America*, off the Italian coast, launched aircraft to hit targets in Tripoli and Benghazi, Libya's second city. F-18 Hornets armed with anti-radar missiles were to attack radar sites near Tripoli, with F-14 Tomcats providing top cover. F-18 Hornets and A-7 Corsair fighter-bombers were to hit radar sites in and around Benghazi, with top cover provided by F-14s and F-18s. A-6 Intruders would attack the Al Jumahiriya barracks and Benina military airfield.[3] Throughout the attack a Boeing E-3 Sentry AWACS 'flying radar station' patrolled the coast of Libya, providing airborne control and warning of any Libyan aircraft.

It was later learned that another nine F1-11 bombers, with six flying in reserve, also took part in the raid with the specific task of assassinating Colonel Gaddafi.[4]

For pinpoint attacks on precision targets the F1-11 crews used the 'Pave Tack' system mounted underneath their aircraft. A laser beam is 'shone' on to the target and the bombs are guided down the reflected beam to a direct hit. The laser designator is mounted on a turret which remains locked on to the target as the aircraft overflies, illuminating the target throughout the flight of the bomb. Eight aircraft in the strike carried 2,000 lb laser-guided bombs; others had cluster bombs.

At 2 am local time, the F1-11 force screamed overhead, taking the anti-aircraft defences by surprise. Two waves of aircraft hit three main targets, running north to south across Tripoli, and turned for a second run. The first bombs landed in the Al Azizza/barracks, Gaddafi's headquarters, and where terrorists are thought to be trained. Seconds later bombs hit the Sidi Bilal port facility, followed by the military side of Tripoli's airport, where the control tower and several aircraft were hit.

Despite the sophisticated aiming devices, several bombs fell in a residential area and 66 people in Tripoli were killed or injured. Gaddafi's 15-month-old adopted daughter was killed and two of his sons injured. His home was hit but he himself was unhurt.

Infra-red Intelligence photographs showed that the American bombs, guided by the F1-11's sophisticated on-board system, left a line of craters from Gaddafi's two-story stucco house past his tent. Perhaps what saved him was the fact that the laser guidance on four of the nine F1-11s attacking his quarters broke down, eliminating the possibility that at least 16 more bombs could have struck.[5]

While the US Air Force was attacking Tripoli, Navy planes hit Benghazi. A-6s bombed the barracks and Benina airfield, where up to 12 MiG-23 fighters were destroyed on the ground.

Libyan air defence went into action, mostly after the American planes had departed. One plane crashed into the sea with its crew but it is not thought to have been hit. Pointless sporadic anti-aircraft shooting went on until daybreak. The 'action' had lasted just 11 minutes but it was a war nonetheless.

Military conflict and armed attack by a superpower, even over as short a period as 11 minutes, is of vastly greater importance than a war which goes on for many years but involves only minor nations. Whatever the United States or the Soviet Union does affects, in one way or another, practically the entire world. Also, while the effects of a war on a small nation may not be discernible to the rest of the world, the effects on a superpower are monumentally visible to all. The US raid on Libya needs to be analysed along several lines. They are: the use and efficacy of military power; political apprehensions and consequences; participation by allies of the Americans and Libyans; effects on the reputation of both parties. In addition, it is necessary to look at the precipitating cause of the raid.

Military Efficacy

The raid was a logistical success in that bombers flew 5,800 miles, being refuelled in flight, and all but one returned safely. However, despite the most advanced aiming techniques some bombs went wildly astray. This failure dismayed senior figures in the European military who felt that it would lessen America's military prestige throughout the world. However, the lack of precision caused more Press comment than professional criticism.

The US raid has important military implications. It means that any small country wishing to harm the United States—or prepared to give refuge to its enemies—is vulnerable to retaliation. This is specially so if the country concerned has a sea coast or a neighbour which will permit overflying. In future any such raid involving great distances and mid-air refuelling, could be made from the US itself; it would not require the assistance of an ally. Europe's refusal—apart from Britain—to aid the US could profoundly influence American attitudes to NATO. As the NATO allies were not prepared to help the Americans will the Americans always feel obliged to help Europe?

The Soviet Reaction

Russian comments on the American raid were milder than might have been expected. In fact, it faced the Soviet leaders with a dilemma. They had intended to hold a second Reagan-Gorbachev summit in 1986. Now they could either go ahead with the summit and gain a short-term advantage; or they could rebuff the Americans over the raid and thus further Soviet political interests in the Middle

East. Gaddafi, soon after the bombing, summoned the Soviet ambassador and gave him a personal message for Gorbachev, in which he pressed for a stronger Soviet commitment to Libya. Ignoring this request, the Russians compromised by deferring rather than cancelling the summit.

Gaddafi's public statements embarrassed the Russians. Tripoli television broadcast the text of an interview between Gaddafi and Soviet journalists.[6] Gaddafi said that Libya had carried out an historic action by 'obstructing the imperialist forces on their way to Moscow.... These aircraft, which took off from Britain, might have been on their way to Moscow'. This fantasy may have helped the Russians to decide that they could give Gaddafi no more than 'additional technical assistance'.

Legality of the Attack

The legal justification was based on the argument that the United States was exercising its 'inherent right of self-defence' after attacks upon its citizens, organized by the Libyan government. This argument was wholeheartedly backed within the US but most of America's allies pointed out that air attacks on suspected terrorists would only add to the cycle of violence. Within a few months, however, many leading commentators were saying that even if the raid had not been entirely legal it had indeed worked.[7] The incidence of terrorism became less and Gaddafi was less frequently implicated.

Libyan Reactions

While Gaddafi and other Libyans denounced the raid, the military response was slight. A small, unsuccessful attack was made on the Italian island Lampedusa, used as a NATO communications base. Two Scud B missiles were fired from Libya but exploded in the sea two miles off the Lampedusa coast. Some Europeans were expelled from Libya.

There was no major military action which Gaddafi could take but he did not need to take any. The propaganda victory was clearly his. The world's media hastened to Libya and the films and photographs of the injuries suffered by civilians and the damage caused to their property created great sympathy for Libya and even for Gaddafi. To the Americans' puzzlement and dismay, European reaction was almost totally hostile to the United States.

Gaddafi's wrecked home has been kept as it was immediately after the raid and is a national monument. Within a few months he had convinced himself that the encounter had ended with a Libyan victory.

Arab and Islamic Reaction

No Arab nation could offer Gaddafi material aid. The Syrian President, Hafez el-Assad, promised 'all possible means of support' but did nothing. The American action embarrassed Egypt, even though President Mubarak very much wanted to see Gaddafi overthrown. He feared that the Arab and Islamic opponents of the Israel-Egypt peace treaty would label him as nothing more than a pawn to be used by the Americans at will. As an Arab he could not condone the American attack—yet he could hardly condemn it too openly because Egypt would starve and lose all military prestige without massive American aid in money and arms. The entire Arab world declared itself shocked, though those leaders who had suffered from Gaddafi's meddling would not have been upset to see him killed. Iran, the most violently anti-American Islamic nation, assured Gaddafi—an ally of Ayatollah Khomeini—that it would support him by attacking American targets. Iran's Prime Minister, Hussein Mussavi, said, 'the USA will receive the due response for its stubborn attitude'. The Syrian-backed PLO breakaway faction's leader, Abu Musa, announced: 'All US and British interests are hostile targets for us, inside and outside the Arab world.'

Political Apprehensions and Consequences

The Americans felt badly let down—some said betrayed—by their European allies. The British Government alone was willing to back the American strike and face the inevitable risks. France and Spain had refused to permit the F1-11s to fly over their territory. The Europeans feared that their economic and other ties with Arab and Islamic states would be damaged if they were to help the United States in this attack—even though they, too, deplored Gaddafi's support for terrorism. A rift developed between the US and its European allies, leading American statesmen to make the caustic statement that the Europeans were 'soft on terrorism'. The British Prime Minister admitted that she had been faced with a highly difficult decision in allowing the use of British airfields. She was, she said, given an assurance that only military targets would be hit. The Opposition parties made much of the death of Libyan civilians.

In effect, the raid gave notice to the Europeans that the US would take decisive action against terrorism if no common policy were agreed. One result has been a marked improvement in the West's combined Intelligence operations. Because of shared Intelligence four big terrorist operations planned by Libya were foiled soon after the raid.

Throughout 1986-87 more information on the movement of terrorists was passed from country to country than ever before. British and American security agencies such as NSA and GCHQ frequently tap international telephone calls and movements of suspects are plotted and circulated. Some government experts believe that Gaddafi will resume terrorist activity when he is under less surveillance and when he has better-trained agents of his own. He announced in April 1987 that he would continue to help the IRA and Yasser Arafat's PLO.

Terrorist attacks against American targets did not decrease in number following the American raid but to the middle of 1987 there had been no major attack, apart from the Karachi hijack and the synagogue attack in Istanbul. The former was only indirectly against Americans and the latter was not against Americans at all. Other state sponsors of terrorism, such as Syria and Iran, also appeared less keen to support big attacks.

The Intercepted Coded Messages

The American administration waged its brief war on the strength of coded messages, which US Intelligence had intercepted, between the Libyan People's

Bureau in East Berlin and Tripoli, concerning the *La Belle* explosion. Nearly all West European and Israeli Intelligence agencies agree that the messages were ambiguous and thorough investigation carried out by a BBC television journalist, Tom Bower, casts doubt on their authenticity.[8] He claims that none of the Europeans 'doubts that the White House and in particular the President's advisers on counter-terrorism in the NSC deliberately distorted the intelligence to frame Gaddafi for the *La Belle* bomb'. Jack Anderson, the well-known American columnist, exposed the CIA's report about a Libyan assassination squad's arrival in the United States to kill the President, as 'a phony'.

While Gaddafi helps some of the most brutal and vicious terrorist groups in the world, there is nothing to connect him to the *La Belle* bomb. The number of American and West European deaths that can be directly attributed to him is small. By far the largest number of his victims are fellow-Libyans. The *La Belle* bomb, European and Israeli Intelligence agencies agree without exception, was a Syrian terrorist act.

References

General: Some of this account has been written from US State Department sources. The author has seen a copy of the Gates Report, referred to in paragraph 2, and the *Operation Rose* plan.
1. Gaddafi, over Tripoli Radio.
2. British Defence sources.
3. US Defence sources.
4. Seymour Hersh, one of America's most experienced investigative journalists, reported on this aspect of the Libyan raid, at great length, in *The New York Times*, 22 February 1987 and in *The Sunday Times*, London, same date.
5. *Ibid.*
6. Tripoli Radio 24 April 1987.
7. *The Sunday Times*, 10 August 1986, published an editorial headlined 'The Raid Did Work.' '... In the past, terrorists have skilfully exploited the divisions in Western counter-terrorist policies and international borders have often provided sanctuary. No longer, and that is the most significant development in the field of counter terrorism for years. President Reagan's raid on Libya, and the essential support Mrs. Thatcher gave him, has made that change possible.'
8. In an hour-long documentary, BBC TV, 3 April 1987. A summary of the programme's research was published in *The Listener*, 2.4.1987. Secretary of State Shultz and Secretary of Defence Weinberger announced that the intelligence intercepts were so perfect that the army's military police in West Berlin had been mobilized and were clearing the bars and discos of American servicemen even before the explosion. Major Ruth La Fontaine, deputy chief of West Berlin's military police, refutes these claims. It would have been her duty to clear the bars but 'I was asleep when the bomb exploded and nobody was alerted to clear the bars. We heard about those claims [in Washington] and they weren't true'. During Bower's programme various American officials discounted the Libyan intercepts.

War Trends

Baluchistan and the Soviet Imperial Plan

The Soviet's far northern geographical position has always limited the Russians' access to the world's oceans and global sea lanes. Some ports are frozen shut for part of the year. Geopolitics restricts the use of others. All this frustrated Russian imperial ambitions—and in more recent times Soviet Union desires—to play an unrestricted maritime role.

For centuries Russian leaders and strategists have longed for a warm water port linked to the Soviet homeland with *direct* access to the sea lanes. The least frigid ports, those on the Black Sea, allow Soviet ships access to the Mediterranean only via the Turkish straits—the Bosphorus and the Dardanelles. Because Turkey is a member of NATO it could easily seal the Soviet Black Sea fleet within these limited waters.

The use of ports and bases on the Indian Ocean figure largely in Soviet strategic analysis. Iran could provide some of them. In Iran the Russians have a neighbour and an increasingly reliant, though unstable, friend. Iran's railway lines are linked to those in the Soviet Union and in time of war could be used to supply Soviet or Soviet-backed forces in southern Arabia, East Africa and Southeast Asia.

There are two major Iranian military sites in the southeast. At Bandar Abbas, which protects (or threatens) the entrance to the Arabian Gulf at the Strait of Hormuz, Iran has a naval base and an air base. A railway line connects it to the north.

In Iran's extreme southeast, in the heart of Baluchistan, is the Chah Bahar naval base and nearby is the Konarak air base. A railway line is being pushed across the desert sands and barren mountains of Baluchistan to link these facilities to the national network. The Shah of Iran had planned to make Chah Bahar into Iran's most important military centre on the Indian Ocean but in 1979, when Khomeini's Iranian revolution forced him to flee, the facilities had not been completed.

Chah Bahar is militarily sealed against intrusion but there are grounds for believing that the base was completed in 1985. An Iranian political scientist, Professor Farzah Kazemi, based at a New York university, claims that he has proof that the base is a huge logistical centre and that it is 'active'.[1]

Soviet interest in Baluchistan is intense. The area covers a large part of southeast Iran and all of western Pakistan. Soviet officers have been systematically studying the Baluchi language at a school in Kabul, Afghanistan, at least since 1984. However, the Baluchi people, who number only 4 million, have been a major Soviet target for influence and subversion for decades. It is believed that Russians have trained a Baluchi irregular force of about 20,000 and armed something like 10,000 of them. This force appears to be wholly dependent on the Soviet Union.[2]

It is a form of insurance for the Soviet High command. Russian aircraft with advanced electronic equipment frequently overfly Iranian Baluchistan on flights from Shindand air base in western Afghanistan to the Indian Ocean, Yemen and

The Soviet Union in Baluchistan

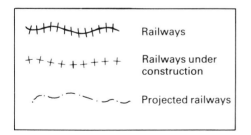

┼┼┼┼┼┼┼┼┼┼	Railways
+ + + + + + + +	Railways under construction
‒ · ‒ · ‒ · ‒ · ‒	Projected railways

Ethiopia. In case of an accident the Russians must be certain of recovering wreckage—and their Baluchi allies are expected to ensure this.

The Iranian government is well aware of the Soviet air and ground operations in Iran. Wholly preoccupied with the war against Iraq, the Iranians are in no position to check the Soviet intrusions but there is no evidence that they wish to do so. According to one source[3] they permit the Russians to do as they wish provided they do not encourage the Baluchis to demand independence.

The Baluchi People's Liberation Front (BPLF) is already active. Mostly Sunni Muslims, the Iranian Baluchis oppose Khomeini, who is a Shi'a Muslim. The BPLF has been infiltrated by Communist agents, though they seem to be under orders from Moscow not to cause disruption at this time.

The Soviet interest is having the complete freedom of use of an Indian Ocean port—by one means or another—is strategically understandable. The Russians already maintain naval and air bases at the former American complex of Cam Ranh Bay, Vietnam; there are other bases in South Yemen, on islands offshore from South Yemen, and in Ethiopia. At the moment Cam Ranh Bay must be supplied from ports in the Far East north of Korea. The Indian Ocean bases can only be fully supplied by ships travelling from the Black Sea through the Turkish straits and then the Suez Canal.

As the Soviet planners see the future their strategy is seriously flawed without the ability to use rail links from Soviet Europe to the Indian Ocean. Control of Baluchistan would solve many problems. Control of Afghanistan is no direct solution; *it has no railroads.*

Soviet plans are well advanced. Russians have been actively running the Iranian rail system since 1981. Soviet-made engines are manned by Russian crews; maintenance is carried out by Russians and they are involved in time-tabling. Some diplomats in Iran say that the Russians 'dominate' Iran's transport system and it is patently obvious that Iran's overland exports depend on links with the Soviet railway system. The number of Russian rail 'experts' working in Iran is estimated to be 5,000.[4]

Russians are also heavily involved in the oil, gas and steel industries and they are building power stations. In December 1986 the Iranian government signed an agreement with the Soviet Union concerning the importing of heavy equipment for steel and aluminium manufacture and for mining.

Other factors concerning the rail system are significant. Iran's rail tracks are standard Soviet gauge. Various lines are being linked. For instance, the Soviet railway station at Dusak in the state of Turkmenia is about 100 km from the border town of Sarakhs; these places are being rail-connected. In eastern Iran the line ends at Mashdad but this too is being linked to Sarakhs. In Azerbaijan the Iranian tracks cross into Soviet Armenia using a bridge over the Aras river; this bridge is one of the most heavily guarded places in the Soviet Union.

Diplomatic sources in Iran and Pakistan believe that the Soviet Union has promised the Baluchis an independent state within the Union of Soviet Socialist Republics—provided that the BPLF assists Soviet expansion. The BPLF cannot speak for all Baluchis but Russian infiltration of virtually all tribes is extensive. Bandar Abbas is far beyond the traditional boundaries of Baluchistan but what one source describes as 'experimental Baluchi agitation' has begun in the Bandar Abbas area. Nobody other than the Russians would have any interest in such agitation.

While the West has had its attention fixed on Soviet activities in Afghanistan the Russians have made great progress in their long-standing plans for their warm-water port and far-southern air bases. They hope to be able to achieve their aims by *fait accompli* rather than by war. The plans are now so far advanced that only war could destroy them, so far advanced that the Russians would go to war to protect them.

References

1. Professor Kazemi disclosed this information during a seminar at New York University, March 1987.
2. Selig Harrison, author of the only major Western study of the Baluchis in recent years.
3. Yossef Bodansky, senior analyst with Mid-Atlantic Research Associates Inc., Washington, 4.4.1987.
4. Assessment by *Early Warning* intelligence newsletter, December 1986.
    Other information from diplomatic sources in Teheran, Islamabad and Moscow.

The War that Nearly was: Greece–Turkey

US MEDITERRANEAN BASES AT RISK

For Greece and Turkey the problem of fixing a clear frontier in the Aegean Sea is complicated by geography. A chain of islands belonging to Greece lies just off the Turkish coast; in a war this could lead to Turkey's access to the open sea being obstructed. Nowhere else in the world does this situation apply and international law apparently does not cover it.

However, the Greeks believe that the spirit of international law favours them. They are so confident of this that for many years they have been willing to allow the International Court of Justice in The Hague to decide the dispute. Turkey prefers bilateral negotiations and settlement. In fact, the court in The Hague may not even have jurisdiction to accept the case.

A coastal state's right to 12 nautical miles of territorial sea is now generally accepted but Greeks and Turks realise that making 12-mile claims would begin a conflict in the Aegean; it is just too congested. Turkey accepts six miles.

The row which came to a head in March 1987 is over the right to exploit oil found under the continental shelf that extends beneath the entire Aegean. Turkey did not accept a UN 1958 convention over the shelf and in 1982 it voted against the adoption of the new UN sea law treaty. The 1958 convention recognised that islands were to be taken into account in determining coastal states' shelf-rights; the 1982 draft, not yet ratified, provides more detail.

At the end of March, Turkey decided to send its oil research vessel, *Sismik 1*, into waters which Greece claims. Both countries alerted their warships and Greece threatened naval action should *Sismik 1* 'trespass'. Both countries are NATO members and the possibility of a war between them was alarming. The personal intervention of Lord Carrington, NATO's secretary-general, induced the Turks not to put *Sismik 1* into a danger area and the Greeks to stop their bellicose talk.

Both countries' Prime Ministers claimed victory and they were feted as if they had indeed achieved a victory. Both gained in national prestige, Andreas Papandreou probably more than Turgut Ozal.

The two countries have been in bitter dispute over Cyprus since the Turkish invasion of northern Cyprus in 1974; 20,000 Turkish troops are still on the island. Greece refuses to hold talks with Turkey on any subject until the troops are withdrawn. There is also a dispute over the island of Lemnos, which the Greeks have turned into a military base. Turkey claims that this violates the 1923 Treaty of Lausanne and the 1947 Paris peace treaties.

The animosity between the two nations goes back to the 400-year occupation of Greece by the Turkish Ottoman Empire. Greece gained independence through an 1830 treaty after the 1821-27 revolutionary war. The rise of Islamic fundamentalism in Turkey has rekindled Greek sensitivity about Islamic imperialism.

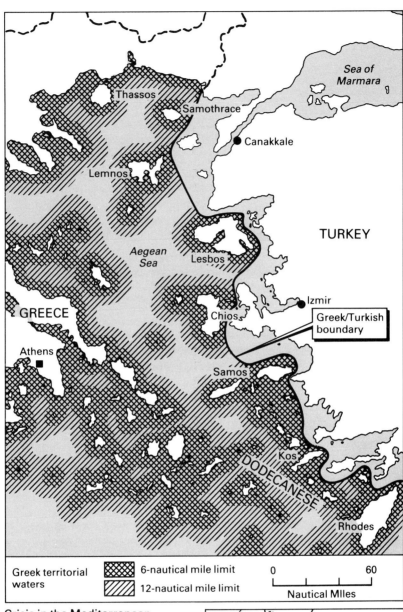

Thassos
Samothrace
Canakkale
Lemnos

*Aegean
Sea*

TURKEY

Lesbos

GREECE

Chios

Izmir

Greek/Turkish
boundary

Athens

Samos

Kos

DODECANESE

Rhodes

Greek territorial
waters

▨ 6-nautical mile limit
▧ 12-nautical mile limit

0   60
Nautical Miles

Crisis in the Mediterranean

U.S.S.R.

RUMANIA

YUGOSLAVIA

ITALY

BULGARIA

TURKEY

GREECE

In late March all the trends were towards war. The Greek government mobilised naval and air forces and newspapers referred to 'the war'. The country's 250,000 civil servants, in the interest of 'national unity', called off a strike set to start on the day the alarm occurred. The Turkish Army enlarged its forces on the Gallipoli peninsula, presumably to seize Lemnos should a war break out.

The foreign general public had by then forgotten that on 19 December 1986 a serious border incident had taken place between Greek and Turkish troops. According to the Greek government's account, an unarmed Greek soldier tossed a packet of cigarettes to a Turkish patrol just across the heavily guarded border at the Evros River. A military report stated that the Greek had laid down his weapons and helmet to answer the Turks' request for cigarettes. In any case, the Turks shot him.

The Turks claimed that a Greek patrol had crossed the border to start the incident. The Turkish troops fired because they thought they were being attacked. The Greek soldiers on the spot called for help and a second patrol, arriving to find one of their men dead, opened fire. Two Turkish soldiers were killed. Both sides played down the episode but it remains a sensitive matter.

At the height of the Aegean and *Sismik 1* dispute President Papandreou demanded the closure of an American communications centre near Thassos, the site of the disputed underwater oil field. He alleged that the US had sided with Turkey. The order was rescinded after high-level negotiations but it indicated the risk to US Mediterranean bases. The Americans have four major bases and several minor ones on Greek territory. The important ones are:

Hellenikon air base, near Athens.
Naval Communications Centre, also near Athens.
Naval Support Base in western Crete.
Iraklion Air Base, central Crete.

The threat which Muslim fundamentalism poses to North Africa, the disintegration of Lebanon, the recurrent traumas of the Iran-Iraq war, continued Syrian hostility towards Israel and other problems, both acute and chronic, affect the entire Mediterranean. Greece—and Spain—feel particularly exposed to dangers. Increasingly they ask themselves, at political, press and popular level, if the presence of American military units helps or handicaps them.

Felipe Gonzalez, Prime Minister of Spain, is challenging some of the key assumptions of the American military presence in Spain. The establishing of four US bases in Spain in 1953 provided the fascist dictator General Franco with international recognition and material support that kept him in power. Elsewhere in Europe the US enjoys the advantage of being identified with liberation of Europe from fascism. This is not the case in Spain.

Mr. Gonzalez specifically wants the US to withdraw its 72 F-16 aircraft from Torrejon, near Madrid, as a condition for permitting the other bases to stay. These tactical combat aircraft are not in Spain to ward off a Soviet threat in Europe, the Spanish strategists say; they are much more likely to be used in conflicts that could erupt in North Africa or the Middle East.

Spain does not want to be dragged into these conflicts and the demand for the F-16s to be withdrawn makes this clear. An American offer to move the aircraft to another base in Spain was rejected in April 1987. A showdown between Spain and the US over the issue could have profound effects in Greece and throughout the Mediterranean.

The near-war between Turkey and Greece was just another indicator that the US is unpopular in the Mediterranean. Much of this unpopularity is unjustifiable but it is real enough to indicate a dangerous trend. Should the next dispute between Greece and Turkey lead to war the effects on Europe as a whole, as well as the US, could be devastating.

War Clouds over Korea?

In its 39-year history South Korea has never had a government which came to power by peaceful means. The country has had a succession of assassinations, coups and street revolts. In addition, it lives under the fear of war imposed on it from North Korea.

This fear has much to do with the way in which South Korea is governed. Its 40 million people have had an impressive unity against North Korea ever since the war of 1950-53. Now many Korean commentators and analysts question why the eternal threat should force them to live permanently under an authoritarian military government, such as that of President Chun Doo Hwan. Some foreign diplomats in South Korea agree that such a regime is no longer necessary.

The country has regular drills against surprise attacks from North Korea. As sirens wail at night, Seoul, which has a population of 10 million, blacks out; all cars and public transport must pull to the side of the road and switch off their lights. The discipline is complete and so is the blackout. Discipline is, perhaps, the most notable aspect of life in South Korea. President Chun makes a virtue of it and not infrequently tells his people that in obeying orders and asking few questions they are working towards a 'great national goal'.

One goal is certainly the year 1988, when Seoul is host for the summer Olympic Games. But even that is not enough to stifle a trend towards dissent. People express their yearnings for a 'fundamental change', though relatively few articulate its form. In the spring of 1986 people took to the streets of eight major cities to protest about Chun's 6-year rule. The overthrow of President Marcos in the Philippines in February 1986 gave South Koreans hope for a less arbitrary form of government in their own land. Radical students have violent fights with the police and Christian leaders speak out against government 'repression'.

The government and the opposition have been trying to negotiate an amended constitution; if they fail to do so their uneasy truce would end. Both sides are in dispute over a successor to Chun, who has promised to step down in 1988. South Korea has the institutions, nominally at least, of a democratic government. But Chun holds all power. As an army general, he seized control after the 1979 assassination of another president-general, Park Chung Hee. The citizens of Kwangju City rose in revolt in 1980 and Chun did not hesitate to send in the troops. The official death toll was 191; reform groups say it was more than 500.

Chun is quick to punish dissent. He will order a publication to be closed down; his secret police question people who visit any office concerned with labour rights and organisation.

Chun justifies all of his stringent controls by the threat from North Korea. In readiness for it South Korea is permanently mobilised with an army of 600,000. War preparations are omnipresent. In the cities all new constructions have a built-in military use; for instance, the public flower gardens are waist-high brick structures which can quickly become machine-gun posts. Vital installations such as oil storage tanks are cleverly camouflaged and often concealed as well. Some railyards are protected from air attack by reinforced concrete shelters and public air raid shelters are always ready for use.

Because the armed forces are strong and are deemed to be so vital they have great social, economic and political importance. This is only in keeping with South Korea's 2,000 years of Confucian autocracy and 35 years of imperial Japanese rule. Military tradition prevents the growth of many aspects of Western life for which younger South Koreans hunger, such as sexual equality. Men and women still eat separately in South Korea.

Chun's political position rejects a style of government which is based on ceaseless projection of possible invasion. It just is not going to happen, they say. The government of South Korea should cease to be authoritarian and become more frank and honest with the people. The high morale which South Korea appears to have, say its internal critics, is artificially imposed and is not 'natural'.

More than 10 million South Koreans are Christians and traditionally social change has emanated from them. Roman Catholic and Protestant leaders publicly press for constitutional amendments which will produce direct presidential elections. The churches, while deeply critical, are reluctant to encourage rebellion.

The university students—South Korea has one million of them—are more volatile. Almost every day police and students are in violent confrontation, almost as a form of ritual. When a student committee calls a lunchtime rally riot police arrive in large numbers. Invariably, violence erupts as students throw stones and occasionally petrol bombs. The police fire tear gas and use their clubs. Many students consider themselves revolutionaries and a few are so extreme that they commit suicide for 'the cause'.

The many generals take no part in day-to-day politics, perhaps because they do not need to do so. They support Chun and approve of his style of government.

What happens in South Korea is crucial to the United States, which has 40,000 troops in the country. In theory, the US is neutral but its resident army would be drawn into any conflict that might erupt. Behind the political scenes, the Americans are influential and they are known to have stopped President Chun from taking drastic steps against his own people. For instance, he proposed to establish 're-education centres' for radical students. The Americans would not tolerate such an authoritarian communist-like step.

The opposition quietly but persistently pressures the Americans to drop Chun, just as they did Marcos. The radicals hate the United States because the Americans—and equally the Japanese—are accused of oppressive control over the nation's economy and government. Yet it was largely American help which has given South Korea its 'economic miracle'.

While President Chun and others may be exaggerating the danger of a war with North Korea—just as they unrealistically minimise the danger of an insurrection—there is in fact, a trend towards conflict. In mid-1987 North Korea has 65% of its armed forces of 840,000 on the border with South Korea. Before 1986 it had always been 45 per cent.

North Korea's military might is impressive. Apart from the 840,000 regulars (from a population of 21 million) the army has reserves of 500,000 and about 5 million men and women have some form of militia commitment. In addition, the High Command claims that it can fully mobilize the nation in 12 hours.

The army has 3,275 tanks compared to South Korea's 1,300 tanks; it has 4,750 guns (South Korea 3,300). Most importantly, North Korea has the biggest commando force in the world—100,000. The country's airpower is also great—854 combat aircraft, all Soviet-built, compared with South Korea's 452 combat planes, all American-made.

The military build up has been at the expense of the general economy. Money is in such short supply that North Korean diplomats resort to black market business activities to help pay for their embassies. North Korea cannot afford its military growth, which suggests that it is not just for show.

There are signs of instability in the North, especially because of the succession problem. Kim Il Sung is grooming his son to take his place but the army's senior leaders oppose the younger Kim as 'unqualified'.

Kim makes strenuous efforts to get support from Moscow and Peking for his son; this has weakened his ability to remain neutral in the Chinese-Soviet dispute. The Soviet has increased its influence over the North Korean government in the last year. It has delivered some of its advanced MiG-23 fighters and they are expected to counter the F-16s of the South Koreans. The Russians have also supplied North Korea with ground-to-ground missiles that can hit Seoul. The Soviet administration will also help North Korea to build a nuclear power plant.

In return, the Russians have been given the use of North Korean ports and overflight rights. Both enhance the Soviet's power projection capability in Northeast Asia.

To counter North Korean and Soviet activity the Reagan administration has urged Japan to take additional defence responsibilities in the area and to give South Korea more economic aid.

The tension between North and South Korea is evident in many ways. North Korea signed a pact with Cuba aimed at disrupting Seoul's international 'athletics diplomacy'. North Korean leaders threatened disruption in various forms, such as boycott and terrorism.

Following North Korean complaints, the International Olympic Committee offered to allow North Korea to stage four events in the capital, Pyongyang, if it permitted free entry of 25,000 associated with the Olympics into the North. This total would include athletes, officials, journalists and spectators. The events offered and accepted are table-tennis, archery, some soccer matches and a cycling race from Pyongyang to Seoul. In March 1987 North Korea demanded a bigger share in the Olympic schedule and insisted that the games should be known as the Pyongyang-Seoul Olympics. This demand was rejected.

Pyongyang was never considered as a possibility for the 1988 Games but North Koreans have been told for years that the city is the chosen venue. Control of the media is so strict that the North Koreans do not know that Seoul was host for the Asian Games in 1986. North Korea is regarded as the world's most closed communist society.

The Korean pensinsula has been a region of tension for decades, which is why the rest of the world has become accustomed to it. The early warning signals which indicate armed conflict are becoming stronger.

The United States' Electric Gun

The US Defense Department is so encouraged by progress on a super-powerful electric gun that it is funding several new prototypes of the weapon. Scientists and military officers associated with the development believe that the 'electro-magnetic cannon' or 'electro-magnetic rail-gun' (EMRG) will have diverse uses, from piercing tank armour to shooting down nuclear missiles.

The weapon uses magnetic fields to accelerate projectiles to speeds of several kilometres per second. At such a speed even a small projectile can puncture heavy tank armour, let alone the relatively thin skin of a ballistic missile.

A prototype small EMRG, made by Maxwell Laboratories Inc., a defence contractor, was used only in indoor tests. Two newer types will, respectively, be tested in simulated battle conditions and be strapped to a tank or other tracked vehicle.

Maxwell's existing rail-gun, dubbed CHECMATE—for Compact High Energy Capacitator Module Advanced Technology Experiment was first fired in October 1985. The largest of about 6 rail-guns in the United States, it had 80 tests and fired plastic projectiles at speed of 3.1 km a second. At that speed the projectile penetrated four 2.5 cm plates of hardened tank armour.

For use against nuclear missiles in Strategic Defence Initiative (Star Wars) projects much greater speeds are needed.

Directors of all rail-gun projects say that the major difficulty is to construct a device that can withstand the tremendous forces and temperatures generated during the firing when speeds of 15 km per second are needed. The maximum speed achieved to date is 11 km per second.

So far rail-guns are one-shot weapons. Kaman Corporation has a contract worth 8.5 million dollars from Defense Advanced Research Projects Agency to build a gun that can fire projectiles at 4.2 km per second, three times a minute.

Another research company is working on a space-based electro-magnetic rail-gun that can fire and re-aim rapidly. SDI Director Lieutenant-General James Abrahamson is encouraging several other projects.

A recent test firing of CHECMATE was designed to measure friction between the projectile and the gun's 5-metre barrel. Engineers triggered the weapon from a distance. The blast made the ground shake and a television camera showed debris whirling inside the test chamber. The plastic projectile had penetrated a 2.5 cm piece of steel. Fired in 20 1-millionths of a second, the 102 gram projectile reached a speed of 2.4 km per second. It was subjected to more than 150,000 times the force of gravity and 'weighs' about a ton.

In mid-1987 Los Alamos National Laboratory completed a US$12 million weapon—for the SDI programme—that is expected to fire bullets at 15 km per second.

While there is much interest in rail-guns in US defence circles the emphasis so

ELECTROMAGNETIC RAILGUN

The Pentagon is building a new generation of electro-magnetic launchers, which use magnetic force to accelerate projectiles. The weapon can be used against tanks on the battlefield and in space against enemy nuclear missiles.

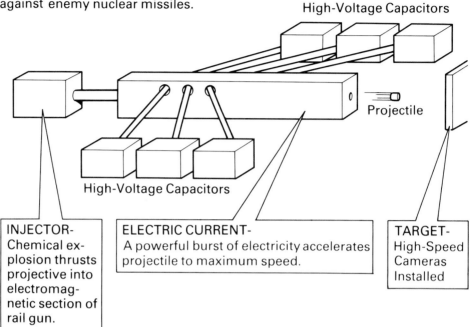

High-Voltage Capacitors

High-Voltage Capacitors

Projectile

INJECTOR- Chemical explosion thrusts projective into electromagnetic section of rail gun.

ELECTRIC CURRENT- A powerful burst of electricity accelerates projectile to maximum speed.

TARGET- High-Speed Cameras Installed

ELECTROMAGNETIC RAILS- Carrying vast amounts of electric current, these rails create a field which passes through a current-conducting plasma 'cloud' following the projectile. The 102-gram plastic projectile reaches a speed of about 2.4 kilometres per second. Under this tremendous acceleration, the projectile is subjected to more than 150,000 times the force of gravity and weighs about a ton.

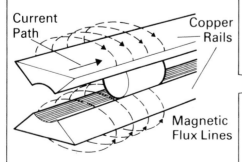

Current Path

Copper Rails

Magnetic Flux Lines

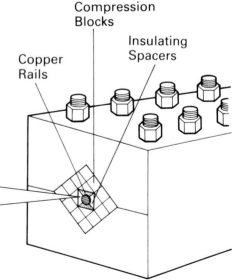

Compression Blocks

Insulating Spacers

Copper Rails

The United States' Electric Gun

far is on demonstrators. More research is needed into fundamental physics. Nevertheless, the trend towards EMRG weapons is strong enough to be talked about as a possible battlefield weapon by 1990.

Background Reading

Afghanistan

Soviet Expansion in the Third World: Afghanistan, a Case Study by Nasir Shansab; Bartleby Press, New York.
The Soviet War by Edward Girardet; Croom Helm, London.
To Win the Children: Afghanistan's Other War; published by Helsinki Watch/Asia.

Angola

Jonas Savimbi: A Key to Africa by Fred Bridgeland; Mainstream Publishing, Edinburgh.

Cambodia

When the War Was Over: The Voices of Cambodia's Revolution and Its People, by Elizabeth Becker; Simon and Schuster, New York.
Cambodian Witness: The Autobiography of Someth May; Faber, London.
Dynamics of the Cambodian Conflict by J.M. van der Kroef; Centre for Security and Conflict Studies, London.

Central America

Out of the Ashes: The Lives and Hopes of Refugees from El Salvador and Guatemala; published by El Salvador and Guatemala Committees for Human Rights, London.

El Salvador

Mirrors of War, translated by Keith Ellis; Zed Press, London.
Witness for War by Charles Clements; Fontana, London.
Promised Land: Peasant Rebellion in Chalatenango, El Salvador; published by Latin America Bureau, London.
El Salvador the Face of Revolution, by Robert Armstrong and Janet Schenk; Pluto Press, London.

Guatemala

Garrison Guatemala by George Black; Zed Press, London.

Holy War

Muslim Fundamentalism by Anthony Hyman; Institute for the Study of Conflict, London.

Holy War–Islam Fights by John Laffin; published by Granada Books, London.

India

Amritsar: Mrs. Gandhi's Last Battle by Mark Tully and Satish Jacob; Jonathan Cape, London.

Iraq-Iran War

Iraq and Iran: The Years of Crisis by Jasim Abdulghani; Croom Helm, London, and Johns Hopkins University Press, Baltimore.

Security Constraints in the Gulf by Anthony Hyman; Institute for the Study of Conflict, London.

Kurdistan

The Search for Recognition by R. Sim; Centre for Security and Conflict Studies, London.

Lebanon

Syria under Assad edited by Moshe Ma'oz and Avner Yaniv; Croom Helm, London.

Middle East

Arabia Imperilled: The Security Imperatives of the Arabian Gulf States By Mazheer A. Hameed; published by Middle East Assessments Group, Washington, D.C.

Morocco

Conflict in the Maghreb: The Western Sahara by D.L. Price; Centre for Security and Conflict Studies, London.

Namibia

Namibia: The Violent Heritage by David Soggot; Rex Collins, London.

Nicaragua

David and Goliath by William I. Robinson and Kent Norsworthy; Zed Books, London.

The Jaguar Smile: A Nicaraguan Journey by Salman Rushdie; Picador Press, London.

South Africa

The Border Wars: South Africa's Response by S. Menaul; Centre for Security and Conflict Studies, London.

Sri Lanka

Terrorism in Sri Lanka by Penelope Tremayne; Institute for the Study of Terrorism, London.

Sudan

Sudan: Threats to Stability by P. Woodward; Centre for Security and Conflict Studies, London.

United States at War

To Arm a Nation by Richard Halloran; Macmillan, New York.
The Defense Game by Richard A. Stubbing; Harper & Row, New York.

General

World Military and Social Expenditures 1986 (annually); published by Armament & Disarmament Information Unit, University of Sussex.